Dear Hal

Wishing you a Merry Christmas

2009

and an excellent 2010, 2011, 2012,
2013 and every year after!!

Love David, Sarah & Ellen

25 December 2009

ONE AMONG EQUALS

England's International Rugby Captains

STEVE LEWIS

VERTICAL EDITIONS

www.verticaleditions.com

First published in the United Kingdom in 2008 by
Vertical Editions, Unit 4a, Snaygill Industrial Estate,
Skipton, North Yorkshire BD23 2QR

www.verticaleditions.com

ISBN 978-1-904091-31-8

Cover design and typeset by HBA, York

Printed and bound by Biddles Limited, King's Lynn

CONTENTS

ACKNOWLEDGEMENTS

Only one name appears on the cover of this book but to suggest that the work be credited to the named author alone is foolish in the extreme.

To begin with there are the 122 players who have captained England without whose endeavours there would not be a story to tell. In particular I would like to thank Rob Andrew, Fran Cotton, Paul Dodge, Phil de Glanville, Mike Harrison, Richard Hill, Dickie Jeeps, Jason Leonard, Colin McFadyean, Nigel Melville, David Perry, John Pullin, Budge Rogers, John Scott, Richard Sharp, Steve Smith, John Spencer, Roger Uttley, Mike Weston and John Willcox each of whom found time in their busy schedules to discuss their experiences of playing for and captaining England. Their assistance is greatly appreciated.

The recording of statistical information in any sport is an essential exercise but unfortunately all too often the records available through various publications and sources will differ which leaves the researcher wondering which direction to follow—heads or tails. Fortunately rugby union has the benefit of one of sports' finest statisticians to fall back on and all this author can suggest to others who may find themselves in the same predicament is to go with John Griffiths. It must be added at this point that any errors found in the following pages are the author's alone and will have been lost in translation from the source material.

All followers of the game will have had their own particular heroes at some stage in their life and I am particularly grateful to Bernard Cornwell for confirming his interest in Richard Sharp and that he named his well known fictional character after the England outside-half.

Once the words are written somebody has to take over the responsibility of the publishing process before the book is completed. Karl Waddicor of Vertical Editions controlled much of this and my thanks go to him and editor Diane Evans for ensuring that the complex procedure ran smoothly.

My good friend Keith Erickson was kind enough to drive me to some appointments which was an enormous help in my hour of need.

Finally my thanks must go to my wife Catherine who yet again went through the nine months of grief and angst that represents the nearest a man can get to having a baby—at least what you the reader are holding in your hand is quiet!

Steve Lewis
Newport, August 2008

INTRODUCTION

It all began at the Pall Mall Restaurant in central London on 26 January 1871. Representatives from 21 rugby clubs met with the sole purpose of founding a union, a governing body which would be instrumental in the administering of a game that was struggling to find its identity. From the day in 1823 when a young scholar at Rugby School by the name of William Webb Ellis is reported to have picked up a football and run with it, other educational establishments introduced their own variation on the new concept and almost 50 years later the time had come to bring these differing interpretations together.

With the formation of the Rugby Football Union it was only a matter of months before a set of Laws had been drawn up and the first international match played. England met Scotland at Raeburn Place in Edinburgh on 27 March, the first in a series of matches that had extended to 125 by the end of the 2007–08 season. It wasn't long before Ireland entered the fray followed by Wales and in 1883 the first Championship was contested between the four countries. France joined the tournament in 1910, Italy in 2000 and of course much interest in the game was seen in the southern hemisphere. New Zealand and South Africa both toured Britain in the first decade of the twentieth century, Australia would follow.

Rugby union is now a global sport and to date England has played capped matches against 18 countries and it is these capped matches that are the focus of this book, more specifically the captains involved. At the end of the 2008 Six Nations Championship England had played 606 capped matches and when Steve Borthwick led the team out at the Stadio Flamino in Rome on 10 February 2008 he became the 122nd captain. Fred Stokes was the first in a list which contains many of the great names of English rugby, players who became household names and some who didn't.

The story of the men chosen as captain is also the story of the development of rugby union in England. It illustrates how the game evolved from its public school origins to the professional sport it now is. How once Blackheath RFC and Richmond RFC were the biggest clubs in the land and how Oxford and Cambridge Universities were so instrumental in the development of many an England leader. No club can lay claim to the number of captains associated with the London clubs and no educational establishments can match the number who passed through the two universities. That neither Blackheath nor Richmond can lay claim to an England captain since 1971 or that the regular contribution of Oxford and Cambridge has all but dried up clearly indicates the game has undergone a massive transformation both geographically and socially. How best then to approach the subject? Thoughts of treating the captains simply in chronological order were quickly abandoned so how should they be discussed? Several options were available but it was decided that by looking at the players on a geographical basis, where they were playing their club rugby at the time of their appointment, a natural clockwise journey around England could be allowed to unfold.

Start in Blackheath, move across south London then continue down to the West Country. Up through the west Midlands to the north-west before crossing the Pennines to the north-east, returning via the east Midlands into north London—perfect. Unfortunately, some players managed to escape this crude rugby map of England and are grouped together in a chapter appropriately called *The Misfits*, but these players apart, the structure worked. Worked that is until players were found to have captained England from two or more clubs; where to put them? For purposes of continuity these will be found at the club where they were playing when originally appointed regardless of what may have transpired later—Wavell Wakefield isn't to be found in the chapter on the Harlequins, Nim Hall at Richmond or Phil Vickery with the London Wasps.

Anomalies aside, the journey begins at Blackheath, one of the clubs behind the founding of the RFU and also home of the first England captain. It ends at Rugby House in Twickenham with a man who is one of the English game's leading movers and shakers in the twenty first century—a most appropriate place to finish.

In between there are another 120 men who experienced the highs and lows of international sport. Among them knights of the realm, leading figures in industry and commerce, outstanding members of the Armed Forces, politicians, Test cricketers and much else besides.

It is unlikely that the collective curriculum vitae of these 122 individuals could be equalled within the game or indeed by any other sport, such is the quality of the men involved. For all that, rugby union remains a team sport in which the sum is only as good as its parts and while 15 men continue to take the field with a common objective, the captain should never be viewed as a man apart. A leader most certainly but always a member of a team—one among equals.

1

THE CLUB
Blackheath

Where should a journey that runs the length and breadth of England begin? Common sense dictates it should start at the very beginning before letting licence to roam. The book should start with the first man to captain England which would lead us to Blackheath RFC founded in 1858 and one of the oldest clubs in the land (some would claim the oldest). Here is a most suitable place to begin the journey as not only does the club count the first man to captain England among its ex-players but includes 11 others on the Roll of Honour. Ten are found in this opening chapter with two discussed elsewhere having first led England from other clubs. But the total of 12 players is a figure only great rivals Richmond can equal.

Blackheath is 150 years old but it was 1933 when the last England captain to come from the Rectory Field appeared. Whilst the old saying, 'What goes around, comes around' should not be forgotten, it is difficult to rationalise that a club currently playing in National Division Two will at some future date be able to count an incumbent England captain among its playing staff, such is the dictate of the professional era. However, and regardless of what the future may hold, the history of Blackheath does provide a plethora of talented and distinguished individuals who played the game at the highest level. Heading the list is the name Stokes.

Old Rugbeian **Frederick Stokes** was 20 years of age when together with Benjamin Burns he represented Blackheath at the meeting held in the Pall Mall Restaurant on 26 January 1871, the outcome of which saw the founding of the Rugby Football Union. Two months later both men represented England in the first international which took place at Raeburn Place in Edinburgh. This was a sometimes chaotic affair with the English visitors and their Scottish hosts clearly used to different interpretations of what at the time were far from clearly defined Laws but it was a start.

Fred Stokes was chosen to captain the team, thereby ensuring himself a permanent place in the annals of English rugby. He led England a year later when Scotland arrived at the Kennington Oval for a return fixture and again in 1873 when England travelled to Glasgow. After three matches, each country had won a first international with the Glasgow fixture ending in a scoreless draw and as could be expected, both teams witnessed many changes in personnel. Only three England players appeared in each match. Fred Stokes was one who kept his place in the team and he remained captain. But this was a short international career that ended four months before his 23rd birthday and it was two years before the name Stokes reappeared in the England team.

The influence brought to the table by former pupils of Rugby School during the early years of the RFU cannot be underestimated. While Fred Stokes was guiding England on the field of play, equally sterling work was being administered off it; Old Rugbeians, Algernon Rutter, E.C. Holmes and L.J. Maton were responsible for the drafting of the first set of Laws. Rutter was also elected the first president of the RFU, remaining in office for three seasons. Frederick Stokes succeeded him. At the time of his appointment, he was 24 years of age and remains the youngest holder of the office to date.

There were six brothers in the Stokes' family all of whom played for Blackheath but only **Lennard Stokes** followed Fred into the England team. Six years separated them and rugby aside Lennard and his elder brother had very little in common. Most noticeably, Rugby School played no part in Lennard's education, Sydney College, Bath proving a more than adequate alternative. After completion of his studies, rather than follow Fred into the legal profession he chose to pursue a career in medicine. Their talents were similarly diverse on the rugby field where Fred played among the forwards while Lennard excelled in the three-quarters. It was with much justification that he was hailed as the greatest player of his day. Ireland was added to the fixture list four years after the first match in Edinburgh and it was against Ireland that Lennard Stokes made his England debut. He was a noticeable absentee for the next two matches but won his second and third caps in matches of singular importance in the development of the game.

International rugby football was originally played between teams of 20 players but this was about to change. England recalled Lennard Stokes to the side against Scotland in 1876, the last international before teams reduced in number, and a year later he played against Ireland in the first 15-a-side match. For someone with Stokes' pace and flair the change in the number of players proved to be for the better. Over the next five seasons England lost only one out of 11 matches which coincided with a period in which Blackheath, now captained by Lennard Stokes, reigned supreme. His elder brother led the club in the 1873–74 season but between 1876–81 Blackheath enjoyed an extraordinary sequence of results; of 83 matches played they only lost six. Stokes played in all but one of the matches, scoring 56 tries as the club swept all but the very best opponents aside, suggesting the club had benefited more than most from the reduction in the number of players. An England captain in the making then and Lennard Stokes duly led his country for the first time against Ireland in Dublin in 1880. His five match tenure began with victory and ended with a draw in Edinburgh a year later. Between this time England won three matches, notably a victory over Wales in the first match played between the two countries (using modern scoring values the outcome equates to 82–0!)

Lennard Stokes ended his international career with 12 caps to his name which for a short period made him England's most capped player and most successful captain. He followed his elder brother into the administration of the game and the RFU elected him as the eighth president in 1886. He held office for two years and remained on the RFU Committee for over 50 years. Both brothers played significant roles in the formative years of English international rugby. Their contributions on and off the field were critical to the foundations on which today's game was built. But life must have been tough for such young men during the final decades of the nineteenth century. There weren't enough hours in the day for whatever careers players pursued outside rugby whether in the legal profession, medicine or finance. For many, no sooner had the rugby season finished then the cricket season began. It was a case of out with the whites, oil the bat, turn over the arm a few times and head off to the county cricket ground. There they would spend the summer in the most idyllic fashion; work and all the demands that went with it would just have to wait.

Fred and Lennard Stokes were competent cricketers and both played for Kent CCC. For most players living and working in London the choice usually came down to Middlesex or Surrey—Lord's or the Oval. Middlesex

CCC had the good fortune of securing the services of **Andrew Stoddart**, as had the Harlequins during his early rugby days. But while he remained true to the county, Stoddart left the Quins to join Blackheath. He excelled at rugby and cricket to such a degree that if no documentary evidence existed to relate his many achievements in the two sports there would be doubts cast over them. He won the first of 10 caps against Wales in 1885. His international career spanned nine seasons during which a disagreement over how to structure a proposed International Board saw the RFU withdraw from the Championship in 1888 and 1889. This was a time when Stoddart was arguably at his peak but no matter, events elsewhere kept him out of the country for much of those two years.

Running parallel with his blossoming rugby career was an equally impressive record as a county and Test cricketer. In the winter of 1887–88 Stoddart toured Australia with an invitation team and rather than return home after the six month sojourn he elected to stay on and joined up with the first British rugby side to visit Australia and New Zealand. Alfred Shaw and Arthur Shrewsbury were two entrepreneurs who instigated the cricket tour and once in Australia decided it would be appropriate that a similar rugby venture followed. Without the official sanction of the RFU there could be no international status attached to the visit. This meant the team played no Test matches but had an arduous itinerary of 35 fixtures of which only two games were lost. The Australian sector had barely got under way when tour captain Robert L. Seddon met a sudden death, drowned sculling on the Hunter River in New South Wales. In the aftermath of this tragedy, Andrew Stoddart was selected to take over the captaincy and led the party for the remainder of the tour which ended when the players arrived back home on 11 November, eight months after their departure. A long time, but even longer for Stoddart who had been out of the country a year having left England with nothing other on his mind than a few months spent playing cricket in sunnier climes. Now he was a man with a unique captaincy experience, one that would stand him in good stead for what was to follow.

Blackheath picked up on it first when appointing him captain for the 1889–90 season in which he also led England for the first time but after two matches Stoddart disappeared from international rugby resurfacing three years later when he was again appointed captain against Wales and Scotland. Both games were lost and but for his exceptional sporting ability

Andrew Stoddart's England days would surely have been over. The RFU may have decided to dispense with his services but in the winter of 1894–95 he returned to Australia and as W.G. Grace's successor led England to victory in cricket's greatest contest. Stoddart played 16 Test matches ending with a respectable run average of 35.57 and continued playing for Middlesex until 1900, hitting 221 runs against Somerset on his final appearance at Lord's.

Following his retirement from cricket Stoddart suffered an extended period of ill health and in 1915, at the age of 52, took his own life. Rugby and cricket joined together in mourning a man who had captained England in both sports added to which were his experiences with the British rugby team, now accepted as the forerunners of the British Lions. This unique treble has secured Andrew Stoddart a record in English sport which is unlikely to be equalled, the demands of both sports in the professional era allowing no time for diversification.

While Stoddart was putting bat to ball in Australia in the 1894–95 British winter, storm clouds were gathering over English rugby. The strict amateur ethos of the game was under serious threat and by the end of 1895 the rugby union map in England looked very different. Professionalism had arrived with the decision of a group of northern-based clubs to disregard the strident attitudes of their counterparts in the south by agreeing to compensate men for any wages lost when playing rugby.

A Cambridge undergraduate born and educated in Yorkshire must have wondered what might have been if he hadn't shown the academic wherewithal to go with his great athletic skills. Would he have laboured in industry and been grateful of the opportunity to supplement a lowly wage by taking advantage of his ability as a rugby footballer? We shall never know because **Frank Mitchell** had plenty of grey matter to accompany the brawn which helped him win athletics, cricket and rugby Blues.

He was introduced to the England pack against Wales in 1895 and retained his place for two seasons chosen to lead the side in his sixth and final game, the 1896 Calcutta Cup match which was won by Scotland for a fourth successive year.

Then cricket took over, in particular Yorkshire CCC. He toured the United States and there were visits to South Africa with Lord Hawke's invitation teams but the county benefited most from his skilful batting. In 1901 Mitchell scored 1,801 first class runs for Yorkshire, enough to see him head the averages with 46.17 and earn him recognition with his inclusion as one of Wisden's cricketers of the year. Here was a Yorkshireman and Englishman who had played cricket for his county and rugby for his country yet had failed to convince the England cricket selectors of his worth but a move overseas led to an unexpected finale to this sporting biography.

Business interests took Mitchell back to South Africa in 1902 where he continued to play cricket at provincial level. For those still to be convinced that the relocation of players and their sometimes dubious eligibility to represent a particular country arrived with the advent of professional rugby union the closing chapter in Frank Mitchell's story may come as a surprise. In 1904 and again in 1912 he led the South African cricket team on tours to England and finally got to play Test cricket at the famous grounds in the land of his birth. The case of Frank Mitchell is not unique, there are examples across sport of similar stories and although some may find such circumstances difficult to reconcile with perhaps there is some consolation to be gained from the knowledge that the migration moves both ways.

In 1908 **Leonard 'Bruno' Brown** played for Queensland against A.F. Harding's Anglo-Welsh tourists. Two years later a Rhodes Scholarship to study medicine took him to Oxford University where he quickly established himself in the first XV and played in three Varsity Matches, captaining the team in 1912. An abrasive forward, Brown's ability was not wasted on the England selectors and in 1911, he won the first of 18 caps in an international career which spanned 11 years to the day. On 21 January 1911 Wales beat England 15–11 at St Helens, Swansea and on 21 January 1922 a more convincing 28–6 outcome saw the Welsh triumph in Cardiff, the day Brown had his only outing as England captain.

He won eight caps as an undergraduate before moving to London to begin a career in medicine. This move took him to Blackheath where he stayed for the remainder of his playing days. 'Bruno' Brown was the only forward to feature in the nine matches played during England's Grand Slam winning campaigns in 1913, 1914 and 1921, by which time he was in his 33rd year, an age when most players of the day had long since retired. But when the time arrived for Brown to hang up his boots, his greatest contributions to the game were ahead of him.

One of only seven England players to appear either side of the First World War, Leonard Brown served with the Royal Artillery Medical Corps in France and Belgium. He was awarded the Military Cross in 1917 before again being mentioned in Despatches a year later. Following the war, he continued in medicine becoming a recognised ear, nose and throat specialist and a Fellow of the Royal College of Surgeons. However, there was another 'career' running in tandem with his chosen profession—rugby administration.

'Bruno' Brown never lost sight of his Colonial roots and he focussed his duties on behalf of the RFU on the southern hemisphere countries. He represented New South Wales on the RFU and chaired the Member Dominions Conference in 1947 at which time he was also England's representative on the International Board. It was during this period that he successfully fought to grant equal IB status to Australia, New Zealand and South Africa. After serving as junior vice president and senior vice president in 1947–48, Brown was elected to become 40th president of the RFU in 1948–49.

Never having lost sight of his roots, in 1949, Leonard Brown was one of the prime movers in the formation of the Australian RFU. Sixty years earlier Andrew Stoddart had played rugby union in a country for which Australian Rules and Rugby League would always prove to be more popular. In the years that followed Australian rugby union needed some men of vision to take up the banner on the sport's behalf. For his significant part in this development Aussie followers of the game remain indebted to Leonard Brown.

It is becoming obvious what a big part Oxford and Cambridge Universities play in the story of the England captains. Of the five men discussed so far, two attended one or other of the great centres of learning, a pattern which will be repeated throughout the following pages. In fact, of the 122 men honoured with the captaincy, 40 attended either Oxford or Cambridge Universities—a staggeringly high figure. In the world of politics, statistics are used to tell as much or as little as is deemed prudent at the time, more often than not leaving it to the individual to search for the truth but in sport things are quite different. In sport, statistics are beyond dispute. And that the figure representing the impact of the universities on English rugby will inevitably become a victim of the law of diminishing returns is an irrelevance.

Anthony Gotley studied law at Brasenose College and won his Blue at scrum-half in the 1909 Varsity Match that saw Oxford register the biggest score in the series to date. Nine tries helped make up the 35 points, all scored by the men on the wings, and all seven Oxford backs on the day would play the game at international level. At this stage, Gotley was yet to be capped but three months later he made his debut for England at the imposing Parc des Princes in Paris.

After four years spent playing friendly matches, France entered the Championship in 1910 and four teams became five. The previous meetings between the two countries ended with comfortable victories for England and perhaps it was with this in mind that the selectors decided to introduce eight new caps for the visit to Paris. Earlier in the season, England had beaten Wales and drawn the match with Ireland, results hardly warranting a knee jerk reaction so perhaps there was an element of confidence reflected in the selection. England prevailed, winning the closest match yet between the two countries, but it was a much stronger looking team that headed for Inverleith for the final match of the season with only three players introduced in Paris included, Anthony Gotley continuing at scrum-half.

In 1911 England were an indifferent team, neither good nor bad. They won two matches and lost two with little to suggest what the next three seasons would produce. Gotley assumed the captaincy in the final match, a home victory over Scotland, but only five of the players selected featured in the back to back Grand Slam triumphs that England would soon claim. For Gotley the result brought a satisfactory end to his international career and within 12 months he was in Rhodesia not destined to return to England on a permanent basis for almost 25 years.

When war broke out in Western Europe, the impact went far beyond the immediate boundaries of the major protagonists. Germany had long since harboured desires to colonise parts of southern Africa. In 1914, there were large military and civilian German populations in South West Africa and German East Africa (now Namibia and Tanzania). Gotley spent the war years in East Africa where British Forces joined ranks with Boer regiments to keep rail links and trade routes open and the German Protectorate was eventually reclaimed. In the period of stabilisation following the armistice Gotley was appointed Assistant Political Officer and later District Commissioner of Tanganyika. He relocated to South Africa in 1926 and established business interests in Durban. He remained there for a decade before beginning to make his way home via an educational appointment at a Dublin College and finally returned to England in 1936. With another

European conflict inevitable, Gotley joined the RAF Volunteer Reserve serving as a Flight Lieutenant with Fighter Command before becoming Squadron Leader in 1941.

Anthony Gotley had a legal background, not ideal preparation for the military campaigns in which he acquitted himself so well. For **Anthony Novis** however, a chosen career in the Army ensured that he would be among the first to see action. That the two men shared a Christian name is almost insignificant when considering other factors that link the pair; certainly, there was an age disparity but by attending Brasenose College, winning an Oxford Blue, joining Blackheath before going on to represent Surrey, the Barbarians and England, Novis followed a path well trodden by Gotley 20 years earlier.

First capped in 1929, Tony Novis played for England seven times over a four year period appearing on both left and right wing and in the centre after being introduced to the game as an outside-half. In 1930, he starred on the British Lions tour to Australia and New Zealand playing in three of the five Tests where he was top try scorer with 16 tries. Whether his army career interrupted his rugby isn't clear but on returning from the tour he was not selected for England again until 1933. Fellow tourist Carl Aarvold was captain during much of this period but following a home defeat to Wales, lost his place to Novis who not only earned an overdue recall but also assumed the captaincy. Ireland were accounted for with some style and the new captain celebrated his return by scoring two of the five tries. A month later at Murrayfield the momentum could not be maintained and Tony Novis together with five other England players had won their last caps.

Novis captained the Army and led the Combined Services when they played the All Blacks in 1935 but on each of his England appearances he is listed as a Blackheath player. The Army and the Royal Air Force cannot claim any direct affinity with an England captain largely because, like Novis, many of the players associated with the Services played their club rugby elsewhere. We shall see in a later chapter that the Royal Navy fared rather better largely due to the United Services, Portsmouth and Devonport Services—clubs with very competitive fixture lists. Aldershot Services and the Royal Air Force College, Cranwell regularly appear in the fixture lists of the day but the level of competition was generally not of the same standard and any player with international aspirations inevitably went elsewhere to play his club rugby. A perfect example of this is Tony Novis, a career soldier until he retired with the rank of Lieutenant Colonel in 1954 but he played for Blackheath and all records relating to his international appearances read—A.L. Novis (Blackheath).

For much of Novis' playing career the Army's representative on the RFU was **Major-General Sir Basil Alexander Hill**, KBE, CB, DSO. Basil Hill attended the Royal Naval Engineering College at Keyham and played rugby for the United Services, but it was with the Army that he began to build an outstanding military career. This was a move that necessitated he find a rugby club, one which would appreciate the arrival of a strapping second-row forward, and it was at Blackheath that the search ended.

It would be futile to attempt to do justice to the military exploits of such a highly decorated individual within the context of this book but suffice to say that Basil Hill gained three mentions in Despatches during the First World War and during the Second World War he was Colonel Commandant of the Royal Electrical Mechanical Engineers.

What we must try and do justice to however are his international rugby exploits which began with a first cap against Ireland. To say that England was an indifferent side in 1903 would be an extreme understatement. The year started with a comprehensive defeat at Swansea following which Hill received his telegram but there was little improvement seen in Dublin or at Richmond where Scotland made sure there was no end to the misery. In truth England were in the middle of a cycle of matches that over a period of nine years showed that when two of the Championship matches were away the team struggled. In 1899, 1901, 1903, 1905 and 1907 England lost all three Championship matches, seasons in which the team had take to the road twice.

It was a time for players to keep their heads down, get on with the games and hope that when the selectors wielded their axe, they would be granted another chance. Hill had nine chances spread over five seasons and was captain for the last two. Against France in 1907, England ran up a record score since the introduction of a points system. Hill had yet to make his mark on the score sheet but his elevation to captain allowed him to determine who should be responsible for goal kicking. By allocating the task to himself he garnered some international points converting five of England's nine tries but it was very different a week later. Wales scored six tries in a 22–0 victory that marked the end of Hill's international rugby. Twenty years later, he made his name as a leading administrator, a role in which Basil Hill excelled. In addition to representing the Army on the RFU he was elected junior vice-president and senior vice-president before becoming the 36th president in 1937; a more appropriate end to a life in rugby than leaving the field at St Helens, Swansea following a comprehensive defeat.

Readers can be forgiven for thinking that joining Blackheath meant a player had to come armed with a degree from either Oxford or Cambridge, be a lawyer, doctor or stockbroker or serve his country with distinction when duty called and in all likelihood end up in a senior administrative post within the RFU. That many achieved one, two or even three of these criteria has been confirmed but no captain achieved all four. It is something of a relief to come across one who doesn't lay claim to any of them. His name was **Murray Wyatt Marshall** and he attended Wellington College in his formative years. He became a timber merchant and because he was born in 1853, was too old for active service in 1914. It was Surrey CCC that benefited from any administrative inclinations he might have had.

Murray Marshall was the sixth man to captain England, his opportunity coming at Lansdowne Road on 11 March 1878, the occasion of his 10th consecutive cap. For Marshall the role of captain was a new experience but there is a perfectly logical reason for the appointment. For the match in Dublin the selectors introduced eight new caps and of those with previous international experience Marshall appeared to be the more suitable candidate. Behind the scrum, A.W. Pearson and Albert Hornby were the only previously capped players but the selectors were yet to allow a back get his hands on the controls, while the four forwards who had been included before could only jointly claim two more caps than Marshall so who better to lead the team? Murray Marshall is one of 31 players to have captained England once but his achievement, and that of the other 30 players, is none the less for that. What does stand him apart from his contemporaries however is his record of 10 consecutive appearances over a five year period, something that no other player bettered for 36 years.

Reflecting on England's wretched away form during the early 1900s one is also left wondering about the home performances which between 1900 and 1909 only produced six victories. Perhaps the term 'home' is slightly misleading as at the end of the 1909 Championship England had entertained visiting teams at no less than 11 different venues. The RFU recognised the need to play all fixtures at the same location but finding somewhere suitable was proving difficult.

In 1907, the RFU decided to purchase 10¼ acres of land at Twickenham, far from convinced about the location which was 12 miles from the city with only a rail link providing public transport. A certain Billy Williams was nothing if not a persuasive individual and he convinced the committee that in years to come the purchase would prove to be a sound one. The land may have been acquired but there was much to be done and it was three years before rugby was played on what became known as 'Billy Williams' cabbage patch.'

Three years earlier the RFU took the unprecedented step of appointing a full-time secretary. This was a salaried position in which Percy Coles became the first man paid to assist in the running of the Union from offices located near the Strand in central London. In 1907, **Charles Marriott** succeeded him and remained in office for 17 years, a period during which the purchase and early development of the famous ground was completed. The RFU eventually moved the offices to the new facility and while building work continued, it was not unusual to see the new secretary riding around the plot on horseback or taking an afternoon nap in a pile of straw. Who was Charles Marriott? What was the background of this larger than life character now helping to guide the RFU into a new era?

Educated at Blackheath Proprietary School and later Tonbridge School, Charles Marriott went up to Cambridge University in 1881 and played in three Varsity Matches for the light blues but even the inclusion of this particularly abrasive forward did not halt a period of extended Oxford supremacy and the Cambridge team lost all three matches. In 1884, he won his first cap against Wales and retained his place through a Triple Crown winning season. Absent in 1885, he was included for the start of the 1886 Championship and another meeting with the Welsh, this time at his club ground in Blackheath. E.T. Gurdon led England to eight consecutive victories over the previous three seasons but was unavailable and Charles Marriott captained the team against Wales and again in Dublin. England won both matches extending the unbeaten run to 10 but Gurdon returned to reclaim the captaincy for the trip to Edinburgh.

Marriott was variously described as a schoolmaster, professional secretary, landowner and lord of the manor. But perhaps it is for one of his lesser-known contributions to rugby football that students of the game, the press and the man on the terrace should be most grateful. In 1913 he founded *The Rugby Football Annual*, a publication full of statistics and much other invaluable content. It continued life as *The Playfair Rugby Football Annual* and later as *Rothman's Rugby Yearbook*. More recently the *IRB International Rugby Yearbook* and the *IRB World Rugby Yearbook* have been published in an attempt to keep a statistically based annual record going. But it was Charles Marriott who originally instigated the concept without which one suspects much of the game's statistical data would be lost.

After travelling around the country for 40 years English rugby now had a home. Twickenham would gain stature in the years that followed and eventually become one of the game's greatest arenas. England played the first international at Twickenham in 1910 and after 40 years of moving matches around the country, it is interesting to note that England did not lose a home Championship match until 1926. Joining England at the new location were the Harlequins, bringing to an end 42 years in which the club had travelled London in search of a home and it was at Twickenham that the Quins would remain until another move in 1963 saw them relocate a mere stone's throw away from what had become known quite simply as HQ.

2

CITY SLICKERS

The Harlequins

What began in Hampstead in 1866 arrived at Twickenham in 1909 via the most circuitous of routes. The Hampstead Football Club played on the famous Heath before relocating to Highbury, the first of several bases that saw the club gradually move south. Swiss Cottage, Catford, Wimbledon Park and Wandsworth Common also played host to the renamed Harlequins Football Club and when the RFU invited former player Billy Williams to find a suitable piece of ground where a permanent home for English rugby could be built, he almost certainly would have had thoughts of incorporating the Harlequins in the project. Cabbage patch it may once have been and there were probing questions to answer regarding transport links, drainage and funding but Williams was a man of vision and time would prove him to have argued his case well.

So Twickenham became a permanent home for England but some months before the gates were opened for international rugby, the Harlequins entertained Richmond in the first game played on the ground. By allowing the Harlequins to take up residency, Twickenham became recognised by the public much quicker than if it had relied on two internationals a year. For the opening game played on 2 October 1909 an estimated 3,500 attended with little more to complain about than a 10 minute walk from the station and the length of the grass. Harlequins defeated their near neighbours and the player credited with scoring the first try at Twickenham was Quins' centre, **John Birkett**. For those members of the press corps in attendance there was a story to be taken from Birkett's endeavours. Though Scotland beat England in the first international, the team did register a try scored by Reginald Birkett. Reginald Birkett was a forward who was capped later as a centre in a team that also included his brother Louis at full-back but more interestingly, he was also the father of John. Reginald Birkett won four caps but there were no more tries whereas for John the try line beckoned rather more frequently.

The move to Twickenham coincided with the first great period in the history of the Harlequins. The club played an enterprising and entertaining brand of rugby which appealed to the public who reacted with their feet; attendances were good wherever they played and the support continued following the relocation to Twickenham. The names of three men in particular became synonymous with this successful era, men who also played for England and went on to captain their country—John Birkett, Adrian Stoop and Charles Hammond.

When John Birkett turned up at Wandsworth Common in 1905 for the Harlequins' trials he was eager to make his mark as a half-back. He was a big man with an ideal build for a position that saw a lot of confrontation with opposing forwards but unbeknownst to him, his future lay elsewhere. The template on which back play had traditionally been based was about to be thrown away, discarded for a new approach, one which would see the ball moved across the three-quarters at speed, the wings given their head and the crowds entertained like never before. The brainchild of Adrian Stoop, this new concept relied on safe hands and accurate passing beginning with what Stoop called the scrum-half, continuing through the mid-field out to the wing. John Birkett's role in this innovative style of play would be in the centre. It was Stoop who saw something in Birkett that leant itself to his radical rethinking on back play and like it or not he was included at his new position in the opening match of the season.

The 1905 Championship saw England in woeful form. All three matches were lost convincingly and after New Zealand won at Crystal Palace later in the year, Wales and Ireland laid to rest any hopes England may have entertained in the 1906 tournament and the losing run now extended to seven matches. This was probably not the time to be called up for a first cap but for John Birkett the opportunity to play for his country came with the announcement of the team to play Scotland. His debut was hardly the stuff of legend but with Adrian Stoop recalled at half-back, the intent to move the ball was clear and tries by both wings helped England to a long overdue victory.

Inverneith to Paris could not have been the easiest of journeys in 1906 but five days after defeating the Scots, England played a first international against France and after being denied success for two years, the team now won a second match within a matter of days. Not yet primed to the demands of international rugby, England beat the French easily allowing Birkett to reflect on a season that had started with his aspirations of becoming a club half-back shattered but ended with him winning two caps in his newly adopted position of centre.

John Birkett was never elected captain at the Harlequins but led England five times; once in 1908 and after a two year break, in four consecutive matches during the 1910 and 1911 Championships. That first outing as captain saw him become England's fifth in as many games but a Welsh victory in Bristol meant the search for a suitable leader continued. The selectors scrutinised four more candidates over the next four games at the end of which the number of rejections increased to eight, Bob Dribble retained throughout the 1909 Championship. This was not quite a recipe for disaster but certainly not a foundation on which to start building a winning team. Captain or not, John Birkett was one of the few players to hold his place and when his international days came to an end in Paris in 1912 he was his country's record cap holder with 21 appearances and no other player had scored more tries for England than Birkett who had 10 to his name.

As Twickenham neared completion within the RFU there was growing concern that England would not have a team worthy of the new facility. Apart from friendlies with France, England won only three matches in the five seasons preceding the grand opening. For the Harlequins there were no such concerns. The players gradually embraced **Adrian Stoop's** revolutionary philosophy and the results followed. Off the field Stoop had worked equally hard to ensure that the Harlequins could take up residence at the new ground. He and Billy Williams became allies, their case strengthened by the support the Quins built up because of the style of rugby now associated with the club. Williams knew that Twickenham would struggle to establish itself purely on the strength of international rugby whereas by subletting the ground to the Harlequins, followers of the game would soon forget all the arguments voiced regarding its location. For an annual rent of £100.00, the Harlequins secured the use of Twickenham for all home matches during the seasons 1909–11 and lest there should be a change of heart by the RFU, Stoop ensured that an application for an extension was quickly submitted.

Who was Adrian Stoop? In a short period, this man had become one of the game's great thinkers on the field. Where had he come from? The smart money would be on Rugby School followed by Oxford University and it would be right. It was at Rugby that Harlequins first spotted Adrian Stoop when they sent a second team to play the school first XV. That was in 1900 and a year later Stoop played his first game for the Quins where he remained for the rest of his days, finally hanging up his boots in 1938 but continuing his association with the club in an administrative capacity. His commitment was total and when the Harlequins moved from Twickenham to a new ground across the road it was a mark of the high esteem in which the club held him in that the Stoop Memorial Ground should bear his name.

Stoop was a law student but he was also a very fine rugby player and he had to divide his time between lectures and training. He won three Blues and was captain for the 1904–05 season at the end of which he won his first cap, the only time he represented the university while on England duty. This was against Scotland and Stoop had to wait a year before being invited back, a pattern which would recur during his seven years of international rugby. Injury and inconsistent selection policies restricted the number of caps he won to 15 but he grabbed every opportunity that came his way with relish. He had a huge impact on the English game best demonstrated by 60 seconds of magic that gave the new ground at Twickenham the best possible introduction as the new home of English rugby.

In 1906, Adrian Stoop first became captain of the Harlequins and remained so until the outbreak of war in 1914. At the start of the 1909–10 season and the move to Twickenham, his visionary ideas for three-quarter play had started to reap rewards. In addition to John Birkett the club recruited other players to fit into his master plan and the first season at the new ground proved to be the Quin's best to date, only four of the 24 matches lost. Stoop was playing regularly again after two broken collarbones had sidelined him for much of the previous two seasons which obviously restricted his England appearances—he had last played for his country in 1907. Fit again, the new season and new ground saw him strike such a rich vein of form that his international recall looked imminent.

Twickenham began duty as an international rugby stadium on 15 January 1910. Wales were the visitors and in front of a crowd of 18,000, which included the Prince of Wales, Adrian Stoop led England for the first time. The officials delayed the kick off as spectators searched for their seats or jostled for the best vantage point on the packed terraces. There were certainly many who would later boast, 'I was there,' but not all of them saw what happened when Welsh forward Ben Gronow got the game underway.

Stoop fielded the ball and appeared to prepare himself to do the expected—kick for touch. Throughout his long and successful career the one thing that Adrian Stoop could never be accused of was playing the percentages, taking the safe option and on this auspicious occasion he certainly didn't disappoint. From the right of the field an arcing run quickly took him over to the left leaving a wrong-footed Welsh defence in his wake. A cross-kick collected in mid-field followed by three quick passes back to the left put Fred Chapman over for the first international try scored on the famous ground—it hadn't been a minute in coming. Wales were beaten and a month later, England returned to Twickenham, Stoop leading his men again in a hard fought match against Ireland. The game ended scoreless much to the dissatisfaction of many of the RFU bigwigs who were all too quick in pointing an accusing finger at the captain. Next up were France. But not for a friendly match, the French included for the first time in an expanded Championship. The selectors didn't disappoint. They did what they did best; wielded the axe—eight new caps, a new captain and a 'rested' Stoop, with only five of the team that played against Wales a matter of weeks earlier included. England delivered the expected result. But what was going on? What exactly was the rationale behind team selection?

The match in Paris saw Anthony Gotley make his debut at scrum-half and for the final game of the season at Inverleith he was partnered by Stoop in the first of five consecutive matches to feature the pair at half-back. The selectors' prevarications may have seen Stoop recalled but they handed back the captaincy to John Birkett two years after he first held the responsibility. By beating the Scots, England won the inaugural Five Nations Championship and only the team's draw with Ireland prevented its first Grand Slam. This was a successful season by any standards and the selectors would undoubtedly have considered it a job well done but that only four players appeared in all four games suggests the results were achieved by accident rather than by design. Stoop never captained England again but the RFU weren't quite so reticent when electing the men to represent the governing body and after making his way through the accepted path to the top—junior vice-president, senior vice-president, member of the International Board and national selector—Adrian Stoop was elected president of the RFU in 1932.

Adrian Stoop and John Birkett enjoyed great success with both club and country. They played in the same England side 14 times, Stoop with the player he converted from half-back to centre waiting outside him for the well timed pass that would unleash the men out wide. This was all very well in principle and on the training field the movement of the ball through five pairs of hands could be practised until it was perfect. When the exercise was completed, Stoop's 'scrum-half' could grab another ball and begin the process again…and again…and again. Of course, transferring a routine that had become second nature during training sessions onto the field of play presented problems—first the backs had to get their hands on the ball.

Rugby union has always been a game for forwards—in its infancy there were 13 forwards on the field but it is doubtful that even that number was as much of a nuisance in open play as the eight we see today. The game belongs to the big men, it is theirs to win or lose; a team can always determine the outcome of matches if they have good forwards and poor backs but rarely the reverse. Adrian Stoop obviously had other ideas and it surely took all his persuasive skills to convert the men up front to his way of thinking. However, in **Charles Hammond** he had the best of allies.

Today 'Curly' Hammond would be termed a loose forward—particularly mobile and a ferocious tackler. His days at Oxford University ended as Stoop's were about to begin but they were frequently selected together for the Harlequins. When Stoop came down from Oxford in the spring of 1905, he was chosen as club vice-captain for the following season, with Hammond re-elected for a fourth successive term as captain.

Earlier in the year, the pair made their international debuts against Scotland at Richmond in the final Championship match of the season. It was an ignominious start with England losing and picking up another wooden spoon, something to which the team was becoming uncomfortably attached. The selectors kept faith with Hammond throughout the following season but it took a further three defeats before Stoop was recalled for the games against Scotland and France, the only occasions on which the three distinguished Harlequins' played together for England.

After Birkett's first outing as captain in 1908, the selectors next invited 'Curly' Hammond to take over what was becoming something of a poisoned chalice. Ireland were the visitors to Richmond looking for a fourth consecutive victory over England but under Hammond, the men in white prevailed. Did the selectors rejoice in a rare success? Did they congratulate Hammond and his men for a job well done and invite them en bloc to go and repeat the deed a month later in Scotland? Did they heck as like! They made multiple changes to the team including new caps at full-back and outside-half together with the almost mandatory new captain. Charles Hammond was replaced in the team by a man who may have deserved a chance to represent his country but who was never invited back. Neither was Hammond.

English rugby would soon embark on a period of unprecedented success in which wooden spoons would be replaced by Grand Slams and but for the outbreak of war how great might the team have become? Between them Birkett, Hammond and Stoop captained England eight times and the four victories they engineered were about par for the course during what was certainly a turbulent era. The RFU's opening of Twickenham is recognised as the beginning of a new dawn for the international game in England. Records will always substantiate such claims but in recognising what followed the Wales game of 1910 we should not lose sight of what went before. Before this the England team suffered years of little success on the field but this lack of success laid the foundations for a team that would do justice to the arena they were soon to enter. John Birkett, Charles Hammond and Adrian Stoop were all key in establishing these foundations.

Twickenham will celebrate its centenary during the 2009–10 season. It is unrecognisable from the twin stands and open terraces that introduced the now famous ground to the rugby public; unrecognisable because of the rugby public which has grown beyond all expectation. Over 50 years have passed since the Harlequins relocated to The Stoop on the other side of the busy A316. As the final stage in the redevelopment of Twickenham got underway so were the builders packing up their tools across the road having completed a major upgrade at the home of the Quins.

Bob Hiller arrived at the Harlequins at the time of the relocation and continues his involvement half a century later in his role of club president. Fresh from a year at Oxford University where he won cricket and rugby Blues, Hiller made a commitment to the Quins after turning out for the club while a student at Birmingham and Oxford Universities. He was soon recognised as a goal kicking full-back. Unfortunately for Hiller the 1960s was a decade which saw the emergence of some outstanding players who were prepared to put their bodies and reputations on the line in the most exposed position on the field. Hiller was more likely to be included at outside-half for the Harlequins while England full-back **John Willcox** remained in residence at full-back.

John Willcox was an all round sportsman who arrived at rugby largely thanks to the concerted efforts of a master at Ratcliffe College. Football, cricket, hockey and even the noble art all featured in his time at college but when he arrived at Sandhurst for two years National Service he made his final choices with rugby and boxing taking priority. Then it was up to Oxford for a three year degree course which ultimately became a four year course, a direct result of Willcox's prowess on the rugby field.

I did spend four years at Oxford. I went to Worcester College to study modern languages which effectively meant French, but also included Latin and medieval French. I was due to sit my finals in the summer of 1962 but there was a suggestion that I would be invited to tour South Africa with the British Lions and I looked into the possibility of delaying the exams. I found out that Balliol College had given Richard Sharp permission to go on the tour so I asked if I could put my finals back a year. Initially I got a negative reaction but when I mentioned that Sharp was being allowed to tour the college decided I could come back for a fourth year with the proviso that I spend one of the terms in France which I was delighted to do.

The 1962 British Lions may not have been a success in terms of the Test series which the Springboks won but for Willcox it proved a personal triumph. He played in 15 matches including three Tests, finishing the tour as top scorer with 67 points. Next up was the promised term in France and what proved to be a totally different rugby experience.

I look back on my three months in Paris with great affection; I met some wonderful people, it was great fun. I played for Le PUC, Paris University Club, which was an open club—anyone could play for them. The fixture list was strong; we played all the major teams that meant a lot of matches in the south of France necessitating long overnight train journeys in couchettes with no windows, smelly bodies and so on. That wasn't so great!

I remember playing in a cup game in Paris. A scrum was formed in the middle of the field and suddenly it erupted, the forwards fighting like hell. Then the two three-quarter lines squared up to each other and to my horror I saw their full-back running at me from 50 yards away. It was like a car crash in slow motion but the referee blew up and it stopped almost immediately. The upshot of it all was that the opposition hooker who was selected to play against England the following week was banned and couldn't take his place in the team.

We had a lovely chap playing in the second-row who I only remember by his nickname Fifi; something I never could understand. We'd travelled to the south for a match and were waiting on the platform for the train to take us back to Paris when the team suddenly burst into song at which Fifi proceeded to strip off. There were a couple of policemen there but they just laughed along with passers by. Fifi was a hideous sight, going bald with some horrible black body hair but it was all done in such good spirit. Then there was the occasion when I had been playing for England at Twickenham. Le PUC won an important cup match on the Sunday afternoon and when my plane arrived at Orly late that night, the players all came out on the team coach to meet me. Somehow two air hostesses became involved and they were gathered up and taken onto the bus and to this day I've never discovered whether they were meant to come with us or not.

John Willcox was forced to miss England's tour to New Zealand and Australia in 1963. 'I couldn't go. The university would not have let me go a second time. I didn't even ask, there was no point. I had to sit my finals but remember listening to the Tests on the radio and thinking how well Roger Hosen was playing and wondering if I would get my place back.' Not only did Willcox reclaim his place but he was also asked to captain England against the fifth All Blacks when they visited Twickenham in January 1964.

In hindsight I feel quite guilty about it. Mike Weston had obviously done a really good job on the tour but the selectors invited me to captain the team against New Zealand. Of course I was delighted but looking back I can't help feeling the thing was badly mismanaged. There were changes in the forwards after the pack had played so well earlier in the year and Malcolm Phillips was moved out to the wing where he had never played before. Malcolm was a wonderful centre, one of the best in the British Isles, one of the few who could make a good outside break; he should never have been put on the wing. Mike Weston kept his place in the centre and Phil Horrocks-Taylor played at outside-half. There was a point during the game when it crossed my mind to swap them around for a few scrums and let Mike launch some of his big up and unders to put full-back Don Clarke under pressure. Mike had a wonderful boot and I felt it could be put to good use from stand-off but I didn't dare make the change; I didn't have the nerve to tell Phil to swap with Mike for a bit which I still regret. A week or so later Mike was playing stand-off for the North-Eastern Counties against the All Blacks and he did exactly that; put Clarke under pressure with some of his huge kicks and within a few minutes the counties were 11–0 up after scoring two tries because the full-back had been caught out.

I can tell you quite categorically that full-back is the last position you want your captain to play, certainly at international level where communication is extremely difficult. You can probably get away with it in club rugby but at Twickenham, for example, the noise is deafening and you can't hear anything from the full-back position where you seem to be miles away from the action making it impossible to exert any control. I think it is amazing that players such as Gavin Hastings and Andy Irving both captained Scotland from full-back with enormous success but how they did it I just do not know. I suppose nowadays the full-back links up much more but when I was playing we were expected to stay deep in defence which effectively cut us off from the team.

These comments are interesting when talking about New Zealand, a country yet to appoint a full-back as captain in a capped match. If the selectors ever gave the issue any serious thought Don Clarke might have been asked to break the habit but the offer never came.

A few years ago I had the chance to meet Don Clarke again; we'd swapped jerseys after the England game but I'd no further contact with him. I was playing in an annual golf tournament in Bolton and met a chap from Cheshire who had hosted Clarke on the tour and they'd kept in touch. He told me Don was coming over to be inducted into the Rugby Hall of Fame and would be coming to stay with him for a few days—would I like to meet him? At this time, I was teaching at Ampleforth College and suggested the two men and their wives join me for lunch. The four of them came and later in the day I took them home for tea before they headed back—I gave Don a lift and the others followed. We had the usual reminisce and then I asked him what he had done after he retired from the game. It materialised that he took up golf and as I was no mean golfer, I decided it was my chance to get the better of bloody Don Clarke. I manoeuvred the conversation around to golf and asked how much he had played, waiting for the opportunity to find out what his handicap was. I used to play off a single figure handicap and was confident that this would better him but when I finally asked the question he told me he had played off plus two! Because of rugby he'd competed with the likes of Nicklaus, Palmer and Player and in one particular year had played 214 matches—I couldn't believe it. If he'd taken up cricket or some other sport I don't doubt he'd have been outstanding.

Willcox retained his place in the team for the 1964 Championship but after a draw with Wales and defeat by Ireland the captaincy went to the Northampton prop Ron Jacobs. Wilcox remained at full-back but there were undermining factors which effectively saw his international career finish at the end of the season.

When I got the job at Ampleforth College they were good enough to let me continue playing for the Harlequins which invariably meant leaving early on a Friday afternoon. It was a hell of a long way to travel and after a couple of years. I decided I couldn't do it any more. I ended up spending a season at Headingley. Then the headmaster asked me when I was going to stop playing. I was responsible for the school team but never saw them play which was far from ideal so the time had arrived when I had to call it a day. I suppose you could say that my job stopped me playing but I wouldn't blame the headmaster for that, he had his responsibilities and had been more than accommodating in the past. This change did however give me the opportunity to spend a couple of seasons playing for Malton but only during the holidays. I played half a dozen maybe eight games a season but I was allowed to play fly-half which was thrilling because I always believed I would make a wonderful fly-half!

As well as playing golf, Willcox also boxed during his time at Oxford:

It was a very painful business. I had to fight at heavyweight for Oxford because there was a light-heavyweight who had fought in the previous year. I had six bouts and quickly became known as the 'Horizontal Heavyweight'. The last competition before the Varsity Match was against the Channel Islands and at last I came up against a chap who was slightly shorter than me but he turned out to be a real pro. He hadn't shaved and as we parted after the first clinch he took all the skin off my face and then he hit me straight on the break, knocked me flat out. Much to my astonishment as I clambered to my feet the referee asked me if I was all right and to my even greater astonishment, I said yes—then he hit me again. I woke up a couple of minutes later surrounded by people in white coats with the strangest feeling. I wasn't in any pain but I was just ashamed that I had performed so badly in front of all these people in Oxford Town Hall. They took me to the Radcliffe Hospital and wouldn't release me until I signed a form to say that if I died it was my own fault. I woke up the next morning and the room was still spinning. It wouldn't be allowed now but three weeks later I fought a chap from Cambridge called Butch Hill and came second again. That was enough.

With Willcox removed from the equation, Don Rutherford and Roger Hosen both enjoyed extended runs at full-back but the team struggled to find any consistency despite the selectors showing a greater level of patience than so often seen in the past. When England lost to New Zealand at Twickenham in 1967, it marked the end of seven international careers: five forwards including the entire front row; a debutant at scrum-half; and full-back Don Rutherford. For eight years Willcox, Rutherford and Hosen had monopolised the full-back berth but when the team to play Wales in the opening fixture of the 1968 Championship was announced, included among eight new caps was **Bob Hiller** and a new era of English full-backs was about to begin.

Between January 1968 and February 1972 Bob Hiller won 19 caps, scored in every match and ran up a total of 138 points making him England's most capped full-back and record points scorer after a century of international rugby. He led his country seven times, the highlight coming at Twickenham in December 1969 when England recorded a first victory over the Springboks. Two months later England beat Ireland in the opening match of the Five Nations. These were the only games won under Hiller's captaincy despite his prolific goal kicking which gave some much needed respectability to several otherwise embarrassing results, perhaps most notably a 14–14 draw with France, Hiller scoring all England's points in his last match as captain.

Following his first season of international rugby, he toured South Africa with the British Lions scoring 104 points in eight appearances. Three years later, he made a second tour, this time to Australia and New Zealand where he clocked up 110 points in 11 matches. That he didn't play in any of the Tests is down to the presence of Irish full-back and Lions' captain Tom Keirnan in 1968 and the irrepressible J.P.R. Williams in 1971 but his contribution to both tours was enormous. In New Zealand, he was given the honour of leading the mid-week team against Wairarapa-Bush.

If his record of being on the losing side only once in 19 outings in a Lions' jersey could have been replicated during his 19 appearances for England there would have been much to celebrate. Looking at the team sheets of the period many great names jump off the page leaving one to question why so much talent fared so badly. On this occasion the reasons are not to be found within but rather by looking elsewhere; to France and Wales which were the Championship's dominant forces at the time leaving the rest to contest the minor positions and hope they would avoid the wooden spoon. This balance of power was reflected when the party of 30 players to represent the 1971 British Lions was announced with only five Englishmen included. Hiller, David Duckham, John Spencer and John Pullin could not be denied their places on past form but **Peter Dixon** was yet to play international rugby, his first cap won against the RFU President's XV in a match played as part of the centenary celebrations that took place shortly after the touring party had been named.

Dixon was approaching his 27th birthday when he won his first cap. The rugby public must have wondered what he had to do to gain recognition but the truth of the matter was that while the selectors may have had problems finding the right players in several positions, the three back row berths were not among them. David Rollitt, Bob Taylor and Charlie Hannaford were the players recently favoured at number 8 leaving Dixon to bide his time. To suggest a 27 year old player who had started out as a schoolboy prop before moving back into the second-row and later converting to number 8, was still to find his best position seems ridiculous.

This was the case for Peter Dixon.

A student of social anthropology, Dixon spent three years at Durham University followed by five years at St Edmunds Hall, Oxford. It was at Oxford that he moved to the middle of the back row winning four Blues at number 8. When the elusive first England cap finally came, he succeeded Bob Taylor in the same position. But all 21 caps that followed were at number 6, as a blind side wing forward following the reinvention of a most talented player

The final positional change came about on the 1971 British Lions' tour. Competition for places in the back row was fierce. Mervyn Davies, John Taylor and the uncapped Derek Quinnell from Wales together with Ireland's Mick Hipwell and Fergus Slattery joined Dixon in the search to find the right balance necessary to make the perfect back row, one which would upset the All Blacks in an area of the game where they were traditionally at their strongest. The six players mentioned above were all worthy of inclusion in a Test 15 but when injury prematurely ended Hipwell's tour a week before the crucial first Test, it was Peter Dixon who packed down alongside Davies and Taylor. The unit played together in three of four Tests in a memorable series that saw the Lions victorious for the first time in New Zealand and on his return the England selectors never considered Peter Dixon as anything other than a blind side flanker.

For English rugby, the 1972 Championship was memorable, not because of a Grand Slam or even a Triple Crown but rather as a campaign that was best forgotten; if any season could be removed from the record books then the 1971–72 season would probably get the vote, it really was that bad. In 1910, the International Rugby Championship included France for the first time. Since when, England had always managed to secure a win or at the very least a draw—until 1972. For the first time England lost all four Championship matches and against France and Scotland, Peter Dixon led the team after taking over from Bob Hiller. Two comprehensive defeats brought this most miserable of seasons to a welcome end but out of the wreckage one positive did emerge—1972 saw the introduction of one of the best back rows ever to play for England. Playing alongside Peter Dixon was open side wing forward Tony Neary who already had six caps to his name. And a rangy, long haired number 8 from Rosslyn Park who was the complete antithesis of anyone who had previously worn an England jersey—Andy Ripley. Outstanding though this trio most certainly was they were unable to reverse England's woeful Championship performances which continued throughout a decade of largely Franco-Welsh domination.

Harlequin's lost their man in 1972 when Dixon relocated to Newcastle and joined Gosforth where he remained for the rest of his career. He helped Gosforth to enormous success during a period that saw few matches lost and culminated in back to back cup victories in 1976 and 1977 which may well have been his best days at Twickenham. Peter Dixon was unfortunate not to have enjoyed more international success with England but his standing in the game is none the less for that. Some back row combinations just roll off the tongue, brilliant individual players who together form a dynamic unit; Neary, Ripley and Dixon were the Back, Dallaglio and Hill of their day. Such combinations come around all too infrequently but when they arrive are worth the entrance money alone— English rugby is waiting.

The back row consists of three specialist positions, Peter Dixon more than capable in two of them. Each position has designated responsibilities but at the same time, the three forwards have to combine to make a unit that is as effective in attack as it is in defence and most importantly there has to be a balance. Far too often players are considered able to play anywhere in the back row and there are some who have proved capable of doing so but they are few in number and a very special breed indeed; think Lawrence Dallaglio and to a lesser extent Richard Hill.

On the resumption of international rugby following the end of the Second World War, the selectors had to pretty much start from scratch. The first back row selection consisted of Mickey Steele-Bodger (an out and out open side flanker), Don White (a traditional blind side) and Australian born Basil Travers at number 8. Following a rout at the hands of the Irish who scored 22 unanswered points, there was a new face in the middle of the back row for the home match against Scotland.

Robert Weighill was from the north-west. On leaving Wirral Grammar School he joined the local constabulary and played his club rugby at Birkenhead Park and Waterloo and but for the outbreak of war he may well have remained in the police force. When he joined the RAF things changed and Bob Weighill found his true vocation in life, but first there was a war to get through before he could entertain any thoughts of a full time career. A pilot in Fighter Command, Weighill was awarded the Distinguished Flying Cross in 1944 and attained the rank of Flight Lieutenant as the war entered its final stages. Now, he could commit to a future in the RAF with the chance to resurrect his rugby career. Bob Weighill represented and captained the RAF in 10 consecutive Inter Services matches from 1948–52 but it was with the Harlequins that he played much of his senior club rugby and where he first attracted the attention of the England selectors who included him for a first cap against Scotland.

England ended the first post war season on a high beating the Scots and France but a disappointing series of trials later in the year saw Weighill replaced by Brian Vaughan for the matches against the Australian tourists and Wales and Ireland in the Championship. Then it was a case of déjà vu, England recalled Weighill for the game against Scotland and retained him for the trip to Paris where he also led the team. Unlike 12 months earlier, both games ended in defeat and after winning four caps, Bob Weighill's international rugby came to an abrupt end.

He continued to serve in the RAF until 1970, a career that saw him command several operational units both at home and abroad. In 1968, he became ADC to Her Majesty the Queen and retired with the rank of Air Commodore. He was still only 50 years of age and in 1971, Bob Weighill succeeded Robin Prentice to become the sixth full time secretary of the RFU, a position he held for the next 15 years.

It took England 41 years to play 114 international matches, a number matched by the country's record cap holder whose career spanned the years 1990–2004. Nowadays England plays a minimum of 10 internationals each year. With the game firmly entrenched in the era of the 22 man squad, players can win caps as replacements even if their time on the field is a matter of minutes. It doesn't take long for a player to rattle up 30 or 40 caps. For some players much of their international rugby has come about because of their introduction from the bench; be it as a blood replacement, cover for a more serious injury, or as a tactical substitution, the oncoming player gets his cap and the total grows. **Jason Leonard** has to put his hand up—he won 11 caps as a replacement but as he has another 103 caps to his name the whys and wherefores of his time on the bench are of no significance. Here is a player who over a 15-year period gave his all to the cause from a position where men are men and the rest are simply heroes—Leonard falling into the second category.

The front row is no place for the feint hearted. It is an area of the game where most commentators admit ignorance, suggesting a complete understanding of its ramifications can only be gleaned from first hand experience. When the arguments are raging on the terraces, in the stands or in pubs regarding who was responsible for a scrum collapsing or any other of the front row offences that can be leapt on by the referee, don't listen to anybody who hasn't been there. The chances are they won't know what they are talking about. Jason Leonard would know what he was talking about, he would be worth listening to. Leonard has forgotten more about front row play than the 'knowledgeable' pundit will ever learn.

I didn't follow rugby as a kid; it was all soccer and scoring the dream goal at Wembley. A new games master arrived at my school, took one look at the curriculum and asked, '...why aren't you lot doing rugby?' He divided us up into the small and fast ones; those who could kick and pass; the tall, lanky lads; and the short fat ones, which included me, and I ended up in the front row. I suppose I always thought I'd grow out of the position but I stayed the same height and only got wider, but I enjoyed it. For a boisterous young lad with lots of energy to spare, it was a great sport to play. You could actually go and knock lumps out of the opposition and instead of the teacher telling you off you'd get a pat on the back and a 'Well done, keep going'. I loved it but couldn't get my head around the idea that if you did the same thing in the schoolyard you would be up in front of the headmaster; that was what I first liked about the game. Later it would be the camaraderie, the social side and also the respect and the discipline that came with it; rugby looks to be a very ill disciplined sport but it isn't, players have to be very disciplined both technically and mentally. The referee is sacrosanct, you don't abuse or question him and even in my last international I was still calling the referee 'sir'—not many sports compare to rugby in that respect.

If you show a bit of ability at school you start playing up the grades. I was 14 when I first turned out for Barking Rugby Club Under 16s, played for the Under 19s at 15 and the firsts when I was 17 or 18. The Saracens were the big local side and I had the occasional game for the Under 21s coached by a local butcher called Ted Roberts. He would bring sausages and pies for us which we ate standing around the back of his car after the match—I enjoyed it. When I played for England Under 19s all the big clubs had their scouts out watching—Saracens, who already knew me,

Harlequins, Wasps and Blackheath all expressed an interest. I needed some advice so I spoke to three guys at Barking who had played some senior rugby. They all suggested that a season spent playing for Barking firsts would be more beneficial than playing for an Under 21 side where I was unlikely to be pushed. If I stayed at Barking I'd come up against some real old gnarled props who would teach me a thing or two—I would be a better player for it. It was some of the soundest advice I ever received so I stayed a year and then moved to Saracens.

I was very much the baby at Saracens; 19 years of age and just hoping to get some second team rugby. I could have played for the Under 21s but I think I was a bit better than that; then I had my lucky break. One of the first team props went away on honeymoon in the middle of the season. It was a big mistake but it gave me my opportunity to play for the firsts against Bridgend. I was chosen at tight head but the loose head prop pulled out so I switched and another player took over on the tight; he was torn to pieces. The coach couldn't believe it, couldn't understand how a player who had stood up to some of the best props in the country was taken apart by an absolute nobody; nine months later that Welsh nobody was on a Lions' tour—it was Mike Griffiths. It was a lucky break because I've no doubt Mike would have crucified me but I had a reasonable game and kept my place playing sufficiently well so that when Ritchie Andrews came back from honeymoon he couldn't get back in; the coach wouldn't drop me.

The start of my England career was similar really. Paul Rendall was coming to the end of his so I was taken to Argentina, the attitude being to introduce me to the side, give me a bit of experience and if I had a bad game Paul could always come back in. It was a tough tour but the players helped me enormously; Brian Moore, Jeff Probyn, Wade Dooley and Peter Winterbottom were all seasoned internationals and they told me just to get on with my game, not to worry about any mistakes. I was like a sponge on that tour, taking in as much as I could but I thoroughly enjoyed it, what a great opportunity. In the second Test I came up against Diego Cash, one of the best tight heads in the world at the time; I didn't struggle but have to say there were a few scrums where I was a bit wobbly. A couple of months later Argentina came to Twickenham and he didn't give me any problems; my game had come on a lot in a short time. Late on Federico Mendez was sent off for punching Paul Ackford but I was well on top by then.

The two caps Leonard won in Argentina came while he was at Saracens but starting with the match at Twickenham, he won the 112 caps that followed while he was with Harlequins, the club he joined at the start of the 1990–91 season.

When I got back to Saracens after the tour there was an issue that ultimately led to my move to the Quins. We were doing some pre-season training and with the first and second team coaches away on holiday the sessions were taken by the guy who ran the thirds. The Saracens' ground at Bramley Road was either concrete or mud; there was never any grass on it. The coach decided we should do some scrummaging, the firsts against the seconds, but it was obvious that we couldn't get any decent purchase with the ground being so hard. Scrum after scrum collapsed and with the players trying to get one over on each other it was like world war three. I told him it was ridiculous trying to scrummage in boots and he finally agreed but told us to go and put trainers on which obviously wasn't going to make any difference, Anyway, we put the trainers on and the same happened by which time I'd had enough. I told him he was having a joke, didn't know what he was doing and he started blaming me for the problem saying it was down to my binding; that was the reason the scrums kept collapsing. Like a proper diva I told him that I had recently been part of the best front row in the f***ing world and he was saying it was my binding; I told him if my binding was f***ing good enough for Brian Moore and Jeff Probyn it was f***ing good enough for him. I walked off and that was the last time I trained with Saracens.

On the tour some of the Harlequins lads asked if I would consider joining the club and I'd said no but a little spat like that makes you think again. I joined the Quins and settled into a pack full of internationals— Brian Moore, Andy Mullins, Paul Ackford, Troy Coker, Mickey Skinner, Peter Winterbottom and Chris Butcher. One season in that pack fast tracked me by four or five years and I knew how much I was coming on when I faced Cash at Twickenham, a guy who had given me a hard time a few months before but not now.

There was a time when, just like a good wine, prop forwards matured with age but since rugby became a professional sport such attitudes have become outdated. Jason Leonard is an exception and his introduction to the England front row at the age of 21 in many ways pre-empted what would follow. Jeff Probyn and Paul Rendall were still playing for England in their mid-thirties, as was Leonard, but at the end of his career he was usually introduced from the bench. With modern training techniques, the correct use of weights and the introduction of greatly improved conditioning, diet and nutrition management the age levels at which front row forwards peak have come down.

So much has changed. Not necessarily in the scrums where technique is as important as ever, but around the field. The work rate these guys have to maintain is huge; prop forwards have to be able to run and pass like a three-quarter, make tackles—when I started out you were expected to make tackles but only when someone ran into you. As for handling the ball, we were actively encouraged not to do it; told to keep out of the way. I used to get up from a scrum, plod along to a ruck, lean on it and when the ball came out make my way to the next ruck and lean on that. Now they sprint from scrum to ruck and blast into them. If the fly-half is caught up in a ruck you will often see a prop step into his position telling the scrum-half to give him the ball. Those are significant changes.

Despite all the changes and the impact they have had on the game some of the basics do need looking at. I'd like to see the ball put in straight at the scrum, something I understand the IRB are looking at. You can have a lineout where the throw in is marginally not straight and the ref blows up and OK, it might have been a bit wonky but when the ball is put into a scrum and its obviously not straight nothing happens and the ref is usually standing right behind the scrum-half. I think there is probably an element of safety in mind and player safety must come above all else but the best way to keep the scrum safe is to keep it up, stop the collapsing because that is when the injuries are going to occur. If a scrum is going to go down there is nothing you can do to stop it, whether it takes one or five seconds if it's going down it's going down. It has got to be sorted out because we don't want the game following rugby league where there is no real contest at the scrum.

As his record suggests, Leonard was not overly troubled by injury but in 1992 he did have a problem that highlights the stresses and strains front row forwards have to put their bodies through.

It was after the game against Wales. Something went pop in my neck. It was a ruptured disc which impacted on all the others and ended up putting pressure on the spinal cord; general wear and tear that had built up over the season. The press started to write me off but I didn't pay much attention to what they said—they hadn't seen my medical records. A guy called John Johnson had and he just happened to be the best spinal injury specialist in the world. He told me that if I wanted to make a complete recovery I had to follow his every word to the letter; if he said I wasn't to do anything for five weeks or not to pick up a weight for three months then I didn't. He was concerned that at my age I might feel I was invincible and be tempted to start playing around with weights and not only undo all the repair work but possibly put myself in a wheelchair for the rest of my life so I listened and I didn't have the problem again. Sure I'm still a bit stiff in the neck but ask any prop what he feels like after 20 years of rugby. I was relatively injury free apart from that although I did break my ankle once and tried to run it off—not a very bright thing to do.

In December 1996, England played Argentina at Twickenham, Leonard leading the team on the occasion of his 50th cap. Dominated by penalty kicks the game did produce one try scored by the England captain. This was the only one he would claim in international rugby. Mike Catt kicked five penalties for England and Gonzalo Quesada responded with six for the visitors and the 20–18 final score confirms how important Leonard's effort was. Seven years later he led what was seen as a second string side against Wales in Cardiff. This was a warm up match before the Rugby World Cup and many of the players were still hoping to be included in the squad to travel to Australia. England won the match comfortably. And that none of the players who started the match in Cardiff were in the team that took the field against Australia in the final three months later confirms how much strength in depth there was in English rugby at the time.

We struggled against Argentina. It was one of those days when the forwards did really well, won a wealth of ball for the backs but they couldn't string two or three passes together. Will Carling was still playing and he kept insisting that we gave them the ball but with 10 minutes remaining we were losing and I had to tell him they weren't getting any more, I was going to keep it in the forwards. We had a run of lineouts and mauls up the East Stand side and the only way Argentina could stop us was by infringing so eventually we got over the line. It wasn't a purist's try run in from 60 yards; it was run in from more like three yards and in saying that I'm probably flattering myself.

We'd learnt a lot since the 1991 World Cup final when the inability to change a game plan probably cost us the match and I wasn't going to let it happen again; we'd tried something for 70 minutes that hadn't worked so it had to be changed. The team I led against Wales was extremely fired up, all the players still in with a chance of making the squad for the World Cup. We were used to playing Wales in the winter and now the sun was shining and the pitch was good; we hit the ground running and caught them cold. The players couldn't believe how easily we won.

Jason Leonard played in his fourth World Cup in 2003. He didn't start in the final but was introduced from the bench for the crucial period of extra time. He was the only player from either England or Australia who had also played in the final at Twickenham 12 years earlier. The two finals all but coincided with the start and end of Jason Leonard's record breaking career in which he was a cornerstone of the front row in four Grand Slam winning teams. An obvious selection for the three British Lions tours of 1993, 1997 and 2001 Leonard won five Test caps and had the responsibility of leading the mid-week team in three matches in South Africa in 1997.

The clock had been ticking for a while. Popping up at outside-half when that player was engaged at the bottom of a ruck was beginning to take its toll and after the World Cup final and an emotional last run out at Twickenham, England's most capped player called it a day. His is a record to admire and it will be some time before it is equalled, if that day ever comes, but for now Jason Leonard sits at the top of the pile. At the time of writing, there isn't a member of the current England squad remotely near him.

John Birkett did it five times, Charles Hammond and Bob Weighill only the once. Adrian Stoop had two cracks at it as did Peter Dixon and Jason Leonard with John Willcox getting a third chance while Bob Hiller led his country seven times. Eight players who between them captained England 23 times. This brings us to the last player in this chapter who could surely justify a chapter to himself such is the measure of his record as England captain. Space will not allow such extravagancies but in that which is available justice must be seen to be done in the name of **William David**

Charles Carling.

Sedburgh School, Durham University and the Royal Military Academy, Sandhurst are three renowned establishments that all played their part in the academic and formative years of Will Carling. But the outcome would not see a son following in his father's footsteps. Unlike father Bill, the life on offer in the British Army did not hold the same appeal for Will and when he returned from England's summer tour in 1988 he resigned his commission, bought himself out of the Army and set about becoming one of the most famous rugby players on the planet—it was as simple as that.

England played nine matches in 1988. The first was at the start of the Five Nations and a trip to Paris that saw the international bow of Will Carling. Against Australia in the last match of the year, Carling won his eighth cap on the day he captained his country for the first time. It was England manager Geoff Cooke who saw something that escaped most observers when he appointed Carling, not just against Australia but also with the long term in mind. Strong claims could have been made on behalf of Rob Andrew, Simon Halliday or Rory Underwood among the backs with Brian Moore, Wade Dooley and Dean Richards the stand out candidates among the forwards. However Cooke was looking for someone who could hold on to the job for a while and of those players mentioned, only Moore would be there with Carling for the duration of his tenure.

A month short of his 23rd birthday Will Carling led England to victory in a thrilling encounter, the start of a journey that would run until March 1996. England played 61 matches in that period and Will Carling led the team in all but two of them. After five games, a leg injury prevented him playing in Bucharest and during the 1995 World Cup he was rested for the group stage match against Italy. Between these two matches was a run of 44 consecutive appearances as captain, a run that seems unlikely to be bettered. For the trip to Romania Jeremy Guscott replaced Carling in the centre and celebrated his international debut with a hat-trick of tries.And it was against Fiji at Twickenham later in the year that England introduced the Carling-Guscott partnership to the rugby public, a partnership that represented England on 44 occasions.

Will Carling's record is impressive: three Grand Slams and four Triple Crowns; the Championship won outright four times; England reached the final of the 1991 World Cup and the semi-final four years later; and there was a tour with the British Lions. But perhaps the most lasting contribution the Carling era gave to English rugby was the way in which Twickenham became a stadium no country relished visiting. Under Will Carling England lost only one home Five Nations match and if Australia, New Zealand and South Africa all enjoyed their day at HQ so too did they experience defeat at the home of English rugby during the Carling years.

There was also a down side—there has to be in sport or it wouldn't hold our interest. For Will Carling, referring to '57 old farts' when discussing the merits of committee members probably tops the list. This is closely followed by his refusal to talk to the media after leading the team to victory in Cardiff in 1991, the first English success on Welsh soil for 28 years. His personal life also came under scrutiny which was par for the course for someone with such a high public profile. But he survived and what became obvious through all the contentious issues was that he never lost the backing of his team, the players always stood by him. What more can a captain ask?

Will Carling led England 59 times, a world record equalled by Australia's George Gregan in 2007. Under his leadership England won 44 matches, there was a 12–12 draw with Scotland and 14 defeats. His run of 72 caps was only interrupted twice which is an extraordinary statistic for a player competing week in, week out in one of the most physical sports. Carling's loyalty to his club, his country and perhaps most importantly to his players is beyond doubt. He grew into a job which at the outset some felt he wasn't ready for or not good enough to hold down but he soon proved the doubters wrong (and in some style). Few words are required to sum up an engaging man who led English rugby out of the mediocrity for which much of the 1980s are remembered into a decade in which mention of England and Twickenham made even the southern hemisphere countries tread warily. Few words indeed; Will Carling—Harlequins, England, Captain.

The Harlequins can lay claim to the two most lauded records in English international rugby. In Jason Leonard they have the record cap holder and in Will Carling the player with most appearances as captain. Neither record is under threat. The club still continues to dine at the top table of the domestic game whereas Blackheath, once so dominant a force has fallen away in recent years. The same thing can also be said of the Quins' near neighbours Richmond, only the history books continue to remind us of the time when all roads led to the Cricketers, the Orange Tree and then over the way to the Athletic Ground.

3

GOING FOR BROKE

Richmond

Richmond RFC was the first major casualty of rugby's professional era and therein lies a cautionary tale. The National League system introduced into English club rugby for the 1987–88 season saw Richmond drafted into Division Two. Occasionally relegated then promoted, the seasons 1987–96 saw the club spending its time in either Division Two or Three but these years of mediocrity were about to end. When the rugby union equivalent of the Klondike gold rush arrived in August 1995 everyone involved in the game thought they had hit the jackpot—and there were some wealthy individuals outside it who also wanted a piece of the action.

Ashley Levett, a commodities dealer based in Monaco, made a financial commitment to the club which reportedly ran into millions. Players suddenly attracted to the Third Division club based in south-west London included Alan Bateman, Ben Clarke, Adrian Davies, Scott and Craig Quinnell; others would follow. The rewards were instant, the club gained immediate promotion to Division Two where it maintained the momentum and in the following season earned a place in Division One.

Then life got tough. No longer a big fish in a small pond, the club had to play the cream of the English game, clubs that also enjoyed the backing of a wealthy benefactor. Richmond didn't look like challenging for honours. Neither was there any real threat of relegation but by 1999, Levett was expressing a desire to reduce his considerable investment. When the funds dried up the club reluctantly took the only realistic course available and went into voluntary administration.

Who was right or wrong? Could the timing have been better orchestrated? Should the club have battled on? These are all imponderables. The fact was that overnight Richmond had become persona non grata, surplus to requirements in a division the size of which was already under scrutiny. Other than bailing the club out (a dangerous precedent to set), the RFU had little choice other than to stand back and watch the demise of one of its founder members.

Richmond did not compete during the following season, but allowed the club to retain its status as an amateur club and it reappeared in Herts and Middlesex Division One at the start of the 2000–01 campaign. Richmond then earned promotion in four consecutive seasons and can now be found in London One. But the chances of seeing the famous gold, red and black jersey in the Premiership in the near future are remote—**Edward Temple Gurdon** would turn in his grave!

Temple Gurdon and younger brother **Charles Gurdon** were the standard-bearers of Richmond FC (as it was known then) during the 1870s and 1880s. Only 18 months separated the brothers but it seems that wherever elder brother Temple went Charles would surely follow. Haileybury College led to Cambridge University where both studied law before setting out on what would become successful legal careers—then there was rugby football.

Between 1874-76, Temple Gurdon won three Blues while Charles continued the family interest in the Varsity Match winning his Blue in 1877. On the completion of their studies the brothers both headed for London and elected to join Richmond where they soon settled into what must have been a formidable pack of forwards, happy to spend Saturday afternoons in Old Deer Park, entertaining the crowds with their great dribbling skills. Often working in tandem, they would control the ball at their feet, take it through the opposition forwards and then terrorise the half-back and three-quarters with their delicate footwork.

Temple Gurdon was first selected to play for England in 1877. Unfortunately the university would not release him from his studies and prevented him from playing. A year later, he was an employee at the Public Record Office and there were no such obstacles to overcome when he was chosen to play against Scotland at the Kennington Oval. Charles won his first cap two years later against Ireland at Lansdowne Road and in the final match of the season the brothers were included in the team that defeated Scotland in Manchester. This was the first of 10 internationals in which the Gurdons played alongside each other for their country.

Temple Gurdon won 16 caps, Charles 14. The elder brother might have been the first to be capped but the captaincy was handed to Charles for one match before Temple got his hands on it—the only occasion when the younger sibling appears to have stolen a march on his elder brother. A drawn game in Dublin in 1882 marked the beginning and end of Charles Gurdon's brief flirtation with the captaincy but Temple was selected to lead the team against Wales later in the year, in a match heralding the start of what has evolved into the Six Nations.

The first International Championship is attributed to the 1882–83 season. England's defeat of Ireland, Scotland and Wales meant the team became the first winners of the mythical Triple Crown and in the following season England won it again. Temple Gurdon led the team throughout the two campaigns and continued in the role in 1885 when, but for a disagreement that had raged on from the previous year, England may well have claimed another Triple Crown. In 1885, Scotland refused to play England. In a nutshell, when England beat Scotland at Blackheath in 1884 the try that decided the outcome of the match was hotly disputed by the Scots and the argument raged on long after the final whistle was blown. Watching the game in the twenty first century it is not easy to reconcile how rugby football was once played. This particular try was awarded to England after a Scot knocked the ball back towards his own line only for it to be gathered by an English player who scored, a frequent enough occurrence in the modern game. In the 1880s, such problems arose primarily because of the varying interpretations of the Laws. On this occasion, some good did come from the ensuing contretemps. Just as the inconsistencies among the clubs led to the formation of the RFU, when it came to the international stage there were also differences of opinion that had to be rationalised. That the RFU may have taken upon itself a degree of stewardship to which it was not entitled certainly raised hackles north of the border but the eventual outcome saw the formation of a body which would oversee such disputes and much else besides; the International Rugby Board as we now know it had arrived.

Temple Gurdon won his first cap two years before Charles was awarded his but in 1886 they brought the curtain down on their international careers in the same match. Scotland prevented another Triple Crown by holding England to a scoreless draw bringing to an end a period of outstanding success for the men in white; of the 20 matches played when a Gurdon was in the team England lost only one and neither brother experienced defeat when captain.

With 16 appearances Temple Gurdon was England's most capped

player, a record he held for 25 years before it was claimed by John Birkett. He captained Richmond for a record 10 seasons and on his retirement went on to become a leading administrator serving on the newly formed International Board. In 1890 he became the 11th president of the RFU, serving a second term after his re-election in 1891. Only 18 months separated Temple and Charles Gurdon at birth and with their passing in 1929 and 1931 respectively, both aged 75, Temple maintained his senior status by predeceasing his sibling; the only known instance of Charles gaining an advantage over his elder brother was in becoming England captain first.

The Gurdons attended Haileybury College in Hertfordshire before going up to Cambridge. Founded in 1858 the college was, and remains, one of the leading public schools in England. The same can be said about Wellington College, located to the south-west of the capital and founded a year later by Queen Victoria and the then Prime Minister, Lord Derby, in honour of the Duke of Wellington. In addition to Temple and Charles Gurdon, Haileybury counts Rudyard Kipling, Clement Attlee and Sterling Moss amongst its alumni while Wellington was the preferred choice of another motor racing world champion in James Hunt, writer Sebastian Faulkes and impressionist Rory Bremner. Then there were **Henry Lawrence** and **Frank Adams**, lesser known names maybe but men who are inextricably linked with the captaincy of the England rugby football team.

Henry Lawrence became England's third captain in the first match played against Ireland which took place at the Kennington Oval in February 1875. On a pitch described as a quagmire upwards of 3,000 spectators saw England gain the expected victory and among the nine players winning first caps was Frank Adams who joined Lawrence in the forwards. Also included in the team was Murray Marshall, another Wellington product but while he headed to Blackheath, for Lawrence and Adams it was Richmond that beckoned. With the opportunity to win caps few and far between due to the lack of regular and varied competition it is understandable that it took Lawrence three years to win his four caps with Frank Adams needing an additional season to claim seven. Lawrence and Adams each captained England twice, both men leading teams against Scotland at Raeburn Place and Ireland at the Kennington Oval; neither did the similarity end there, the captains enjoying the same measure of success, drawn matches with the Scots and victories against Ireland.

We have already seen examples of captains who took up office within the RFU during their playing days or soon after. Henry Lawrence was elected vice-president for the 1875–86 season and re-elected a year later but when he looked the obvious candidate to succeed Charles Heatley in becoming the fifth president he decided to stand down citing business commitments as his reason for not pursuing the higher office. Baron may be the lowest rank in the nobility but as the son of the Rt Hon the first Baron Lawrence, Henry would undoubtedly have had his own functions to perform and his involvement with rugby appears to have come to an end following his resignation from the RFU.

Frank Adams enjoyed several more seasons with Richmond after his international days ended. A member of Temple Gurdon's undefeated team of 1886–87, he was once described as '…worthy of his place, being very keen and energetic, and a valuable player by reason of his weight, strength and vigorous following up'. All prerequisites for a forward of the day. However, like Lawrence, he too was lost to the game when his interests as a shipping insurer took him firstly to Australia and New Zealand and later to the USA. Unlike his contemporary who died aged 54, Frank Adams lived to the ripe old age of 79. Together with Henry Lawrence and others who guided England through the early years of international rugby these are names to remember at a time when much else about the union game as it once was is fast becoming forgotten.

Henry Lawrence was only associated with rugby football when teams were made up of 20 players but Frank Adams was a forward whose services were still called upon after the reduction in numbers. It is difficult to imagine 40 players on a rugby field; the dimensions of the playing area as we now know it should not exceed 100 metres by 70 metres excluding the dead ball areas, much the same size as in the 1880s but with 10 fewer players vying for space. When teams were reduced to 15 the game opened up considerably and it was only a matter of time before some innovative individuals among the backs began to assert their influence in ways never previously witnessed. Adrian Stoop, his concept of a 'scrum-half' and a clearly defined three-quarter line lay in the future but a move toward that ideal can be identified some 20 years earlier.

It may well all have started at Oxford in the early 1880s when the university enjoyed an unprecedented run of four consecutive victories over their greatest rivals. Harry Vassal's leadership influenced the teams, and despite being a forward, he encouraged the backs to play a much more expansive game. During Vassal's three seasons as captain, Oxford were unbeaten in the 70 matches played and instrumental in seeing this diversification used with such dramatic effect was half-back **Alan Rotherham**.

When teams reduced to 15 players, a period of experimentation followed before a combination of forwards and backs was arrived at. Oxford favoured playing nine forwards and six backs and the national selectors, after six seasons during which various options were considered, adopted the proven format for the first time when England met Wales in December 1882, taking the field with two half-backs, three three-quarters and a full-back. If the scheme had an element of risk involved the selectors went some way to eliminating it by taking the precaution of including seven Oxford University players in the team but they need not have worried.

A comfortable victory in Swansea heralded the start of the Temple Gurdon era, a time of Triple Crowns and near misses, and at half-back for nine of the 11 matches played between 1882–86 was Alan Rotherham. His education completed, Rotherham moved to London to pursue a legal career and took his considerable skill and experience to Richmond where he joined forces with the Gurdons. His appointment as England captain came in 1887 when he succeeded Temple Gurdon but after four seasons in which the team remained unbeaten, there was only one way it could go. Drawn matches with Wales and Scotland couldn't hide the disappointment of a first defeat to Ireland, achieved at the 13th time of asking; then followed two seasons in which England didn't turn up, preferred to stay at home and did not compete in the Championship.

The formation of an International Board had been high on the agenda since England's controversial victory over Scotland in 1884 now, with a deal about to be struck between the four home nations it was the RFU who threw its toys out of the pram. The oldest union wanted more than an equal share of the cake and with the other unions not prepared to make any concession that would effectively leave the RFU running the new venture negotiations came to a halt the outcome of which was England's absence from the Championship for the next two seasons. Whether he would have added to his tally of 12 caps is not known but when the dust settled and England resumed her place after accepting the conditions laid out by the other unions many new names appeared on the team sheet for the opening fixture in 1890. Noticeable was the absence of Alan Rotherham.

One has to be particularly careful when referring to the England team sheets of the latter part of the nineteenth century. Accuracy is needed when considering the Gurdons and more so perhaps when Jas Davidson was joined by Jos Davidson in the team. Then, against Scotland in 1898, the inclusion of A. Rotherham at half-back encourages the reader to double check that which has gone before. But fear not, the records that can so often be misleading on occasion are right in this instance—enter **Arthur Rotherham**, cousin of Alan.

Unlike his older relative who favoured the law, Arthur Rotherham studied medicine which took him to Cambridge University and then St Thomas's Hospital, London. He won two Blues in 1891, fog causing the postponement of the 1890 fixture until March and toured South Africa with the British team in 1891 playing in 16 of the 20 matches including two Tests. An experienced player then but one who would see seven years pass before he was finally selected to play for England by which time his 29th birthday was fast approaching.

A draw in Scotland and home victory against Wales was a definite improvement on recent performances with nothing to suggest what lay in wait. It was the misfortune of Arthur Rotherham to lead England in its worst season to date in 1899 when all three matches were lost for the first time, a solitary try against a rampaging Welsh team the only score registered. Although the blame for the unacceptable return was largely attributed to a poor set of forwards, 10 players in the losing team against Scotland were not called upon to play again for England including the captain. The next England team to take the field included 13 new caps; the selectors were not happy!

One of only two forwards to survive the cull was **Frank Stout**. As with the Gurdons, Rotherhams and Davidsons extracting statistics concerning Stout needs care as he had an elder brother named Percy who also played for Richmond and England. Unlike the others who were linked by position, Percy Stout played among the three-quarters but in any event, he was one of the 10 players summarily dismissed in 1899.

The family home was in Gloucestershire and it was at the Gloucester club that Frank Stout began his rugby after a brief flirtation with association football. He won seven caps as a Gloucester player and became the club's first British tourist when he visited Australia in 1899. Led by the Rev Matthew Mullineux of Blackheath, a half-back with no experience of international rugby, the British team were surprisingly beaten in the first

Test and the need for change was very apparent. For the second Test, six players were brought into the team and there was one positional change that saw C.Y. Adamson of Durham move from the wing to half-back in place of Mullineux who admirably decided to stand down knowing full well that he was not good enough to play the game at Test level. Frank Stout assumed the captaincy for the remaining Tests, and the team won all of them, but despite his obvious qualities as both a player and leader, he did not appear in an England jersey again until 1903 after an absence of four years.

On his return from Australia, Stout moved to London and joined Richmond. His recall came in the last match of a season in which the selectors appear to have been clutching at straws, England already beaten by Wales and Ireland. Scotland arrived at Richmond in search of a fourth Triple Crown and for the third time in five seasons England lost all three matches. Having added only one more cap to his total Stout went on a second overseas tour, spending the summer in South Africa with Mark Morrison's British team. Yet to be called Lions these tourists found life much tougher than those that had gone before and the British team lost the three match Test series. Stout played in 20 of the 22 matches including the three Tests but even this high figure pales when compared to the contributions made by Wales' Reg Skrimshire and Scotland's Bill Scott who both played in all 22 matches. Frank Stout was now a seasoned international footballer with seven Test appearances making him the most capped tourist of his era but his England career had somehow gone off the rails and it was time to put the record straight.

Captaincy first came his way in Australia since which time no opportunities to build on the experience had presented themselves. This changed in 1903 when he was elected club captain at Richmond and when he was included in the team to play Wales at the start of the 1904 Championship his appointment as captain was not a surprise. What did come as a surprise was that after leading the team to a creditable draw and outscoring the Welsh by three tries to one, though retained in the team for the next game the captaincy went elsewhere. This was scant reward for having helped restore pride to the jersey after the previous season's whitewash. Perhaps Stout should have called it a day, retired from international rugby with his 11 caps and the honour of having captained his country once. But who would turn down the chance to do it again? Nobody in their right mind, so when he was asked to lead the team in 1905, Frank

Stout was up for the job.

Unfortunately for Frank, England didn't have much of a team to lead. A total of 27 players were called upon for the three matches but it was to no avail, England never recovering from a 25–0 hiding at Cardiff Arms Park. When Ireland won 17–3 in Cork the time seemed right for wholesale changes. But the selectors defied all logic, introducing only three new caps against Scotland and inviting Stout to continue. Alas, there is no happy ending. England were beaten and once again laid claim to the wooden spoon—if such a thing existed then it would surely have been England's to keep considering the vice like grip with which it had been grasped in recent years.

Frank Stout was the ninth Richmond player selected to captain England in the 34 years since the formation of the RFU and the start of international rugby. The 10th would not appear until 1948. The war years brought many playing careers to an abrupt halt but just as seven men won caps before and after the First World War, three men did return to international duty following the Second World War.

Outside-half **Tom Kemp** won the first of his five caps against Wales in 1937 and the second four weeks later when Ireland were the visitors to Twickenham but it was two years before he won an elusive third cap in what proved to be the last match before the war. He won his first cap when he was studying at Cambridge but by the time of his third Kemp had moved on to St Mary's Hospital. After spending the war years in the Middle East he returned to St Mary's before taking up a variety of appointments at leading London hospitals and serving time as an examiner in medicine at the University of London. He was elected a Fellow of the Royal College of Physicians in 1947 and became a Doctor of Medicine in 1953 but busy schedule or not, there was still time for the occasional game of rugby which he now enjoyed at Richmond.

The first post-war Championship saw Nim Hall introduced at outside-half. Hall had taken over from Kemp at St Mary's and would eventually succeed him as Richmond's playmaker but when the team to play Australia in the following January was announced there was a recall for Tom Kemp who won his fourth cap 11 years after the first. Australia beat England and when the team to play Wales two weeks later was announced it showed two changes and a new captain, Tom Kemp replacing E.K. Scott, another to have studied medicine at St Mary's. Kemp was now into his 33rd year and could only have been viewed as a short term appointment. After leading

England to a draw Tom Kemp joined the ever growing list of captains who led their country once but this time the decision was of his own making after he declined the opportunity to continue against Ireland and was not called upon again.

After retiring from all levels of rugby in 1949, Tom Kemp served on the RFU as the representative for Cambridge University. In 1968, he was elected vice-president and a year later became a senior vice-president making him a likely candidate for the higher office in 1970–71, the season in which the RFU would celebrate its centenary. Generously, he chose to stand down leaving the way clear for William Ramsey to become president in the landmark season having previously held the position in 1954–55. Ramsey was a most popular choice after giving many years of stalwart service to English rugby. This was duly recognised when he received a knighthood in the New Year's Honours List. Kemp's magnanimous gesture was also rewarded when 12 months later he was chosen to succeed Ramsey and became the 64th president of the RFU.

The centenary season began with a gathering of rugby men from around the world. The Centenary Congress held at Cambridge University saw delegates from 43 countries assemble at the invitation of the RFU to witness firsthand how the English game was run and administered at all levels. Dr Tom Kemp chaired the congress which was an unreserved success. It is pleasing to see that some of the countries represented, which were relatively new to the game in 1970, now compete in the final stages of the Rugby World Cup. Many events were organised to ensure that the centenary would be one to remember and the off field celebrations were in full swing long before the Five Nations Championship got under way. On 16 January, all roads led west, to Cardiff Arms Park where England would begin the campaign against a most talented Welsh team, one on the verge of greatness—everything was crossed.

Oxford won the 1966 Varsity Match 8–6, scoring two tries in the process. Wing forward **Tony Bucknall** scored the second try early in the second half when he collected a cross-kick to score under the posts only to see the simplest of conversions missed. The Oxford captain would not have been happy at such a waste of valuable points in what was always going to be a tight game but his team prevailed and the celebrations undoubtedly went on late into the December night. Captain on the day was Tommy Bedford, a South African international of some standing and destined to become one of his country's finest number 8s. At Twickenham three years later he had to take second best when England registered a first victory over the Springboks with a team that included five new caps, Tony Bucknall among them.

South Africa was the first of 10 consecutive matches Bucknall appeared in which came to an end against Scotland on 27 March 1971, 100 years to the day after the first international took place. Bob Hiller was the preferred choice as captain during the 1969–70 season with Bob Taylor taking over in his absence for the final game against France but when the team to play Wales in the centenary season was announced it was full of surprises. Perhaps several new caps introduced together might help produce a positive result. The five that played against South Africa suggest there is some merit in the policy, but when the selectors decided to include seven for the visit to Cardiff many an English eyebrow was raised while in the valleys, the celebrations had started long before the English team crossed the Severn Bridge. And who should be elected to take this team into the dragon's den? Tony Bucknall.

As he was a stockbroker in the City, Bucknall knew quite a bit about risk and would have been the first to appreciate the size of the one the selectors were taking. Strange things sometimes happen on a rugby field but there was nothing strange or surprising about the events in Cardiff after Bucknall led his team out and the formalities were completed; Wales winning the first match in what would be a Grand Slam season. It was to the selectors' credit that they didn't panic. They made only a couple of minor adjustments, their conservatism rewarded with a win against Ireland, a draw with the French and a one point defeat by Scotland and although the captaincy was passed back to Hiller, Tony Bucknall retained his place in the team until England had completed 100 years of international rugby— practically to the minute.

Against Wales, Tony Bucknall became the 12th Richmond player to captain England. Blackheath can also lay claim to 12 captains, a record waiting to be broken by another club, the chances of either Blackheath or Richmond adding to their tally being remote. It will be for Harlequins, Leicester, Wasps or another of the big names that feature in the Premiership to improve on the figure. But after 100 years two of the principal clubs behind the formation of the RFU were responsible for more England captains than any other. Almost 40 years later, Richmond and Blackheath still head the table.

4

GO WEST YOUNG MAN

Bath, Bridewater and Albion, Bristol, Exeter, Gloucester, Penryn, Redruth, Wellington

The West Country: Devon and Cornwall, Gloucestershire and Somerset; cream teas and pasties, cheese and cider; Dartmoor and Lands End, the Cotswolds and Roman Bath. Altogether much removed from the hustle and bustle of the capital city but none the worse for that. And this is rugby country—serious rugby country!

Gloucestershire has won the County Championship more than any other and Devon appears on the honours board seven times. For Somerset there are three runners-up places to add to the title won in 1923—and for Cornwall? Well, they reckon the county damn near emptied in 1991 when an estimated 40,000 headed for Twickenham and a final showdown with Yorkshire that saw the Cornishmen come from behind to grab a famous victory in front of the competition's biggest crowd. So, to say that they take their rugby seriously in the West Country is understating the reality—they take it very seriously!

In **Sam Woods** we come to the first example of a player who captained England from two clubs. Woods was a sportsman and scholar from Australia. Born in New South Wales in 1867, he attended Sydney Grammar School, arriving in England to continue his formal education at Brighton College before going up to Jesus College, Cambridge in 1888 where he excelled at rugby and cricket, winning a combined total of seven Blues. Despite being a more than able forward on the rugby field perhaps it was as a cricketer that Sam Woods is best remembered. He had a long association with Somerset CCC both as a player and later in an administrative capacity and played Test cricket for Australia and England. He represented Australia in three Tests against England in 1888 and seven years later was a member of Lord Hawkes' England team that toured South Africa where he also featured in three Test matches. Be it with bat or ball Sam Woods was equally at home. At Cambridge he is credited with taking all 10 wickets in an innings and on one occasion playing for Somerset against Sussex he scored a double century in a little over two hours. Impressive statistics but there is sufficient evidence to suggest that his prowess on the rugby field did in fact match that seen on the cricket square.

Sam Woods was described by E.B. Holmes as having '...a style peculiarly his own. If given a 'roving commission' Woods is one of the most dangerous of forwards. His strength, pace and dash cause his individual play to be of a most determined character, and though he cannot be called a scrummager, he has been selected for England on account of the extraordinary pieces of play he is continually bringing off. His tackling is wonderfully sure and exceedingly severe...he has frequently been brought out as an extra three-quarter to strengthen the defence...'

In the 1890s there was little specialisation among the forwards—the old adage of 'first up, first down' still applied when it came to scrummaging—but surely Holmes is talking about the nineteenth century equivalent of an open side wing forward, '...extraordinary pieces of play...tackling is wonderfully sure...an extra three-quarter...' This could apply to Peter Winterbottom, Neil Back or any number of open sides seen in recent years and in Woods we don't appear to have come across a typical forward of the day.

Sam Woods played his early club rugby for Wellington, a market town in north Somerset, but he won the first six of his 13 caps while still an undergraduate at Cambridge. In the Triple Crown season of 1891–92, he was given the captaincy for the Ireland match, taking over from Fred Alderson who was unavailable. He repeated the task 12 months later, leading England to another victory over the Irish and it is because of these two matches that Wellington is linked with the captaincy of England. After missing the 1893–94 season Woods returned to the team a year later and enjoyed an extended run of three matches as captain. Now a Blackheath player he led winning teams against Wales and Ireland before Scotland won a second Triple Crown in what proved to be Sam Woods' final international appearance and the only defeat among his five matches as captain.

By the very nature of the two sports it is clear that subject to a clean bill of health one's days spent at the crease can long exceed those in the scrum and this was certainly the case for Woods where records confirm he continued playing for Somerset until 1911. The county ground at Taunton is 10 miles east of Wellington and 10 miles further away is Bridgewater, the home of Bridgewater and Albion RFC. As Woods played out his final years with bat and ball so was a rugby career beginning at this famous old club.

Robert Dibble is something of an enigma. Here is a man reported as having served in the Boer War which began in October 1899 and ended in May 1902; was a member of the England pack 19 times from 1906 to 1912; and was still playing club rugby for Newport in the 1920–21 season during which he made 20 appearances for the Welsh club. So how old was Bob Dibble in 1921? Assuming he was at least 16 years of age in 1902 when he fought in South Africa that would make him 35 but in all probability he was two or three years older. That he was first capped in 1906 is a matter of record; he played against Scotland and France and later in the year was in the team which drew with the first Springboks. Although he was absent throughout the 1907 Championship he was ever present the following year and in the summer toured Australia and New Zealand with the Anglo-Welsh team.

Bob Dibble of Bridgewater and Albion first captained England in 1909. He led the side throughout the Championship and in the friendly with France and enjoyed a second bite of the cherry in 1912. By this time, he was a Newport player having joined the club in 1911. If the strength of rugby in the West Country at that time needs confirmation, we only have to look at the England team that played Scotland when Bob Dibble won his first cap. In addition to Dibble and his Bridgewater connection also included were players from Bristol, Devonport Albion, Exeter, Falmouth and Plymouth; a significant move away from London and the north of England, regions traditionally recognised as the backbone of English rugby.

Tom Kelly was the Exeter representative in the team. Another abrasive West Country forward, Kelly won 12 caps between 1906 and 1908, the games played in London, Swansea, Edinburgh, Dublin, Paris and Leicester—all of which involved a considerable amount of travelling for a player based in Exeter. It must have been frustrating when the RFU decided to play Wales at nearby Bristol in 1908 as this was the only match Kelly missed between winning his first and last caps. Two weeks earlier he had led England to a comfortable victory in Paris but after nine games in the second-row, against France he was selected at prop allowing Lancelot Slocock to move from the back row into the second-row. Bob Dibble also returned at number 8 having won earlier caps in the front row.

England were beaten in Bristol and Kelly was recalled to partner Slocock against Ireland and Scotland in teams which bore little resemblance to those he had been introduced to two years earlier. English rugby has seen several prolonged periods of indifference when selecting eight, nine or more new caps at the same time became a frequent occurrence but on the resumption of fixtures following two world wars, the introduction of many new faces was unavoidable.

Fourteen new caps were included in the England team that played Wales in Cardiff on 18 January 1947. There was representation from Oxford and Cambridge, Devonport Services, Bedford, Coventry, Northampton, Otley, Sale and Waterloo but what made this team selection quite different from those which had gone before was the inclusion of three medical students from St Mary's Hospital, London who made up the midfield—the outside-half and centres. Nim Hall would win future caps as a Huddersfield and Richmond player; Norman Bennett later represented the United Services but on qualifying as a doctor **Edward Scott** returned to his native Cornwall and played his club rugby at Redruth from where he won four caps, three of them as captain.

The Championship may not have resumed until 1947 but in the 1945–46 season the four home countries together with France and a New Zealand Army team took part in a series of matches arranged to mark the end of the war. No official status was granted, neither did the participants play the same number of games but like everything else at the time, rugby union was in desperate need of a fillip and these matches proved a great success. England played six Victory Internationals and Edward Scott featured in them all so despite not having any caps to his name when he was selected to play in the first Championship match in 1947 the experience gained ensured that he was ready for the demands of the bigger stage.

England defeated Wales but the selectors did not invite Scott back during the season. It was against the Australian tourists a year later that he won his second cap and led England for the first time. An Australian team had travelled to Europe for a similar tour in 1939 only to immediately return home following the outbreak of war. The eight year delay was overlooked when they ran out at Twickenham in front of a crowd in excess of 70,000. The Wallabies proved much too strong scoring three tries in an 11–0 victory. For the England captain it appeared to be a case of 'thank you very much' when he was included in the team to play Wales two weeks later but saw the captaincy handed to Tom Kemp. After one match, Kemp declined the invitation to continue against Ireland, which reopened the door for Scott, but two more defeats brought an end to his international rugby.

There aren't many examples of a father and son both playing rugby football for England but Edward Scott and father Frank are included in this small number. Frank was born in Australia but on qualifying as a doctor, he upped roots and made for England and the West Country. He then set up in practice, played rugby for Bristol and was capped by England in 1907, one of a collection of players rather unflatteringly referred to as one cap wonders. Forty years later Edward followed his father into the England team and also began his career in medicine setting up practice in the pretty little village of Portscatho, located on the South West Coast Path, a few miles from St Mawes. It sounds idyllic—someone should make a television series about it.

As the crow flies, Portscatho is less than five miles from Penryn but Falmouth Bay and the Carrick Roads determine a much longer journey to get to the home town of **Victor Roberts**. Penryn was always going to be Roberts' preferred choice of club while Edward Scott made the longer journey to Redruth. Although both played for England in the seasons immediately following the war it was never in the same team. Vic Roberts won his first cap against France in the final match of the 1947 Championship, the first of 12 caps won over five seasons which make him Penryn's most capped player. If not for work commitments, it is probable Roberts would have been content to play all his rugby in Cornwall. But come 1956, when he received a rather belated recall to the national team following a five year absence, his employees at HM Customs and Excise had transferred him to London and he played his club rugby with the Harlequins from which club he won a further four caps.

London and the Harlequins were a long way off when Roberts won his first cap. He replaced Don White and enjoyed a try scoring debut in a winning team, a dream start but it was two years before he got another chance. During the 1948–50 seasons, Roberts established himself in what was an ordinary England team but his individual performances were good enough for him to be included in the British Lions party that toured New Zealand and Australia in the summer of 1950, one of only three English representatives in the squad of 30 players. The competition for Test places was strong and Roberts had to content himself with 10 appearances against provincial opposition. But rarely does a British Lion not return from a tour a much improved player and Vic Roberts was no exception. The England selectors concurred, inviting him to captain the team against Wales in the opening match of the 1951 Championship and although well beaten, Roberts retained his place throughout the season but not the captaincy. Then came five years in the wilderness.

The England team that played Wales in 1956 included 10 new caps. Among them were Peter Jackson and Peter Thompson on the wings, scrum-half Dickie Jeeps, Ron Jacobs at prop, John Currie and David Marques in the second-row, Peter Robbins on the flank and Alan Ashcroft at number 8. These players would form the nucleus of the team in the coming seasons. Jeff Butterfield and Phil Davies were an established partnership in the centre while hooker and new captain Eric Evans first played for England in 1948 meaning Vic Roberts joined a team picked with the future in mind. It proved to be his swansong. A year later England won a Grand Slam but Roberts was not there to enjoy it, his place in the back row taken by Reg Higgins, a player six years younger.

In terms of international players Wellington, Bridgewater and Albion, Exeter, Redruth and Penryn have probably had their day. The clubs may still produce some talent but rest assured it will be snapped up by the bigger fish in the pond, gravitate to the leading clubs, and any such young men will ignore the dictum and go east. Time now to concentrate on three West Country clubs that compete at the highest level of the domestic game in England, clubs between which there is certainly no love lost—Bath, Bristol and Gloucester.

Rugby football in the ancient Roman city of Bath dates back to 1865 when the forerunner of what is now Bath Rugby was founded. For much of its history the club could never claim to be one of England's finest, 120 years would pass before that happened, but there have been England internationals gracing the Recreation Ground since the club moved there in 1894. Frank Soane in the 1890s, Vincent Coates before the First World War and Ron Gerrard played in the 1930s. Alec Lewis arrived at Bath in the 1950s, winner of 10 caps and a future England selector and in the 1960s, Lawrence Rimmer ensured the club continued to gain international honours. Then in the 1980s and 1990s there was such an explosion of talent at the Rec, there was probably a case to answer with the Monopolies Commission if any envious club had decided to pursue it. John Horton, John Palmer and David Trick; Stuart Barnes, Simon Halliday; Roger Spurrell and Tony Swift; John Callard, Gareth Chilcott, Graham Dawe,

John Hall; Ben Clarke, Jeremy Guscott, Victor Ubogu, Nigel Redman, Andy Robinson and Jonathan Webb. These were part of the English connection to which could be added Dave Hilton, Andy Nicol, Eric Peters and Andy Reed of Scotland; Ireland's Simon Geoghegan and Ieuan Evans from Wales—a far from complete list but surely one to make the connoisseurs purr, rub their hands together and head for Bath. And they did so in ever increasing numbers as the club collected much of the silverware on offer during the period; between 1983–96 Bath won the domestic cup no fewer than 10 times and with the introduction of national leagues, Bath won seven titles. There is no doubt that over two decades Bath produced some of the best teams ever to play the game at club level. Absent from the names above but ever-present in the success story is the man who cajoled and encouraged the forwards; decided when and when not to release the potent energy of the backs: chose whether to kick or pass. This was the scrum-half, the general—this was **Richard Hill**.

I was born in Birmingham but the family moved to Salisbury where I attended Bishop Wordsworth School which has a good reputation for rugby. David Egerton and I were there together and funnily enough, when I was in the sixth form the other Richard Hill was in the first form— he was a little dot at the time. I went to Exeter University where I studied PE and in due course was made captain of the first XV. In March 1983 we played an evening game against Bath, which ended in a 6–6 draw, and shortly after I was asked if I'd be interested in joining the club which came as a bit of a shock. I played three games at the end of that season. Maesteg, Cardiff, where I came up against Terry Holmes for the first time, and Bedford.

Rugby Union was some years away from joining the ranks of professional sport but it was the professional way in which Bath approached the game that helped the club stand out from the rest during the 1980s and beyond.

There was a very professional set up at Bath: not paid but not unlike that seen at international level today. Jack Rowell was the head coach and under him were a variety of specialist coaches. Dave Robson took care of the scrum and doubled up as an analyst, taking time to go and see future opponents returning armed with copious notes on them. Dave Alred, who

64

later joined England and assisted the Lions, was the kicking coach. Tom Hudson had previously worked with Carwyn James at Llanelli and when he became Director of Sport at Bath University he joined us as a fitness and motivational coach. A little later Brian Ashton came on board as skills coach.

Bath was the first club to go on warm weather training breaks. We would be in Lanzarote for a week in January when the rest were training in the cold and wet which helped us a great deal in the second half of the season. We were also the first club in England to have the liquid refreshments at half time in place of oranges; nobody could believe it when we produced these huge crates. So in every respect Bath were great innovators and that was the reason we stayed ahead of the game; the players were in particularly good physical shape after working with a proper strength and conditioning coach, we were fitter and stronger than anybody else and we were more organised than anybody else. Added to which there was a very good recruitment network that picked up the likes of Andy Robinson who arrived from Taunton and Nigel Redman from Weston-Super-Mare. The club also developed a very strong Cornish connection, which saw the likes of Roger Spurrel, Chris Martin and Andy Reed come on board, a connection that continues to bring players in. All in all, Bath at that time was as well organised as it was possible to get in the amateur era.

Between 1983 and 1994, Richard Hill played in eight cup winning sides and throughout the six seasons that saw Bath win league titles. He was club captain in 1985–86 and again in 1986–87 when a notable cup and league double was delivered. It wasn't long after arriving at the Recreation Ground that the selectors invited Hill to join England on a summer tour to South Africa where he won his first cap. Then followed two seasons on the bench as those responsible deliberated over the merits of Nigel Melville and Richard Harding, a period when he won three caps as a replacement. Then in 1987 the man currently leading the best team in the land was reunited with the number 9 jersey and given the added responsibilities which go hand in glove with captaincy.

I'd played for England in 1984, 1985 and 1986 during which time we had been booted around by every team we came up against; it was pretty awful. The game could be brutal in those days, very much a case of survival of the fittest, but we just didn't seem to have that bit of fight in us. I'd played behind a pack that had been constantly battered so when I was appointed captain we sat down and decided that whatever happened we were going to go down fighting, try and re-establish some respect for the England team rather than not retaliate when kicked or punched which would only ensure that we would be on the receiving end all afternoon.

Ireland beat us 17–0. Marcus Rose was laid out late in the second half and had to leave the field but nobody did anything, we continued to be bossed about and it was following that defeat we decided enough was enough. Next up was France and from the kick off they were in amongst us but this time the forwards stood up, piled into them. I wouldn't condone it but we laid our store out from the off, there was claret everywhere in what turned into a very brutal game. At the after match dinner at the Hilton, Jacques Fouroux, the great French scrum-half, captain and coach came up to me and said '…you English, you were very dirty today…' then he smiled and added, '…just like the French used to be…' He knew the score. He knew it was a case of tit for tat after all the stick we had taken over the years.

Then it was Wales in Cardiff and we decided same again. There was a bit of niggle at an early lineout. Steve Bainbridge and Steve Sutton had to be spoken to and when the ball was thrown in a second time there was a lot of elbowing and shoving before it spilt out and went about 10 yards downfield. Phil Davies had a tug at John Hall and Wade Dooley stepped in and floored him. Davies had to leave the field and the crowd went mental.

We lost the game but it was interesting afterwards sitting down with Martin Green, the England coach. He was happy because even though we had lost to Ireland, France and Wales a bit of respect had been established, the England pack had stood up and I was quite pleased. I felt that we were making some strides forward. Two days later I got the call saying that four of us were being disciplined and I'd lost the captaincy; a hell of a shock. Martin rang to say he'd been told it was either him or me and as he had always wanted to go to the Great Barrier Reef (the first Rugby World Cup was in the summer and England were to be based in Australia) I realised I had no chance. But I do think that was the watershed for the England pack which never took another backward step; teams stopped messing about with them. It's unfortunate, but that's how it was, once the two packs respect each other the trouble stops. England hadn't been getting that respect.

The RFU disciplined Richard Hill and Bath colleagues Gareth Chilcott and Graham Dawe together with second-row Wade Dooley. The RFU also banned the players for one match but for Hill the disappointment of losing the captaincy hurt most.

My big mistake was doing the team talk with an RFU official standing in the back of the dressing room. England were meant to be whiter than white in those days and any suggestion of foul play was frowned on from above which cost people like Chilcott a lot of caps. Roger Spurrel was another who suffered. He was one of the hardest men I played with. An ex-paratrooper he captained Bath for four seasons but was never capped, much lesser players getting the nod. Roger just didn't fit into the RFU's ideal.

Hill made one appearance in the World Cup. Then at the start of the following season he was sent off playing for Bath against the Harlequins after punching opposite number Richard Moon. It was two more years before he returned to the team against Fiji at Twickenham, retaining his place for the start of the 1990 Championship when he started a sequence of 20 consecutive appearances. This included the 1991 Grand Slam and all six of England's games in the World Cup that followed, Australia beating England in the final, the last of Hill's 29 appearances.

There were three more seasons at Bath before he brought the curtain down on his playing career in 1994 and it was during those final years that things were put in place that would keep Richard Hill involved in the game.

I started going through the coaching awards and the RFU asked me if I would get involved with a new team they were introducing, England's Emerging Players, but it was a little bit awkward trying to coach guys I could come up against the following week. When I finally finished playing, I had no ideas of going anywhere other than Bath where I became chairman of selectors but I got a call from Mike Teague inviting me to coach Gloucester. I took a lot of persuading because Gloucester was a club set in its ways. They always referred to Bath as a cosmopolitan club at the same time selling themselves as the local club with every player born within a mile of the cathedral. They made a big thing of this in the build up to the 1990 Pilkington Cup Final in which we beat them 48–6 and Teague was determined things had to change.

He ended up bashing his head against a brick wall and left for Cardiff but by 1995 he'd returned to Gloucester with a new agenda.

I thought a lot about the offer, it represented the sort of challenge I enjoy so I finally decided to go for it. One of my first tasks was to recruit some non-Gloucester players and then get the club to accept them; Trevor Woodman, Phil Vickery and Mark Mapletoft all signed and Steve Ojomoh came from Bath. Then the club spread the net wider in an effort to bring in some overseas players. This was met with huge resistance, but Phillipe Saint-Andre was so well accepted; the Shed would sing the Marsellaise when he ran out—and then he took my job!

A couple of months after I joined Gloucester the game went professional and I had a decision to make—hang on to the day job or make a full commitment to rugby. Not an easy choice when you are raising a family but I loved it too much to walk away so I took the plunge. I spent three and a half years with Gloucester then went to Ebbw Vale where I worked with Leigh Jones before taking the job at Harlequins on a three year contract. Two years into the contract, Leigh rang to say he had joined Newport and would I be interested in working with him again. This was a lot nearer home so I spoke to the Quins and accepted the offer. Within two months the WRU decided to set up five regions, which meant that there were too few jobs for the number of coaches involved, and I found myself out of work. This was when the position at Bristol presented itself. It was perfect for me—I was very lucky.

In 2003 Richard Hill began his role at Bristol with a blank sheet of paper, a result of the club's efforts to bring about some financial stability. They had sold the Memorial Ground to Bristol Rovers FC with an arrangement in place that allowed the rugby club to continue playing there. All but two players had been released and Bristol were a mid-table side in National Division One.

When I got involved, top of the agenda were plans to get promoted back into the Premiership and to build a squad capable of competing at that level. We won promotion in 2005 and two years later finished third in the league which saw Bristol qualify for the Heineken Cup. When I first started work at Bristol, the club worked and trained out of a cricket pavilion that was part of Bristol University then we moved to purpose built facilities at Clifton RFC in 2006. This now accommodates all the administrative and training requirements we need. The Memorial Ground is due for a major refurbishment that will necessitate finding somewhere to play for a couple of seasons. This will make life extremely difficult, but at the end of it, Bristol will be playing at one of the best grounds in the Guinness Premiership and that will make it all worthwhile. The future looks good and I want to play my part in it by ensuring that the club maintains its place in the Premiership over the next couple of seasons. It's not going to be easy but I have to work through it.

I'm more than happy at Bristol. I've no burning desire to get involved with England at the moment. I watched Andy Robinson do it and the grief he got was unbelievable. Brian Ashton is going through the same now [March 2008] and it's just not worth it, not at the moment. Unless you feel absolutely certain that you can go into the set up with your own management you are on a hiding to nothing and personally, I don't want that hassle. It's a shocker, a hard job to do. England were runners up in the World Cup and Ashton still got slagged down. Warren Gatland has taken over Wales and brought in his own management team and in Shaun Edwards he's got a big ally within the set up. Brian hasn't got that.

Richard Hill played the game at the highest level and now coaches a successful club but he clearly holds no ambition to go that one step further. Unlike when he represented England as a player. When being asked to captain England was the ultimate goal. There was a time when Richard Hill would have found it difficult to relate to Bath's greatest rivals. As a player, he would probably have struggled to find a few good words to say about Bristol but now he lives and breathes the club with a passion that is refreshing to see. We shall return to Bristol in due course but there is still some unfinished business to attend to back down the A4.

Somebody was going to have to do it—but who? Will Carling led England to the Triple Crown in 1996, Ireland defeated at Twickenham in his final game as captain. He would play throughout the following season but was going to have to listen to someone else give the team talk, someone else rally the troops if things weren't going to plan on the field—but who?

Jack Rowell rang and said he would need to speak to me the following day and to make sure I had my phone on. I was playing golf with Henry Paul,

Mike Catt and Jon Callard; I shouldn't have left the mobile on but I had an inkling what was coming. We were playing a short par three when the call came; the others knew who it was and just hung back waiting for me to finish speaking to Jack. I ended the call and told them I was the new England captain—yes! A great moment.

That was in 1996, four years after **Phil de Glanville** won his first cap as a replacement against South Africa. By the time of his appointment, he had 16 caps to his name but of these, he won seven as a replacement, seven when one of the leading contenders missed a season through injury and two in the group stages of the 1995 World Cup. Captaincy material—you bet! When senior players such as Rob Andrew and Rory Underwood were asked to name Will Carling's replacement they pointed to the bench; that was where the next England captain would come from and nobody in the squad disagreed.

The influence of Oxford and Cambridge on the role of England captain has already played a big part in the story and there is more to come. But in fact, this strong association probably finishes with Phil de Glanville, the 40th and most recent captain to have passed through either university.

My parents were both teachers. My early years were spent in Zambia but when we returned the family settled in London and I went to Dulwich Prep School; my mother taught maths there and my father was teaching at the college. Eventually they made a conscious decision to get out of London and we moved to Tavistock in Devon which is right on the edge of Dartmoor; so I went from kicking a ball about in the street to living among all this open country.

I spent a couple of years at a very small prep school in Tavistock and then got a bursary to Bryanston School in Dorset, the start of a brilliant five years. Rarely did a day go by when we didn't do sport; shooting, tennis, rowing, cricket, athletics and of course rugby. I'd played hooker at Dulwich but my parents suggested I got out of the scrum so at Bryanston I switched to scrum-half with the occasional game at outside-half. In the holidays I played a few matches for Tavistock seconds, mainly at stand-off and it was actually my dad who was responsible for me becoming a centre. He'd played for Rosslyn Park in the 1970s with the likes of Phil Keith-Roach and Andy Ripley and the idea came from him, he suggested the move.

In 1980 dad left teaching and with his brother-in-law set up Rhino, a company manufacturing training equipment—scrummaging machines, post padding, tackle bags. He had contacts in Australia so before going to Durham University I spent a year in Queensland playing for the Colts at Western Districts in Brisbane and that was when I really began to develop as a player. It was dry and warm, the backs saw plenty of ball and my ability and performance improved—then it was Durham. There was a guy there called Ted Wood, a chap in his sixties who had been coaching in the north-east for years and I came under his wing a bit in terms of mentoring. He was a selector for England Students and I was invited to take part in the trials which was my first taste of England competition—I was 19.

In his first year at Durham de Glanville came across a player who was going to have a big influence on his rugby career. Will Carling was in his final year at the university and already an England player, travelling to London at weekends to play for the Harlequins. This meant that when he was available for the university he had to fit in where needed and with a successful centre partnership established Carling was invariably included at full-back. During his time at Durham, de Glanville played for the England Students in the Student World Cup held in France in 1988 and moved up to the England Under 21s, the next stage of a natural progression towards the top which continued in the right direction when he went to Oxford for a one year postgraduate course.

I studied economics and politics at Durham and social studies at Oxford. Politics was my main interest and if I hadn't met my wife I would probably have gone into politics—but she forbade me from being a politician! I won my Blue at Oxford and was starting to knock on the door but the Carling-Guscott partnership was well established. With the World Cup coming up Will and Jerry were never going to be dropped, at last there was the continuity which had been badly needed and I certainly don't have any gripes with the situation that existed. The battle between Will, Jerry and myself went on for six years and I probably spent more time on the bench than on the field. It was very frustrating; if you track the form of the three of us over that period there are times when the media suggested I was probably playing the better but it wasn't always a case of merit based selection, there was a bigger picture to consider.

Carling and Guscott played together in the centre for England on 44 occasions. For anyone hoping to break into the side the prospects were not good, the captain seemingly a permanent fixture and Guscott one of the great talents of the day. This was even more difficult to cope with for a player partnering Guscott week in week out at the same club but no matter how good a player waiting in the wings was he would have to be patient—three into two won't go.

After the Student World Cup I started to think about where I should play my club rugby. I was invited to play for Bristol against Clifton on Boxing Day but hardly got my hands on the ball. I received a call from Dave Robson who was involved in the coaching set up at Bath and he suggested I have a run out with the club; he'd seen me play against Clifton and felt that I would fit in. I played for the seconds against Cardiff and it was like chalk and cheese, end to end stuff, plenty of ball and I didn't really have a decision to make. In my first training session at Bath I was introduced to Jack Rowell and it was a case of, 'Sorry, who are you? What do you do here Jack?' He remembers that to this day and has never forgiven me!

The next two or three years saw the physical demands of the game gradually increase and also impacted more on the players' time. In addition to normal training Bath held two gym sessions a week which started at 6.00am; the club always travelled on the Friday night before an away match and Sundays were often spent in London training with England. The weekend was gone—it must have been extremely difficult for the guys with families.

The England squad used to meet on the Thursday before a match then it became the Wednesday, then the Tuesday; I would sit down with my employers at the start of the season and go through the time I was likely to need off. They would give me a certain number of days as their contribution. I would take some of it as holiday and some of it as unpaid leave. Fortunately I had a great boss but the ever growing demands meant it was inevitable that the game would go professional.

From an international perspective a player with de Glanville's versatility was ideal bench material and that was where he sat until an injury to wing Tony Underwood in an autumn international against the Springboks in 1992 saw him brought on for a first cap. When Ian Hunter had to leave the field in Cardiff there was a second cap but it was an injury much closer to home which saw de Glanville win a place in the starting line up.

A few months into the 1993–94 season Guscott was struggling with a groin problem that would keep him out of rugby for a year so when the team to play New Zealand at Twickenham in November was announced Phil de Glanville was included at centre alongside Carling. England recorded a notable victory and he was retained throughout the Five Nations. He also went on the summer tour to South Africa adding two more caps to the total but with Guscott back to full fitness, de Glanville returned to the replacements' bench and it was during this time of relative inactivity on the international stage that he learnt his trade as a captain.

John Hall couldn't play in the 1995 Cup Final so I took over as captain and the following season started my two years in the job. Bath played the most satisfying rugby; it all becomes a bit of a blur after a while but a few games do stick in the memory. We put 70 points on Gloucester in the league, they didn't touch the ball. A couple of their players said after the game that they had just been chasing shadows; every time they tackled someone the ball had gone. We hardly lost a game in that first season as captain—it was a pleasure and goes down as one of my best times in the game. The team spirit was fantastic, we worked hard, spent a lot of time on preparation and it paid off.

Bath won a cup and league double in 1995–96, Phil de Glanville leading a team that were only beaten twice in the league and with Will Carling about to stand down as England captain he was a serious contender to replace him. And so it proved.

Because of Will's involvement in issues off the field the role of England captain had become blown out of all proportion; the sense of what it was really about in danger of becoming lost. When your captain has paparazzi on his doorstep every day, people listening in on his mobile phone, all that sort of stuff, you began to question how anybody could live like that; Will was rarely off the front pages. When I went to the press conference at Twickenham where the announcement regarding my appointment was made, I had to keep my head down in the back of a car and be shepherded in through a side door—it was unbelievable. You have to try to understand the profile the role had taken on at that stage, even in the professional era it is way below what it was then—the press were constantly hounding and there was a moment when I wondered if I really wanted all this. After accepting the job, I made a conscious decision to squash it all, try to take the heat out of it. The press started turning up at my wife's school looking for new angles, wanting to do features on us both, would we do this or that interview but I said no and it pretty quickly went away.

Will played on for a season and people have often asked if it was hard having him in the squad—it wasn't. At team meetings and training sessions, he was happy to take a back seat and there were no problems. We started well beating Italy with a team that included several new caps then there was a match against the New Zealand Barbarians which was pretty much New Zealand but there were no caps awarded. We lost and I picked up a bad dead leg, which prevented my playing against Argentina, Jason Leonard taking over.

My biggest disappointment came in the 1997 Five Nations. England played some brilliant rugby to beat Ireland, Scotland and Wales and win the Triple Crown, scoring 30 or 40 points in each match but against France at Twickenham we let a 20–6 lead slip away. With 20 minutes remaining we successfully defended a series of five metre scrums and cleared the danger but when they got their hands on the ball the French ran in two brilliant tries as only they can do and suddenly the force was with them. That was my biggest regret because we could have had a Grand Slam.

That summer England toured Argentina. The Lions were in South Africa and a lot of the team were with the party. This meant there were some new faces in the squad. Argentina is always a difficult place to tour and we did well to win all the provincial matches and the first Test. We were thumped in the second after losing Mike Catt and Nigel Redman who were called up by the Lions but the real nightmare came later. A month after returning home we set off to play a Test in Australia. The squad included several of the Lions players who would fly straight from South Africa and we all met up in Sydney. They had played a Test the week before after which there had been a good end of tour bash and when they arrived on the Tuesday, they were still suffering and also had jet lag to overcome. That was a huge challenge for me. The guys who had been in Argentina were into their pre-season training, some light work in the gym and long runs, while the Lions were coming off a great high and all the time the RFU committee had been doing their stuff; Jack Rowell finding out two days before the Test that he was being cast aside—he was furious. It was terrible—my lowest point.

Clive Woodward was Rowell's replacement and set about putting his mark on the set up which included appointing a new captain and for Phil de Glanville the following two seasons were a mix of highs and lows. With the next World Cup fast approaching several players were introduced to international rugby as the search began in earnest for those who would make up the squad; in the centre Will Greenwood and a young Jonny Wilkinson providing competition for de Glanville and Guscott. Bath winning the Heineken Cup in 1998 compensated somewhat for another Championship spent on the bench as Greenwood rose to the plate and then a dislocated shoulder ruled de Glanville out of contention for the 1999 Championship which saw Wilkinson score 60 points making a strong case for his inclusion in the World Cup squad.

Greenwood and Wilkinson both made it, as did Guscott and with Wilkinson now preferred at number 10, there was also room for the ex-captain who ended his international career in the quarter-final against South Africa, the country he was first capped against seven years earlier. This time the result was very different; Phil de Glanville along with the rest of the England team and the 80,000 spectators who filled the Stade de France spending the second 40 minutes watching Jannie de Beer practicing his drop kicking skills, slotting five to sink England without trace.

Phil de Glanville retired from international rugby following the 1999 World Cup but continued playing with Bath until the end of the 2000–01 season when he finally called it a day. Since 2003 he has worked for Sport England which is largely government funded with additional monies coming from the National Lottery. Working in conjunction with local councils Sport England helps fund local projects for the benefit of the community which is '...very rewarding. When you find you are able to influence people's lives for the better either through the introduction of money or by advice it is very satisfying.'

Phil de Glanville's international rugby career was to a large extent mapped out around that of a long serving England captain, the longest serving, added to which there was also the competition from Guscott. So how coincidental is it that the third and most recent England captain to come from Bath should experience similar circumstances?

Martin Johnson is second only to Carling in the list of appearances as England captain and for much of that time Danny Grewcock was his partner in the second-row. By the time he arrived at Bath, Grewcock was an experienced international having already won caps as a Coventry and Saracens player. At his new club, he formed a formidable second-row partnership with **Steve Borthwick**, a player on the verge of international honours but now in the same position as de Glanville—unlikely to replace an exceptional captain and being edged out by his Bath colleague. With Simon Shaw and Ben Kay in the mix, for Borthwick the scenario was suggestive of some serious bench work at best—and not the type seen in the gym.

Of course, the average second-row forward is not quite the same animal as a centre three-quarter. There was no chance of Carling or Guscott getting sent off and banned for a couple of matches which would have aided de Glanville's cause no end. When things got a bit out of hand up front Johnson and Grewcock were never going to take a step back and such moments sometimes led to an enforced lay off leaving another door open for Borthwick.

He was first capped against France in 2001. England won comfortably but would have to wait until October to see if they could claim a Grand Slam and everything else on offer, forced to postpone the visit to Ireland due to an outbreak of foot-and-mouth. There was a summer tour to North America on which Borthwick won three caps but even with Johnson injured come the rearranged fixture there was no place for him in the side which went to Dublin in search of the previous season's silverware, only to return empty handed. England quickly recovered from the disappointment by beating Australia at Twickenham. Again, Grewcock and Kay got the nod ahead of Borthwick. He was included seven days later when England scored a record 134 points against Romania. But it was 18 months before he reappeared in an England jersey, as a replacement against Australia in the summer of 2003 in what was the final build up towards another World Cup.

Steve Borthwick didn't make the squad in 2003. The next few seasons saw him in and out of the team until the 2006 Six Nations during which he started all five matches. Even after his longest sequence of consecutive caps to date there was another long wait before he was included in the warm up matches which were England's final preparation before the defence of their title began. This time he did make the squad and played in the group stages but the selectors preferred Shaw and Kay when it got to the business end of the tournament.

Steve Borthwick was club captain at Bath in 2007–08 but when he announced he would be leaving to join Saracens at the end of the season he fell foul of the powers that be. Fortunately this didn't impact any further afield and he was included in the England team that started the 2008 Championship against Wales at Twickenham.

Players become international captains for a variety of reasons and in the case of Steve Borthwick his chance to lead England came when Phil Vickery had to withdraw from the team to play Italy, England's next opponents following a desperately poor second half performance against the Welsh. Under Borthwick's direction, England's season was back on track albeit with a less than convincing win in Rome. The Italians are no pushover in a tournament that has seen them frequently upset the odds and few teams travel to the Stadio Flaminio without a certain amount of caution—for Steve Borthwick then, it was a job well done. At the end of the season, he was appointed England captain for the summer tour to New Zealand, two Test matches that never fail to sort the men from the boys and for England, a team in transition, a tough place to start rebuilding.

How many men have captained England while playing for Gloucester? Ask any follower of the English game to name three or four clubs and the likelihood of Gloucester being one of them is high. It is one of the oldest clubs, dating back to 1873, and it is certainly one of the best supported. So how many England captains were playing for the West Country club when they were selected?

If **Phil Vickery** had moved to London Wasps a couple of seasons earlier than he did the answer would be none and the club would barely have had a mention in these pages which would have been a sad omission. But England's 2007 World Cup captain was a Gloucester player when he was first picked to lead the team against Argentina in Buenos Aires in 2002 and again in the group stages of the 2003 tournament, this time against the Pumas' near neighbours Uruguay.

Phil Vickery joined Gloucester in 1996, staying with the club for 10 seasons before moving to the Wasps. During his time at Kingsholm he not only became Gloucester's first England captain but also the club's record cap holder with 47 to his name before leaving for pastures new. At the end of the 2008 Six Nations the total had risen to 64 but on the back of a surprisingly successful World Cup in 2007 England's performances a few months later were woeful and many pundits began to question whether the captain was worth his place but Vickery held on. It was decided he would spend the summer at home which gave Steve Borthwick the chance to establish himself in the role and Vickery some long overdue R&R; time for the body to recover from the intense pressures it is subjected to in the front row.

The first cap came in 1998. Wales were the visitors to Twickenham on a day that saw England register a record 60 points against the men in red. Vickery replaced Leicester's Darren Garforth following a defeat in Paris but after an hour against the Welsh he was one of three changes made in the English pack thereby setting the tone for the immediate future; both props getting plenty of game time over the next two seasons. Garforth was in pole position during the 1999 Championship but Vickery was selected for the warm up matches before the World Cup and went into the tournament as the man in possession. He played in the group stages but sat out a quarter-final play-off before becoming one of those unfortunate enough to have to stand by and watch de Beer's lesson in the art of kicking drop goals.

Then another factor entered the equation in the shape of Julian White, but 18 months later when Graham Henry and his fellow selectors sat down to choose the British and Irish Lions who would tour Australia in the summer of 2001, Vickery was deemed to have done enough to earn himself a place in the party and in fact played in the three Test matches. These were important times for Vickery and all those with aspirations of playing in the 2003 World Cup. England's ultimate goal was getting ever nearer. By 2002 the ever astute Clive Woodward must have been well on the way to formulating the squad he wanted to take to Australia. When Vickery was chosen to lead England in Argentina during the summer and also played in the three autumn internationals that saw famous victories over New Zealand, Australia and South Africa on consecutive weekends, there was much to suggest that his name was pencilled in. Then injury struck and the chances of Vickery's participation suddenly took a marked downward turn.

In his second term as Gloucester captain Phil Vickery missed much of what proved to be an historic season for the club. Gloucester won the Powergen Cup and topped the Zurich Premiership League only to miss out in the inaugural Grand Final, a contentious event which saw all the season's efforts come down to the outcome of three additional matches involving the top four clubs (two semi-finals and a final). Wasps prevailed at Twickenham in what proved to be a one sided affair that undid all that had gone before. It counted for nothing that Gloucester had topped the league by 15 points and won four games more than the runners-up. Sods law saw to it that Vickery was absent when the club lifted the Powergen Cup in April but included in the team beaten by Wasps on 31 May.

Two weeks later England played New Zealand in Wellington. When Jason Leonard left the field at the end of the second half he was replaced by a rejuvenated Vickery who helped the visitors defy the odds by beating the All Blacks on their home turf. This after being reduced to 13 men for a brief period during which six forwards successfully defended a scrum on their own line. England defeated Australia seven days later, Vickery included in the starting line up and Woodward's jigsaw was almost complete. What happened later in the year is to be found elsewhere but suffice to say that Vickery played a part in all England's games during the 2003 World Cup and experienced that second outing as captain against Uruguay in the group stages—a taste of things to come.

No sooner is one World Cup over then everything becomes focussed on the next. As reigning champions, England became the team everyone wanted to beat. There was nothing new in that but this time there was the added incentive of downing the champions' colours and down them they did. Opponents were queuing up for a crack at a team which by 2005 looked far from world champions and a year later were in freefall losing a record seven consecutive matches—something had to be done. As is the norm, the coach became the fall guy. When Andy Robinson departed, Brian Ashton took his place and, for the first game in the 2007 Six Nations, appointed Phil Vickery as his England captain. Vickery still had niggling injuries to contend with but he did play in three Championship matches and he was present when Wasps lifted the Heineken Cup later in the season but he sat out England's summer tour to South Africa. Another complete rest was prescribed if he was to take his place in the squad and lead England later in the year.

Never before had the defending champions been so readily written off. England were declared no hopers by the media and many felt they would struggle to go beyond the group stages. Such pessimism seemed well founded when South Africa beat them 36–0 and with Samoa and Tonga waiting to deliver the coup de grace all seemed lost. To their eternal credit, the England players rallied together and made it through to the quarter-finals only to be paired with Australia, a nation still struggling to come to terms with 2003. In a titanic struggle, Phil Vickery led his men with great character and conviction despatching the Wallabies and then knocking hosts France out in the semi-final played in front of a hugely partisan home crowd. England were in the final, the outcome of which would have little bearing on the fact that as defending champions this squad of players had already acquitted themselves well.

England walked out at the Stade de France to meet South Africa, a team which had beaten them four times in the last 12 months. Eighty minutes later it became five times. It was not a repeat of the hammering inflicted in the group stages and the final score of 15–6 perhaps suggests a closer game than the final actually was. If not for a miniscule suggestion of a foot in touch that required much deliberation by the fourth official before a Mark Cueto 'try' was rightly disallowed the game may have had a different outcome. The fact that the Springboks were the better team on the day has never been questioned by even the most diehard England supporter and there were plenty of those in Paris.

Vickery's men had restored some much needed pride to English rugby but it was short lived. A disappointing Six Nations saw Ashton come under fire from critics who needed little encouragement. By the time Jonny Wilkinson was dropped following the defeat at Murrayfield supporters had long since forgotten the heroics witnessed in France a few months earlier. Truthfully, any number of England players could (or perhaps should) have been dropped following the Scotland game. It would have come as no surprise if the captain had been among them but Vickery survived to fight another day. Only time will tell whether Vickery, Brian Ashton and several other players who did not step up to the plate in the 2008 Championship continue to play a part in the England set up. As captain he might be more vulnerable than most but whatever the future holds his has been a story of triumph over much adversity and for that he should be congratulated.

And so to Bristol. In comparative terms Bristol are the new arrivals among the West Country trio. Founded in 1888 the club is younger than Bath and Gloucester by some 23 and 15 years respectively. That counts for nothing in 2008 which sees all three competing in the Guinness Premiership. Their close proximity to each other together with the serious rivalry that has long existed between them ensures full houses whenever two meet.

There was a time when Bristol could have fallen victim to the professional game. The club could have dropped down the leagues and become another name famously linked with the past. But thanks to some well intentioned individuals who possessed the necessary business acumen, the arrival of Richard Hill and a draft of quality players two seasons in National Division One ended with promotion to the Premiership in 2005. Currently, Bristol appears to be comfortable and enjoying life among the elite of English club rugby.

It has been 20 years since a player from Bristol last captained England. When the England team summarily dropped Richard Hill following events in Cardiff, Bristol's **Richard Harding** was picked to replace him at scrum-half against Scotland. Harding was first capped in 1985 since when the position had been contested between himself, Hill and Nigel Melville. When Hill fell foul of the authorities, Harding found himself first choice at the first World Cup. Two group games and the quarter-final defeat by Wales brought his tally of caps to seven but Melville reclaimed the jersey after an absence of two years for the start of the 1988 Championship.

Harding did get on as a replacement against Ireland at Twickenham and returned to the starting line up for an end of season game to celebrate the centenary of Dublin. England won both matches and when the selectors announced the tour party to travel to Australia and Fiji in the summer Harding was one of two scrum-halves included. Despite the presence of many leading international players, the tour was a great disappointment England rarely producing anything to suggest they had improved since the World Cup. Both Tests ended in defeat but there was a chance to repair some of the damage with a first Test against Fiji completing the itinerary.

Richard Harding led England against a nation whose rugby players are never less than compromising while at the same time being capable of playing the most entertaining rugby. Fiji consistently produces big, physical players who are all comfortable with ball in hand running in tries from all over the park. The mix of talent, rock hard surfaces and the high temperatures makes playing in the Pacific Islands a testing experience and Richard Harding can take some pleasure in the knowledge that he led England to victory in the face of such difficulties in what was his 12th and final international appearance.

It is only in recent years that Fijian rugby has started to register results which, with the talent and athleticism of the players available, one could have expected much earlier. The biggest upset of the 2007 World Cup came when Fiji defeated Wales in the group stages. This earned the Islanders a place in the quarter-finals but for so long the rugby world has watched and wondered why such skilful and physical players struggled to come to grips with the forward encounters—the scrum and lineout—areas which a team must control if games are to be won. The reason behind this may lie in a hybrid version of the game, one which sees teams reduced in number and that caters for the skill and speed of the Fijians—seven-a-side rugby.

Long before the introduction of the Sevens World Series, Hong Kong was, and remains, the home of international seven-a-side rugby and over many years there have been no greater exponents of this thrilling spectacle than Fiji. In 1990, Fiji beat New Zealand in the final of the Hong Kong tournament, the 20 minute game played in atrocious conditions. At one point from a position deep inside his own half Fiji's Walsale Serevi, recognised as the master of the sevens game, threw an outrageous pass between his legs which led to a try at the other end of the field. Nobody present or watching on television had ever seen anything like it unless they were around 80 years of age, had a particularly good memory and were at Twickenham in January 1923.

Bristol cannot lay claim to an England captain since Richard Harding. Twenty years have passed but that is a mere interlude when one considers it was over 60 years following the foundation of the club before the first Bristol player to captain England appeared. **Leonard Corbett** was a centre three-quarter who received glowing reports in his day. The best receiver and passer of a ball of his time, he was also one of the first players to use the dummy to great effect often leaving despairing tacklers in his wake. He learnt these skills on the playing fields of Fairfield School in Bristol and developed them at Bristol Saracens and Cotham Park before being finally honed to perfection at Bristol.

It did not take long for the England selectors to recognise these skills and in 1921, Len Corbett won his first cap outside stand-off W.J.A. Davies in a three-quarter line that included Cyril Lowe, Ernie Hammett and Alistair Smallwood. The match saw England secure the Grand Slam, but for Corbett it was two years before he earned a recall, playing in two matches of another Grand Slam season. That was in 1923 and a year later Corbett played in all four matches of yet another successful campaign and the record now read seven caps—seven games for England all of which were won.

Corbett was now part of the establishment and played throughout the 1924–25 season but it is a fact of life that great periods of sustained success are followed by a fall from grace. England proved to be no exception to this when some level of mediocrity returned to the team between 1925 and 1927.

Corbett was in and out of the team but for the 1927 Championship, he was installed as captain and led England in all four matches. Wales and Ireland were beaten, the games with Scotland and France lost. Just as a fall from grace is inevitable so too is a rise from the ashes and in 1928 England returned to Grand Slam winning ways but with a new centre pairing and under a new captain. Len Corbett's career had spanned six seasons during which English rugby enjoyed much success. The players around Corbett enjoyed the benefit of thoughtful and accurate distribution by a centre who could present the ball on a platter at precisely the right moment—most of the time.

In 1923 England's first opponents were Wales at Twickenham. The home side won a close match 7–3, the deciding score a drop goal, which at the time was worth four points. In his book *Rugger* co-written with H.P. Marshall, W.W. Wakefield refers to the game and the score which ultimately set England on the road to the Grand Slam. '...suddenly Corbett, who was hemmed in by Welshmen in mid-field, passed between his legs to Smallwood on the wing, and Smallwood, evidently startled, immediately dropped a very fine goal from near the touchline.' This was not a defining moment in English rugby but it confirms that what goes around comes around.

International rugby players are among the most travelled sportsmen. Thanks to the great advances in air travel the world has become a small place which allows players from both hemispheres to spend six or seven days in Hong Kong, play a sevens tournament and move on to the next venue. Be that in South America, South Africa or Europe is of little relevance; the plane will take the strain and globetrotting rugby players move through the departure and arrival halls as a matter of course. Before the 1950s, air travel and rugby had yet to be united. The summer tours to the southern hemisphere undertaken by the British Lions began and ended with weeks at sea aboard ocean liners. For teams travelling to away matches in the Five Nations the journey would be by rail with the added attraction of a short encounter with the English Channel or Irish Sea if France or Ireland were the destination. Rugby players kept their feet firmly on the ground but in 1930, there was a break in tradition and a sign of things to come.

Sam Tucker won his first cap against Wales in 1922. A comprehensive defeat did not bring about the normal knee jerk reaction by the selectors as England had won a Grand Slam in 1921. The upset was accepted as a minor setback but for Tucker it had a more lasting effect as he didn't play for his country again for three years. Five hookers were chosen before he was recalled in the team to play New Zealand, a match that marked the start of a run of 20 consecutive appearances that ended when Ireland won at Twickenham in 1929.

At the start of the next season Sam Tucker was in his 35th year and not included in the team to play Wales. The hooker's berth was handed to Robert Sparks, returning after a two year absence. Many players have had to withdraw from international duty for all manner of reasons and when Sparks came off his motor bike on the eve of the match he became one of that unfortunate number and Sam Tucker found the door to international rugby open once again. The only problem facing the selectors was how to get the replacement to Cardiff in time for the match. Nowadays Bristol is an hour from Cardiff by road or rail but travel wasn't that straightforward in 1930 so when it was decided to fly Sam Tucker to Cardiff on the morning of the match this was a fairly unique experience. He is surely one of the first players, if not the very first, to be transported to a Championship match by air.

An England team including nine new caps defeated Wales and Tucker kept his place throughout the Championship taking over the captaincy for the home matches with France and Scotland and continuing in the role at the start of the following season against Wales. This was the eighth time Sam Tucker played against the Welsh and he only tasted defeat when winning his first cap. The match that saw him win his 27th and final cap ended in a draw giving him the added achievement of not having led England in defeat, a win and two drawn matches his record as captain.

Sam Tucker was equally successful when leading the great Bristol teams of the late 1920s and Gloucestershire during the same period which saw the county crowned champions in consecutive seasons. As captain of both club and county, Tucker had gained a wealth of experience which would stand him in good stead when he was invited to lead England but such experience is not necessarily considered essential as another hooker from the Bristol club demonstrated some 40 years later.

John Pullin began his rugby with Bristol Saracens and it was not long before word got around that a young hooker of some ability was making a name for himself at the local club. Such notices quickly attracted the attention of Bristol and the inevitable happened.

You were 'invited' to play for Bristol. I started in the United because John Thorne was first choice but he picked up an injury and I got a call one Friday night telling me I was in the team to play Newport the next day. I'd never closely followed rugby so the name Bryn Meredith didn't mean a lot to me at the time. [Meredith was a Welsh international of some renown that had been on two British Lions tours when Pullin packed down opposite him.] I took a strike against the head and John Blake dropped a goal to win the match which meant I kept my place against Swansea and then Cardiff and I ended up playing about 14 games on the trot.

We travelled to Northampton who had a hooker called Andy Johnson, the best I ever played against; he took me apart and I was dropped for the next game. Johnson never played for England, the problem being he was so good the selectors were reluctant to pick him because referees thought he must be cheating and he had a lot of penalties awarded against him. Jeff Young of Wales suffered in much the same way. He also got a reputation and was frequently penalised for nothing other than being good at what he did. A referee would come along, see Jeff's name on the team sheet and decide on reputation alone that he would be penalised three times whereas I never had that sort of reputation and could break all the Laws in the book and get away with it.

I won my first cap against Wales in 1966, a game we could have won but Don Rutherford missed a penalty in front of the posts at a crucial time and as a result five of us were dropped and it was two years before I was picked again. Bill Treadwell and Steve Richards played during that time. I remember Richards coming to play in the pre-season trials at Bristol but I saw him off and when we were both included in the England party to tour Canada in 1967 he was the recognised number one but I ended up playing in the major games and that was the end of his international career.

Pullin still hadn't done enough to convince the England selectors that he was the man for the job. They preferred Bert Godwin of Coventry when the time came to select a team to play the New Zealand tourists in the autumn. Godwin was a player last capped three years earlier, but when it came to the opening match of the Five Nations, Pullin was awarded his second cap, the start of a run of 36 consecutive appearances including 12 matches as captain. Following his recall, Pullin, played under nine captains, watching them come and go until his turn finally came when he was asked to lead England on a summer tour to South Africa in 1972.

I'd no real experience of captaincy. I led Bristol on the odd occasion when the appointed captain was unavailable but realistically, you didn't want the England job because in those days it was the first sign that you were on your way out; you tried to stay clear of it. It was desperation on the selectors' part really. If I had said no, I don't know what they would have done but it would almost certainly have been the end of my England career. I suppose it was coming up to my turn and I couldn't side step it any longer but I didn't really want to be captain knowing that if things went wrong I would be out.

We'd had a terrible season losing all four Championship matches for the first time so a tour to South Africa was seen by many as a recipe for disaster as we were scheduled to play seven matches including a Test and some of the stronger provinces. I'd been to South Africa before, with the Lions in 1968 and the Barbarians in 1969, so I knew it wasn't going to be a picnic but we did well. We were held to a draw by Northern Transvaal but won the other matches including the Test which was seen as something of a national disaster. It was assumed we were there for the taking after the performances in the Five Nations and they were supposed to be the best team in the world at the time. The defeat didn't go down well and after the match the coach took his players away and gave them a right going over; he wouldn't let them attend the after match reception and only one, I think it was Piet du Plessis, eventually turned up a couple of hours late. It may have meant a lot to them but it was bad manners really.

Any preconceived ideas Pullin may have had that by taking over the captaincy his England days were numbered were soon laid to rest. England retained him as captain for the game against the New Zealand tourists in January 1973 and for the Championship in which France and Scotland were beaten. These were welcome confidence boosters for the task that lay ahead; another summer tour, this time to New Zealand preceded by a stopover in Fiji. Scraping a 13–12 victory in Suva was not good preparation and when Taranaki, Wellington and Canterbury summarily beat the tourists, the idea that here was a team capable of competing against the All Blacks in Auckland seemed outrageous. What escaped most people's attention however was that England, while conceding seven tries in the four matches had also scored seven with some indifferent goal kicking proving costly.

In front of 55,000 spectators at Eden Park John Pullin and his team rose to the biggest of rugby challenges and defeated New Zealand outscoring them by three tries to two in the process. With away victories against South Africa and New Zealand under his captaincy, John Pullin now had the chance of a unique treble as England were due to play Australia at Twickenham in November. England claimed another scalp meaning the three southern hemisphere giants had all been defeated within an 18 month period, something never achieved before and all the more notable as the victories arrived under the same captain.

With such success it was inconceivable that the selectors would begin looking for a replacement and in 1974 Pullin continued throughout what was a disappointing Five Nations campaign. The following season the RFU appointed John Burgess as England coach and he in turn installed Fran Cotton as captain. Coinciding with these changes was the first real threat to John Pullin's lengthy run of appearances in the shape of Leicester's Peter Wheeler.

I was dropped to the bench after a defeat in Dublin and Peter Wheeler took over for the French game, which we also lost, but he kept his place against Wales where he came up against the famous Pontypool front row. They soon saw him off and I went on to win my only cap as a replacement and remained in the side for the Scotland game. I went to Australia in the summer and when tour captain Tony Neary was injured I led the team for the last time in the second Test which was also my final appearance for England.

The next few seasons didn't see me play much club rugby. If England had wanted me back I would have been ready but after the summer tours I had to make up time on the farm particularly after Lions tours when I was away for three or four months. That usually meant I wouldn't turn up at the club for a couple of months after my return which didn't go down very well at Bristol but I wasn't that bothered to be honest; I've always felt more of a Gloucester man really. I enjoyed playing for the county and there was a time when I nearly joined Gloucester after Bristol brought someone in over me while I was still playing for England. They were going to make him captain and I told them that if they didn't see me as first choice hooker any longer I would move on with Gloucester my likely destination. That all got sorted but in hindsight I do think I was more akin to playing for Gloucester than Bristol; at the end of the day I didn't chose that option. Bristol weren't a bad club but I always felt they would have liked to drop me; I just never gave them the chance.

John Pullin is a Gloucester man through and through. Only he knows what kept him at Bristol when the club's greatest rivals held such appeal but he went some way to getting the best of both worlds with his numerous appearances for Gloucestershire, helping the county to three Championship finals. In 1972, Gloucestershire beat Warwickshire and a year later met Lancashire in the final played at Bristol. Under Pullin's captaincy the county had to accept second best on the day but the disappointment was forgotten a year later when the same teams met again in the final, Gloucestershire reversing the previous year's outcome in winning the title for a record 11th time.

Things became very different once my England days were over. Bristol brought in a young hooker and I settled into playing a few games for the United which was fine but I remember giving training a miss for a week so I could get involved with the kids on Bonfire Night. I rang the club and withdrew from the team blaming an old injury which still gave me the odd niggle. The committee obviously weren't best pleased and when I rang up the following week to say I was fit for selection I was told that as I hadn't been fit the previous week I wasn't needed and they slammed down the phone.

That would have been it but I got a call on the Friday asking me to be a replacement against Lydney and having said I was fit I could hardly refuse. The hooker got a right pasting and wasn't on the field long so I had a game, and ended up seeing the season out. I was becoming ever more aware of my responsibilities at the farm and found myself hanging back a bit in an effort to stay out of trouble. That is the time when you do pick up injuries. I couldn't afford any serious problems so decided to call it a day.

Today we would call John Pullin an elite player. He kept himself fresh and best prepared for the big stage and why not, at a time when players were amateur in every sense of the word and being a self-employed farmer any serious injury would impact where it hurt most—in the pocket. International rugby saw the best of John Pullin. His 42 England caps and

13 appearances as captain were both records at the time of his retirement and he starred for the British Lions in South Africa in 1968 appearing in three Tests and again in 1971 when he played in all four Tests against New Zealand; his place in English rugby's hall of fame is well deserved.

Then there was the Barbarians and a famous day in Cardiff—27 January 1973. The 1971 heroics still fresh in the memory the traditional end of tour fixture saw a Barbarians team including 12 Lions take on the seventh All Blacks, a team intent on revenge. Outstanding match as this most certainly was it will always be best remembered for the most shown try in rugby history accompanied by Cliff Morgan's enthusiastic commentary which ensures that the name Pullin will never be forgotten. '…this is great stuff. Phil Bennett covering…brilliant, oh that's brilliant. John Williams… Pullin, John Dawes, great dummy…'

And the rest, as they say, is history.

5

THE MISFITS

Cambridge University, Cardiff, London Irish, Oxford University,
RNEC Keyham, United Services Portsmouth, Wanderers

The best laid plans of mice and men...Everything was straightforward; list the captains, categorise them into regions based on where they were playing at the time they first captained England and write about each region in turn. A total of 112 players were cooperative, there were no issues other than when two clubs could lay claim to a player's allegiance during his period as captain but on closer inspection the remaining 10 players could not be found a home within the great scheme of things. These players don't conform to a simple north, south, east or west classification so room had to be found elsewhere for them; 10 men with less obvious connections to the captaincy but no less important for that.

The Inter Services tournament was introduced in 1920 with the inclusion of the newly formed Royal Air Force Rugby Union. The Army and Royal Navy had commenced fixtures in the 1906–07 season but the inclusion of the RAF allowed a triangular competition to begin which continues to this day. It is perfectly understandable that the RAF should be last to arrive at the table (as man knew he could walk and swim long before realising he could also fly) but with the resumption of international rugby in 1920, this unique sequence of fixtures found its place in the rugby calendar.

Wavell Wakefield was one of the leading advocates of RAF rugby as both a player and administrator and he played no small part in the founding of the club. It was fitting then that he should captain the team in its first Inter Services match. However, later developments dictate that his is a story to be told elsewhere. This is not so for one of his opponents in that first fixture at Queen's Club London played on 7 February 1920. The RAF lost to a Royal Navy team that would dominate the first three years of the new tournament due in no small part to an outside-half who the best part

90

of a century later, still demands to be included among the greats of English rugby. What possible measurement with any tangible meaning can be found to support such a statement when the game has changed so much? How can we compare like with like? The truth is that we cannot but consider the following and then decide if there is a valid argument to be made.

William 'Dave' Davies was always destined for the Royal Navy. Born in Pembroke—the Welsh still question how he was allowed to get away—Davies served an apprenticeship at the local dockyard. Later his chosen career in naval engineering determined he should spend time learning his craft in a more academic arena. At the Royal Naval Engineering College at Keyham and subsequently the Royal Naval College, Greenwich he proved diligent in his studies and equally successful on the fields of play before eventually relocating to Portsmouth to take up his duties. It was there that his rugby career really began, the young stand-off appearing for the United Services Portsmouth and the Royal Navy.

For three seasons Adrian Stoop and Harry Coverdale had been the England selectors' preferred choices. Both featured in two of the Championship matches in 1912 and looked likely candidates to continue in 1913 when an additional fixture saw the new year begin with a match against South Africa. The Springboks' final game in Britain was against England on 4 January by which time Scotland, Ireland and Wales had all been accounted for but it hadn't all been plain sailing. Newport and Swansea had risen to the occasion to record famous victories as had London, albeit at the second attempt. At Blackheath on 26 October 1912 a London divisional side fought gamely before losing 12–8 and on 16 November, much the same was expected in the second meeting between the teams played at Twickenham, particularly with Stoop and John Birkett unavailable through injury. Stoop's omission opened the door for 'Dave' Davies and as is so often the case, through one player's misfortune another will benefit. In this particular instance so too did the national team. London defeated the tourists 10–8 and seven weeks later Davies was one of five new caps in an England team determined to succeed where the other home nations had failed.

The Springboks prevailed at Twickenham to gain a deserved victory and an alternative grand slam. Despite the disappointing 9–3 defeat the new outside-half had done enough for the selectors to keep faith in him and

Davies was included in a team showing only two changes for the opening game of the Championship in Cardiff. Visits to the Principality had been fruitless for some years. Traditionally the first match of the Championship, England's hopes of Triple Crowns and Grand Slams had often been dashed on previous sorties beyond Offa's Dyke but in 1913 the dismal run came to an end. By beating the Welsh in their own backyard so began 11 years of unparalleled success.

We will never know what might have happened if rugby football had not been put on hold from 1914–1920 but if we consider the seasons immediately before and after the war then there is much to suggest that England may well have enjoyed the greatest decade in her history. In the box seat, controlling game after game was Davies with William Cheeseman as his first half-back partner followed by Francis Oakeley, also of the United Services. These were the half-backs in England's back to back Grand Slams of 1913 and 1914 confirming the ascendancy that had started to gain momentum in 1910 following a decade of mediocrity. But the young men of the land were soon to be called to a much greater cause, one which asked far too many to make the greatest sacrifice.

Davies spent the war years serving aboard HMS Iron Duke and HMS Queen Elizabeth in the Grand Fleet following which he returned to Portsmouth and resumed his career as assistant constructor with the Admiralty. International rugby started again in 1920 but other levels began to pick up the pieces a little earlier and there is record of Davies playing for the Royal Navy against the Rest of Fleet in 1919. His second half-back partner before the war had been Francis Oakeley who was declared lost at sea in December 1914. Oakeley was a lieutenant in the submarine division and it was with another submariner that Davies would soon form a winning partnership.

Cecil Kershaw won his first cap for England against Wales in 1920 partnered by Blackheath's Harry Coverdale who had preceded Davies at outside-half. England suffered a first post war defeat in Swansea but with Davies now available he joined forces with Kershaw and three victories followed. Come the 1921 campaign there was an ominous look of stability and confidence among the England ranks which suggested that the RFU would enjoy a successful jubilee and they were not disappointed. With Davies now captain England ran their opponents ragged conceding only three penalties in the four matches while scoring 14 tries. A third Grand

Slam was a formality despite a stern French effort in the final match. England could now boast three Grand Slams in four seasons, losing only one of 16 matches one in which Davies did not feature. Neither did he play in the opening game in 1922 which saw a resurgent Wales embarrass the reigning champions, scoring eight tries in a 28–6 mauling at Cardiff Arms Park. The selectors reacted by introducing five new caps for another away game, this time in Dublin, and with Davies back in the team it was business as usual. Davies' only blemish on his record in the Championship was a fortunate draw with France at Twickenham, the season ending with a fifth consecutive Calcutta Cup victory.

The 1923 Championship was 'Dave' Davies' last and, as was always the case with this most gifted individual, he went out on a high at the peak of his career. Wales dug deep at Twickenham before losing 7–3; England overwhelmed Ireland at Welford Road, Leicester; Scotland matched England's two tries but failed to convert either going down 8–6; and France lost a player through injury giving England a numerical advantage for much of the game which they fully exploited. England recorded another Grand Slam, the fourth in six seasons with another to follow in 1924 but Davies would play no part in that. His had been a memorable international career; he had been on the winning side in 20 of his 22 appearances and successful captain in 10 of the 11 games in which he led England. Davies' record is almost perfect only South Africa and France denying him victories. His final act on the international stage came courtesy of a drop goal in the dying moments in Paris. But how good was he?

Some observers of the day were of the opinion that Davies benefited hugely from the quality of his scrum-half partners in particular Oakeley and Kershaw but this can be said of many of the great outside-halves and should not be allowed to diminish Davies' undoubted ability. It is best to seek out the opinion of someone who saw him play. In his 1944 publication *Rugger: The Man's Game*, E.H.D. Sewell describes Davies thus, 'What hands! And kicking ability. An elegant stand-off who wheedled his way through with a length of stride incredible but factual. A great nurse of a tiring pack.' Elsewhere in the same book and with the same prosaic style Sewell writes, '"Dave" indisputably ranks very high in the position. I can see him now gliding, or slithering, rather than running along pouching passes when going full bat, or dropping a much needed goal with telling accuracy. His "forward easer", short punts into touch, never overdone, were proverbial, and helped the chances of his side beyond compute.' Much may be lost in translation but the message is clear. There is more, this quote comes from one who played with Davies. In the 1927 publication, *Rugger* co-written with H.P. Marshall, Wavell Wakefield refers to Davies as '...the artist and philosopher.' He continues in reference to Davies' leadership qualities, 'He was a great player and a great leader...at his best when things went none too well. It was then that his philosophy appeared, for defeat never worried him, and the result was the last of his cares. He would come round when a try had been scored against us, quietly encouraging, pointing out our weaknesses, urging us to greater effort. He knew well enough when to blame bad play of any sort, but as an instinctive leader he knew also when to praise. To me he is the best representative of the real spirit of Rugger...'

It is not the purpose of this book to seek out England's finest captain but if it were there can be little doubt that W.J.A. Davies would feature on the short list. For a captain who had a good run in the role over a few seasons and among those who led the team on more than six occasions his record of 10 victories and one match drawn is difficult to improve on particularly when considering the two Grand Slams delivered during the period. Little surprise then that following his retirement from international rugby he should become a national selector and between the years 1925–28 help build a team which would deliver yet another Grand Slam.

The Grand Slam is the ultimate accolade for those competing in what became a Six Nations Championship with the inclusion of Italy in 2000. Obviously all opponents must be defeated in the season and in achieving this it goes without saying that the successful country is crowned champions. And if the winner is one of the four home nations, there is the added bonus of a Triple Crown. Grand Slams are not easy titles to gain. Many favourites have fallen at the most unlikely hurdle proving that a team can take nothing for granted in this finest of international tournaments. Just ask the Irish who have only one to their credit; won in 1948, that single success now hangs over the national team like an albatross.

On 15 March 1913 England won her first Grand Slam. 'Dave' Davies had only just arrived on the international stage which meant the honour of leading England lay elsewhere and it was **Norman Wodehouse** who called the shots from the depths of the scrum. First capped against France in 1910, Wodehouse lost his place for the final match of that season. The selectors reinstated him at the start of the next season from when he was present until retiring in 1913. Wodehouse played all his club rugby for the United Services and Royal Navy. Undoubtedly a fine rugby footballer who enjoyed success at the highest level his rugby career is somewhat dwarfed when one considers the achievements he aspired to in his professional calling.

At the age of 20 Wodehouse was a Lieutenant serving during the First World War following which he was promoted to Commander. He spent most of the inter-war years overseas and by 1939 had risen to the rank of Rear-Admiral and been made a Companion of the Order of the Bath. On his retirement a year later having recently been promoted to Vice-Admiral, Wodehouse became ADC to HM King George VI but this position was short lived, his recall from the retired list taking him back into active service and in September 1941, Vice-Admiral Norman Wodehouse CB was declared missing, presumed lost at sea when in command of an Atlantic convoy.

Wodehouse is not a common surname, you won't find another in the lists of international players and the name is undoubtedly best known through the works of one of literature's greatest comic writers. How ironic then that the only recorded criticism aimed at Norman Wodehouse, albeit indirectly, during his tenure as England captain should come from his namesake, Pelham Grenville 'Plum' Wodehouse, a great follower of the game who was prompted to write a humorous verse or two about the English three-quarter play during the 1913 season and, furthermore, get a leading London journal to publish it.

The problem was that 'Plum' was educated at Dulwich College and on the right wing for England during the 1913 Championship was Cyril Lowe, also an Old Alleynian. Lowe had pace in abundance which he proved on many occasions for the college first XV and more recently Cambridge University but in winning his first five caps he saw little of the ball and failed to score prompting PG to condemn those players inside him in satirical verse. Maybe there was a certain bias. It is doubtful if the great man would have taken such umbrage had Lowe been an Old Rugbeian for example but, whatever the reason, his words received a wide circulation and although Norman Wodehouse retired at the end of the season Lowe continued in the team and went on to win a further 20 caps either side of the war. Following Plum's dig it would appear he saw a lot more of the ball, scoring 18 tries and in doing so becoming England's record try scorer which he remained until Rory Underwood eventually bettered his tally in 1990.

In the years immediately preceding and following the First World War the England selectors were spoilt for choice when deliberating over who should captain the team. W.J.A. Davies and Norman Wodehouse were given their chance and proved to be high calibre leaders. The selectors could also have considered other representatives of the various services. Group Captain Cyril Lowe and Captain Cecil Kershaw RN were both experienced enough and there is little doubt that Captain, later Major, Alfred MacIlwaine would have made a good fist of it. In the end it was down to Davies and Wodehouse to represent the services as international captains but they were not the first.

Ernest 'E.W.' Roberts first played for England in 1901, one of those miserable seasons for English rugby which came along all too often at the start of the century; all three matches ended in defeat and Roberts was replaced in the back row after two appearances. His naval career took him overseas in 1902 and on his return two years later he quickly re-established himself in rugby circles and was one of the founder members of the Royal Navy RFC and a great supporter of the Devonshire county team. Both were extremely successful during the period, Devon enjoying unprecedented success in the County Championship and the Navy immediately getting the better of their military rivals. These were high profile fixtures but it still came as a surprise when Roberts was selected to win his third cap against the New Zealand tourists in December 1905, almost five years after winning his last.

'E.W.' was fated. Defeat was followed by two more disappointing performances against Wales and Ireland and once again, he found himself surplus to requirements. A year later comprehensive defeats in Swansea and Dublin once again left the selectors scratching their heads and when the team to play Scotland in the last game of the 1907 campaign was announced Ernest Roberts was included as captain (RNEC Keyham his named club). There would be no happy end to his England career; the Scots won a fifth Triple Crown and dashed any hopes he may have held of experiencing victory in an England jersey—six caps in six years and all six matches lost.

Ernest Roberts' naval career was a glittering one. Returning from overseas, he was appointed instructor of cadets on HMS Britannia and later

HMS Cornwall. By 1914, he had risen to the rank of Lieutenant-Commander and the war years were spent on destroyers. In 1919 he was appointed to the Admiralty where he held several positions specifically related to physical fitness and sport during which time he wrote sports handbooks for both the Royal Navy and Royal Marines. He was also instrumental in acquiring the Rectory Field in Plymouth as a permanent home ground for Devonport Services and which still serves as the club's headquarters. In 1931 Roberts was appointed Naval assistant to the Second Sea Lord and a year later elevated to the rank of Rear-Admiral.

'He was one of the best forwards England ever had, clever, genuine, with plenty of pace and a football brain. The men of Devon worshipped him and he was intensely popular with all ranks of the Navy.' These words are taken from an obituary that appeared in the 1934–35 edition of the *Rugby Football Annual* and sum up perfectly Roberts' playing and leadership qualities. As an RFU committee member he also embraced the task of England selector and it was while looking at players in the north west that he met a sudden and untimely end. Ernest Roberts was found dead in a hotel bedroom in Manchester on 19 November 1933, a heart attack later determined as the cause; he was 55 years old.

It would be disappointing if any reader were yet to be convinced that this chapter is not fully justified in its own right or that the captains discussed should have been accommodated elsewhere. A Rear-Admiral and a Vice-Admiral join the growing list and it is appropriate that we now concentrate on a man who rose even higher among the ranks and as a full-back played twice for England including one outing as captain.

Admiral Sir George Hamilton D'Oyly Lyon KCB was a lieutenant when first capped by England. Although he was 24 years old at the time, he was of the firm belief that he had been capped too soon. Along with E.W. Roberts, Lyon was another of the founder members of the Royal Navy RFC and would play all his club rugby for the United Services and Navy. In addition to his England caps other representative honours included county rugby for Hampshire and Surrey and he was a member of the Barbarians joining the club on two Easter tours to South Wales. But it was his inclusion in another team which stole the headlines. Speculation and uninformed comment are regularly to be found in the press and it would appear that things were little different 100 years ago. 'Warship chases footballer down Channel' cried the headlines.

Lieutenant George Lyon regularly supervised training sessions on a gunboat which meant spending five days in the English Channel—Monday to Friday. While carrying out this particular duty he was selected to play for London against Australia at Richmond. When Friday came, he was instructed to stay with the training ship and informed the secretary of the London Division by telegraph that he was unable to play. There it would have ended if not for a chance remark made at a dinner on the Friday night; Commander Lord Chatfield on hearing of the situation immediately arranged for Lyon to be replaced in time to get the morning train from Portsmouth to London. Food was taken out to the gunboat daily and an earlier delivery than normal was arranged for the Saturday morning to allow time for Lyon to be brought ashore and catch the London train hence the slightly misleading headline. It was all to no avail however as the tourists swept to a comfortable victory but it didn't end there, the matter later raised in the House where the question of priorities was discussed before the issue was finally laid to rest.

Lyon won his first cap in an away defeat to Scotland at the end of the 1908 Championship and his second against Australia with the added responsibility of captain, England losing both matches. What proved to be a short international career came to an abrupt end largely due to his naval duties. But Australian reports of the match highlight the fact that two of the tries scored by the visitors in the 9–3 victory were as a direct result of mistakes by the England full-back.

As with Norman Wodehouse and Ernest Roberts, George Lyon's naval career cannot receive the attention it undoubtedly warrants within these pages. He was Commander on board HM Monarch in the Battle of Jutland; on the outbreak of the Second World War he had risen to the rank of Vice-Admiral and was a Companion of the Order of the Bath. During that conflict he served as Commander in Chief of the Africa Station and later Commander in Chief of the Nore. In 1940 he was made a Knight Commander of the Order of the Bath and in 1942 promoted to the rank of Admiral, second in command only to the Admiral of the Fleet. This is a very brief resume of a most distinguished career but sufficient to confirm the calibre of men playing international rugby for England in the early years of the twentieth century.

If a rigid geographical structure had been imposed on the chapters of this book where could Portsmouth have been included? It would have been difficult to justify its presence elsewhere as it is rather distanced from the major clubs which dictate the format being used. Reading also falls outside the crude carve up which is annoying because Reading plays host to a club historically associated with the capital but other than on the occasion of an away fixture, no longer plays there. As for Cardiff, there is no getting away from the fact that the Welsh capital falls outside any perimeter one cares to consider. No matter how the rugby map of England is drawn there is no way Cardiff can possibly be included and the same applies to Dublin, even more so perhaps, but visits to both cities are necessary to tie up two loose ends, track down two players who somehow got away.

Lansdowne Road has long since been recognised as the home of Irish rugby. It is the last of the traditional rugby stadia—stands running the length of the touchlines with large exposed terraces behind both sets of posts. Currently the ground is undergoing a makeover which will bring it in line with all the other major venues in the game but while ensuring spectator comforts are improved, the few remaining links with a once amateur sport will be severed.

A cross between a Swiss chalet and a rural English pub, the home of Wanderers RFC once stood proud on the corner of the famous ground but no more. When the bulldozers moved in down came the clubhouse which couldn't be accommodated in the new plans; it's the way of the world. Older than the Irish Rugby Football Union, older than the RFU, Wanderers was formed in 1870 by a group of university students endeavouring to increase the number of clubs and by doing so the number of fixtures. In 1880, Wanderers became joint tenants of Lansdowne Road and played home matches at the same venue as Lansdowne FC, all of which would have certainly helped farm the heavy, carved up playing surface Ireland were so adept on. Not that any of the other international grounds were in much better shape.

The saying 'out of sight out of mind' is as relevant to the game of rugby as it is to any of life's many diversions but in the case of **Peter Young** another old adage, 'once seen never forgotten', proved a more appropriate assessment of a man destined to captain England who all but disappeared from the domestic game. Born in 1927 Young served with the Royal Navy from 1945–48 before going up to Cambridge where he won his Blue from the back row in the 1949 Varsity Match. His studies behind him, Young joined the Imperial Tobacco Co. and during this period played his club rugby with Rosslyn Park. Later he was employed by W.D. and H.O. Wills as a factory manager in Dublin which suggested that any aspirations regarding international honours that Young may have harboured were about to be seriously jeopardised.

By the 1950s, only six players had been capped by England while playing their club rugby 'abroad'. When one considers the clubs involved were Edinburgh University, Edinburgh Wanderers, Hawick and Newport then it is a perfectly reasonable assumption that the selectors had ample opportunity to follow the progress of the players in question. Ireland was a different matter altogether, totally distanced from the English game with little if any contact between English clubs and their Irish counterparts other than end of season tours which would not help in the international selection process. Regardless of the absence of any precedent, Young joined the Wanderers and within two years that club could be added to the list of those outside the country which had fostered a player who went on to play for England.

How Peter Young overcame the obvious problem is unclear but it is known that he represented the Western Counties (Gloucester-Somerset) against the All Blacks in 1953 and was chosen to captain the Rest against England in the final trial later in the year, a game won by the second string selection. This wasn't Young's first experience of the trial process having been chosen for the Colours in the first trial in 1950. It was as a lock forward that he was now included and when the team to play Wales in the opening game of the 1954 Championship was announced there were two new caps in the boiler room—Peter Young and Peter Yarranton. England beat Wales at Twickenham but a fortnight later the All Blacks proved too strong and England's eight match unbeaten run came to an end. The second-row pairing was retained for the remaining games of the season at the end of which Young had five caps to his name and had helped his country win a Triple Crown.

For the first two matches in 1955 Jack Hancock partnered Young, another ex-pat who was playing his club rugby at Newport. Defeat in Cardiff and a draw on Young's club ground in Dublin brought an end to Nim Hall's illustrious international career. Hancock also found his services no longer required, Yarranton brought back for the final two games. With

Hall's departure the selectors needed a new captain and for the remaining games which were both played at Twickenham, Peter Young took over. England succumbed to a French team that was a prototype of the great sides that would soon follow leaving a battle for the Calcutta Cup which had to be won if England were to take anything out of the season. Tries by Frank Sykes and Ian Beer secured a 9–6 victory but the captain would not have known at this stage that he had played his last game for England. Young featured in the three trial matches later in the year but after the selectors considered all the leading contenders and experimented with various combinations they finally decided on two students, John Currie and David Marques of Oxford and Cambridge University respectively chosen to play against Wales. The first of 22 consecutive matches in which they would form a dominant England second-row pairing.

Rosslyn Park is one of those grand old names in English rugby. Founded in 1879 the club boasts a tradition not dissimilar to that of Blackheath and Richmond but whereas both those clubs have a healthy association with the England captaincy, the cupboard remains bare at Rosslyn Park. A career move took Peter Young elsewhere and as the club celebrated its centenary, another man destined to lead England also moved on. **John Scott** moved to the sunny climes of Cardiff and the most famous of Welsh clubs that he headed and where he remains to this day.

If they are good enough they are old enough. Nowhere will a better example of that old chestnut be found than in the case of John Scott, a player for whom age was never a problem. Here is a player who was so young when he began making a name for himself at Exeter and in the county championship that most of his contemporaries are in receipt of a state pension or in the very least have a bus pass.

I was playing for Exeter and Devon when I was 16 and I actually had an England final trial before I played for England Schools, I must have been 17 at the time. There were three of us, two lads from the north east and myself, and we each played senior rugby before being chosen for the England Schools. I'd been on the fringe since I was 14 but was never selected; basically you had to have someone in there putting your name forward and it became pretty obvious that I didn't have anyone. It wasn't a problem because at that time I was playing football, basketball, cricket, doing athletics and generally getting on well. At 14 or 15 I was playing basketball with men and soon after that joined Exeter which admittedly wasn't the highest level of rugby but we did play Gloucester, Bath and Bristol. At 16 I turned out against Gloucester at Kingsholm and had no problem with it at all and at 18 I was in the second-row for the South-Western Counties against the All Blacks, a team that included the likes of Andy Haden, Alex Wylie and Ian Kirkpatrick.

I went to St Lukes College in Exeter and during that time Rosslyn Park got interested. They invited a few players from the college to go on tour and when I finished at Lukes I ended up joining the club. It was a strange thing because all the guys who were my mentors when I was a youngster playing at Exeter told me that if I wanted to get on as a rugby player I had to go to London where I would be seen. That's what everybody said, so in the end I went to London—when I got there I just wanted to get away, I couldn't stand it.

In 1978 I went on the Barbarians' Easter tour to South Wales and played against Cardiff on the Saturday. At that time the club was struggling up front, they just couldn't compete with the likes of Pontypool, and on the following Monday I had a phone call asking if I would like to join Cardiff. When I returned to London I basically packed my bags and moved; been here ever since.

Cardiff once boasted a fixture list to rival the strongest in the land and there was no possibility that the England selectors could overlook John Scott. Now playing at number 8 he had won four caps in the 1978 Championship while at Rosslyn Park but thereafter it was the Welsh club which would come to claim 'Scotty' as one of their own, supporters readily adopting him always excepting that most divisive of annual encounters which sees England and Wales do battle. In his third year at Cardiff he was elected club captain, a role that sat well on the broad shoulders of John Scott as his four consecutive seasons in charge confirm. During that time Cardiff won the Welsh Challenge Cup three times and were crowned league champions in 1981–82. If the England selectors needed any further evidence that the man who had led the Under 23s in 1977 was captaincy material, here it was and in 1983, he took over from Steve Smith for the last two matches of the Championship.

We got a result in Cardiff, drew the game 13–13, the best England had done at the Arms Park for 20 years. Despite that I was asked to take over from Smithy and did it for two matches before the right captain came in which was Peter Wheeler. There were problems that had been ongoing for some time. When I got the call telling me I was going to be captain my first reaction was to question what had happened to Steve Smith and second to ask why Wheeler wasn't being given the job. It was all a bit negative. My first thoughts on taking over the captaincy concerned the atmosphere that surrounded the team but what can you do? Stand before the players and say, 'Look, I shouldn't be here...'?

When we went to South Africa a year later a lot of players were unavailable, Peter among them. Derek Morgan had taken over as chairman of selectors and he got in touch one Friday night and asked to see me. Derek was the only one I had any time for, you always knew where you were with him at a time when some of the others were pathetic. He lived locally so we met in a pub and argued for five hours at the end of which I think the barmaid had the casting vote. In particular we rowed about the makeup of the squad I was being asked to lead, a side I'd had no input in putting together, and much else besides. In the end, I had to weigh up whether I still wanted to be an England international captain and I finally agreed. We didn't do too badly winning four provincial matches and holding Western Province to a draw but the team lost both Tests. We were hammered in the second but South Africa were a good side, very good and I really don't think we got the credit we deserved.

Next up was a game to mark the 75th anniversary of Twickenham. I led an England XV against a President's XV, nothing meaningful, but at the after match dinner the summer tour was discussed and the attitude from committee members seemed to be '...well, at least we went...' I thought, 'No, no, no. This isn't on. This isn't what it's about.' Nobody seemed to know where England was going. Behind the scenes a lot of the guys were trying to tell committee members that if they wanted us to improve as a team, they were going to have to get a bit better organised; it was appalling to be honest. Then I was picked as captain against Australia but I told them where to stick it. I was given 24 hours to think it over but I'd made my mind up. I should have done that in 1983 and I should have done it when we went to South Africa; I shouldn't have got the job either time. I was just the ammunition because they knew I was big enough and daft enough to take the job on but I was the wrong guy; I became captain to the detriment of players much more worthy of it, players in a much better position to do the job. As a captain you're only as good as the other 14 players around you and without their support you haven't got a hope. How many are you likely to drag along with you under those circumstances? Not a lot.

The only time I was an unsuccessful captain was in those four games with England. I was flung in at the deep end, swimming against the tide, undercurrents—the lot. I regret ever accepting it; I would have done a better job captaining Wales! With England nothing was ever planned, it was just thrown together. There were plenty of players about, good club sides at Leicester and Bath and all it needed was a bit of organising, a bit of input from the Peter Wheelers of this world and there would have been good years for England but they just let it drift.

It is not usual for a lock forward or number 8 to get embroiled in discussions about the relative merits of outside-halves but this is an issue which has been known to land John Scott in hot water; one instance in particular standing out.

It's what I've become known for; a comment about an outside-half which I didn't actually make. If you take Alan Old, Les Cusworth, John Horton and there were others, these were good outside-halves, but when they were picked for England, they were expected to do something other than what they did best for their clubs; good attacking players told to kick etc. What still gets my back up is that some comments I made about Rob Andrew when he won his 19th cap against Australia still get misquoted. I was asked what I thought of the England team and mentioned that I thought there were other outside-halves around who would probably have benefited from being allowed to settle into the team in the way Rob had because out of those available I thought he was the worst. What I have been quoted as saying is that Rob Andrew was the worst outside-half ever to play for England but I didn't say that; some of the journalists still use it but it's wrong—I didn't say it.

Now a successful businessman in Cardiff, John Scott has very little to do with the game other than through his weekly column in a local newspaper which has been running for over 20 years. Contentious, argumentative, opinionated; these are words that could be used to describe the content but above all else, his comments are knowledgeable, informed and honest. Listening to John Scott deliberate on a game which he obviously regards with great affection the same words come to mind and one is left with the impression of an adopted Welshman of 30 years' standing who for all that is nothing less than 100 per cent English.

Reading RFC play in South West One of the national leagues which is some distance off Premiership rugby and yet the town plays host to a Premiership club which in 2000 appeared in danger of losing its way. A mile north of the M4 lies the imposing structure of the Madejski Stadium, home of Reading Football Club, and in one of sport's most bizarre examples of a club upping sticks and moving on, it is to this modern all-seater stadium that London Irish decamped from their traditional home in Sunbury-on-Thames. The reasons why are no longer questioned, such has been the success of the move, but in 2000 the club decided to play all home fixtures at Reading, cushioned the impact on its supporters by arranging transport on match days and eight years on the town now lays witness to England's biggest St Patrick's Day party.

London Irish would appear alongside Richmond, Harlequins and Blackheath if it could lay claim to an England captain who played at Sunbury in years gone by. This is not the case for a London Irish player born in Port Elizabeth, South Africa in 1971 who played for the club after the move to Reading. He made his England debut in 1994 and would retire from international rugby 13 years later after winning 75 caps and much else besides.

We don't know if **Mike Catt** was a spectator when John Scott's England team played South Africa in the first Test in 1984 which took place in his home town but we do know that as a player he first came to prominence in the all conquering Bath teams of the mid 1990s. A club which could comfortably field 15 internationals was not the easiest place for a newcomer to make his mark but Catt's versatility stood him in good stead for the challenges which lay ahead and whether it was at outside-half, full-back or in the centre he proved himself more than capable. With squad players becoming more important at international level, having someone on the bench who could cover so many positions was invaluable and when Rob Andrew was forced to leave the field against Wales at Twickenham in 1994 Mike Catt ran on to win his first cap. Later in the year it was Canada who provided the opposition and an injury to full-back Paul Hull presented Catt with the chance to show what he could do from that position and by scoring two of England's six tries he succeeded in convincing the coaching team that he should be retained for the 1995 Championship. England won an 11th Grand Slam with an unchanged side following which it was a return to the country of his birth for the World Cup, the first of four tournaments in which he would feature.

Having seemingly established himself as first choice full-back Catt continued in the role in 1996. But when Italy and Argentina were played later in the year he was selected at outside half and took over the place kicking duties, scoring 34 points ticking another box on an ever improving C.V. Tim Stimpson was given a run at full-back in the 1997 Championship and with Paul Grayson recalled at outside-half Catt was forced to watch on until England imploded against France at Twickenham surrendering a 20–6 lead in the process. His inclusion at outside-half against Wales in Cardiff was a minor triumph, Wales beaten in the last match at Cardiff Arms Park with Catt contributing 14 points to help bring home another Triple Crown.

When the British and Irish Lions party to tour South Africa was announced Grayson was included and Catt had to settle for a trip to Argentina with England until fate played a hand. Injury brought a premature end to Grayson's tour, Catt called upon to replace him; four years later in Australia it would be Catt who was heading home after breaking down in his first match, the start of a difficult time.

The next two seasons were stop-start affairs with injury problems beginning to take their toll. Bath were struggling at the bottom of the table and Catt continued playing when the better option would surely have been to take time out; give his body chance to recover properly. Two years had passed since he last appeared in the England squad and bearing in mind all his problems it was no surprise when he was not included in a provisional group of 43 players invited to prepare for the World Cup. The surprise came later when the squad of 30 players to travel to Australia was announced. One has to be realistic and say that if Charlie Hodgeson and Alex King hadn't picked up injuries which ruled them out of contention then we might have seen the end of Mike Catt as an international player but that wasn't the case and what an inspired selection his turned out to be.

Clive Woodward made no secret of the fact that Catt was in the squad as an outside-half but it was in the centre that he made his mark coming on as a replacement in the quarter-final against Wales and continuing in the role in the semi-final against the French. He took much of the pressure off Jonny Wilkinson at number 10 and introduced new options particularly with the boot and there can be little doubting the part he played in England reaching the final where he was introduced at the end of full-time but with 30 minutes still to play.

The rest is history and recorded elsewhere but for Mike Catt the journey continued. Part of the 'experience' in a less than experienced looking squad he played in both Tests in Australia in the summer of 2006 then nothing until the fourth round of the 2007 Six Nations. Brian Ashton had replaced Andy Robinson as England coach at the start of the year and he didn't have long to stamp his mark on the team before England's defence of the World Cup would get under way in France. He knew the backs well having been Robinson's attack coach and critical victories over Scotland and Italy produced the desired start but when the wheels came off big time in Croke Park, Dublin a mixture of injury and poor form took Ashton back to the drawing board. But where to look for players?

Rumour had it that there was a guy in his 36th year, who was famously hampered by injury, but could still be seen pulling the strings most weekends for London Irish—and he had the best part of 70 caps to his name. It rolls off the tongue a bit like that old Bob Newhart skit about the discovery of tobacco, 'What's that Walt?…Yes, I hear you…You put this leaf in your mouth and you set fire to it…and…and you've bought 50,000 tons of the stuff?'

Brian Ashton not only re-launched Mike Catt's international career he also made him captain against France and Wales in the Championship and later in the year in a World Cup warm up match again against the French, matches in which Catt did enough to convince Ashton that he had a part to play in the tournament. Two group appearances and three more at the serious end of the business took Mike Catt's tally of caps to 75 and how appropriate that the curtain should come down on his international career playing against the country of his birth, a country he could well have represented if events had taken a different course. What a loss to English rugby that would have been!

This chapter has considered the players associated with the England captaincy when they were in the armed forces, those who were playing their club rugby elsewhere and a player who was representing a club that played home matches on the fringes of the regional approach that has been adopted. This still leaves three players who may have been considered elsewhere but who the record books advise were, at the time they first led their country, representatives of significant institutions in the development of many an England captain, Oxford University and Cambridge University. It is fitting that having prepared so many players for international duty and played a big part in the education of 40 England captains these two great founts of knowledge should be able to claim a few as their very own. The score was 2–1 to Cambridge.

John Daniell was an all round sportsman. At Cambridge he won three rugby Blues and three more as a cricketer and on coming down he enjoyed lengthy associations with Richmond RFC and Somerset CCC. His cricket days understandably continued long after his rugby career ended prematurely through persistent injury problems. That was in 1904 but he continued with Somerset until 1912, captaining the county in five consecutive seasons. He was first capped by England in 1899, the only time he turned out without the added responsibility of captain. After his debut, Daniell's international record followed a most extraordinary path; he only led teams against Ireland and Scotland in alternate years, 1900, 1902 and 1904.

Injury most certainly played its part in this irregular pattern, an ankle problem he picked up in the Varsity Match ruling him out of contention for the opening games of the 1901 Championship for which he had already been confirmed as captain. Optimistic about his chances of being fit to face the Scots in the final match and deciding that he desperately needed some game time he played a couple of games for Richmond after which he still felt that he required a little more practice. There was no rugby played the week before the Scotland match so a run out for a local football team was organised. This was a new and ultimately one off experience. Unfamiliar with the round ball game John Daniell soon found himself coming off second best when making an over exuberant tackle that saw him limp from the field and as luck would have it, out of the Scotland game. Injury played no part in Daniell's absence from the team in 1903, a year which saw him working on a tea plantation in India, but on his return he re-established himself at Richmond where his performances quickly brought him back into international contention. He was recalled against Ireland and Scotland in 1904, games which proved to be his final involvement with international rugby as a player.

We don't know who was responsible but John Daniell was referred to as 'the Prophet'. His attention to detail when preparing for a rugby or cricket match was legendary and this, together with his experience of both sports eventually led to his becoming an international rugby and cricket selector. He was involved with the England cricket team for the series with Australia in 1921 and South Africa in 1924 and as an England rugby selector between 1913 and 1939. Daniell and his colleagues were responsible for six Grand Slam winning teams. He was chairman of selectors from 1932–39 and a junior vice-president in the last season before the outbreak of the Second World War. He maintained administrative positions at the RFU during the war years and in 1940, following the death of George Robinson while in office, Daniell became acting president until 1945 when he was formally elected as the 38th man to hold the position, the start of a two year tenure.

By the 1940s the list of past presidents of the RFU was largely made up of men who had not played the game at international level but some of the great names of English rugby were included; Fred and Leonard Stokes, Temple Gurdon, Adrian Stoop and Major-General Sir Basil Hill among them. There was also **John 'Jenny' Greenwood**, the 35th in line who 'the Prophet' had coaxed as a player into captaining the England team. Coaxed, enticed, lured (whatever the correct word) into playing for England never mind being chosen to lead the team would have been far from the thoughts of the recently demobbed Captain in the Grenadier Guards who had been wounded and subsequently mentioned in Despatches during the Great War.

John Greenwood attended Dulwich College before going up to Cambridge in 1910. He won three Blues between 1910 and 1912 and on leaving university began working for a firm of accountants in the City. The rules regarding eligibility for the university team must have been quite relaxed at the time because shortly after Greenwood left Cambridge he borrowed sufficient money to enable him to go back, play for the team until the Varsity Match and then return to his job.

Greenwood won his first cap against France in 1912 when he was still officially at Cambridge. He continued in the team throughout the following season still listed as a Cambridge player, likewise in 1914 which saw the 'student' play in three matches. It was the same after the war when John

Greenwood played in a fifth Varsity Match in 1919 and led England during the 1920 Championship; match details all continuing to link him with the university.

How this came about is quite interesting. That John Greenwood loved Cambridge University and everything associated with it is beyond doubt. He had a particular affiliation with the rugby team so when he heard that there were no previous Blues available to help the university prepare for the first post-war Varsity Match to be played in December 1919 he offered his services immediately. It soon materialised that Oxford would include players who had won Blues before the war and had since returned to finish their studies but for Cambridge there was no such experience to call on. Greenwood had a chance meeting with representatives of Oxford who agreed it was important that the Varsity Match be returned to the status previously associated with it as soon as possible and to this end concurred that if the administrators at Cambridge approved, the Oxford committee would raise no objection to Greenwood's inclusion in the Cambridge team. They confirmed this in writing and so it came about that John Greenwood played in his fifth Varsity Match leading Cambridge to a hard fought 7–5 victory.

Then England came knocking in the shape of John Daniell—would John Greenwood consider playing in the Championship scheduled to commence little more than a month after the Varsity Match? This would be a difficult season for England, as it would be for all the participating countries, with the need to introduce many new caps to the team unavoidable. Daniel also asked if Greenwood would captain England. Greenwood answered yes to both questions with a condition laid down that was readily accepted. Not only was he to lead the team against Wales but, providing he stayed injury free, John Greenwood would remain captain throughout the Championship, which he did. After losing to Wales in Swansea, England beat France, Ireland and Scotland and the 'student' from Cambridge remains the most capped player from either of the universities. He may have detracted from the norm twice but not without having received the necessary approval. This means the records can confirm that from 1912–20 John Greenwood played in five Varsity Matches, won 13 England caps and led his country four times—all as a Cambridge University player.

Greenwood was elected President of the RFU in 1935, attaining the office before John Daniell, and he was re-elected in 1936 for a second term. Beyond rugby, he qualified as a chartered accountant in 1920 before becoming a director of Boots the Chemist and latterly joint Vice-Chairman of the company—an equally successful story to accompany his sporting escapades.

When does a player from either Oxford University or Cambridge University stop being one? Seemingly never in the case of John Greenwood but for the rest, when does one association end and the next begin? Take the example of **John Kendall-Carpenter**. Here is a player who on 10 February 1951 captained England for the first time and is clearly listed as a player from Oxford University; programme notes, the *Playfair Rugby Football Annual* and all subsequent publications specifically devoted to international rugby confirm that on that particular February day Kendall-Carpenter was an Oxford University player.

Two weeks later on 24 February, Kendall-Carpenter led England for the second time. France were the opponents, the match was played at Twickenham and the England captain was listed as hailing from the Penzance and Newlyn club. Now there are two ways of looking at this. If Kendall-Carpenter had not been listed as an Oxford player for the Ireland game then the university would have no direct association with an England captain. If however, he had been listed as playing for Penzance and Newlyn then Cornwall would have provided the England captain throughout the 1951 Championship, Penryn's Vic Roberts, captain against Wales. Realistically, for a man who included MacGregor among his forenames and was reportedly born in Cardiff, one has to question why he ever pulled on an England jersey in the first place but Kendall-Carpenter did and with no small amount of distinction.

Wherever his place of birth it was in Cornwall, specifically Truro that the young Kendall-Carpenter began to make his mark as a rugby player. After attending the local school he secured his place at Exeter College, Oxford going up in 1947 but was unable to gain a place in the first XV having to settle for regular appearances at wing forward for the seconds. When he finally broke into the senior team, it was at prop forward in which position observers felt his broad frame could be used to good effect and his conversion to an international number 8 was put on hold.

The Varsity Match was once a showcase for some of the emerging talent and in many ways it gave the England selectors an additional trial match to assess the leading candidates. There are no shortage of examples of undergraduates rewarded with a cap after an impressive performance in the Varsity Match and Kendall-Carpenter can be included among them but despite being hidden away among the tight forwards in the 1948 fixture it was at number 8 that he was selected to win his first cap.

Defeat in Dublin saw the selectors return to the drawing board. There were changes at half-back, hooker and in the second and back rows but rather than drop the number 8 they followed the lead taken at Oxford. For the next five matches they chose Kendall-Carpenter at prop playing on both the loose and tight heads before eventually returning to the middle of the back row where he remained, and from which position he won 17 caps.

Following his retirement John Kendall-Carpenter excelled in a variety of administrative positions. He was chairman of the International Rugby Football Board and like John Daniell and John Greenwood, elected president of the RFU. In 1989, he was awarded the CBE for services to rugby and was chairman of the Rugby World Cup committee preparing for the 1991 tournament to be hosted by England. Unfortunately John Kendall-Carpenter didn't live to see the efforts of his committee as he died suddenly in May 1990 aged 64.

This chapter has allowed us to tie up all the loose ends because from here on players will sit where they are told. Those who began their experiences as England captain while playing in the north east, north west, for Leicester or wherever will be found in chapters dedicated to the north east, north west, Leicester or wherever. There will be no more anomalies; no more cases of players not fitting into the preconceived pattern. The misfits have all been dealt with but what misfits they were and where would English rugby have been without them?

6

MIDDLE MEN—PART ONE

Coventry, Moseley, Worcester

There can be little doubt that National Division One is the toughest league. The standard of rugby found in the Premiership is obviously higher and the intensity of the matches much greater but that is what the clubs in the lower division aim for; that is what they want. The chance to play at the highest level and compete week in, week out against the best clubs in the land is the prize at the end of the season if a club can top the division, prove itself the best. But there is a catch; with only one place on offer at the end of the season not only does a club resident in National Division One have to prove itself against teams of a similar standing but it will have to better the performance of the club relegated from the Premiership a year earlier—and therein lies the problem.

Relegated clubs want immediate promotion back to the Premiership. The squad of full-time professional players is retained with that very objective in mind and for most; the time spent in the lower division is a short one. In 2007 Northampton were relegated from the Premiership. As the club retained its squad of big name players, it immediately set about returning to the top tier and had achieved its objective some weeks before the season ended. In the preceding seasons, Harlequins and Leeds both gained promotion at the first time of asking after being relegated, all of which makes life very difficult for the clubs in National Division One. But it can be done.

Worcester RFC had never played in the top division before gaining promotion in 2005. This was to be a new experience and despite sailing fairly close to the wind on occasion the club is still there, still holding its own against the more established names found in the Guinness Premiership. The commitment and enthusiasm shown by financial backer Cecil Duckworth has been instrumental in the success story that is

Worcester, a club with first class facilities and a squad of first class players to go with them. Among those recruited was back row forward **Pat Sanderson** who joined the club in readiness for the 2005–06 season, the first in the Premiership, and was appointed club captain.

Sanderson arrived at Sixways from the Harlequins but launched his international career when he was at Sale. One of 20 uncapped players on the ill fated tour to the southern hemisphere in 1998 he made his debut against New Zealand in Dunedin and retained his place for the second Test and again the following week when England played South Africa in Cape Town. Three games in which England were on the receiving end of some high scoring defeats. Twelve of the squad either saw their international careers end after the tour or in some cases never get off the ground. Sanderson could have been forgiven if thinking such was his lot but with the Lions visiting Australia in 2001 he was recalled for England's tour to North America.

In the absence of Neil Back, Martin Corry, Lawrence Dallaglio and Richard Hill, all on Lions duty, Sanderson won three caps coming on as a replacement for Joe Worsley but no sooner had he got used to playing international rugby again than the rug was pulled out from under him and a four year wait began. The recall coincided with his arrival at Worcester and he was included in the autumn internationals with Australia, New Zealand and Samoa and despite not featuring in the Six Nations was chosen to lead England in Australia during the summer of 2006. England lost both Tests but the captain performed well in difficult circumstances and was retained for another round of autumn matches. But again he missed out on the Six Nations—Martin Corry, Lewis Moody and Joe Worsley preferred in the back row.

Another summer tour in 2007, this time to South Africa, brought Sanderson a 16th cap and there can't be many current players who have more experience of playing against the southern hemisphere countries. Pat Sanderson has played against both New Zealand and South Africa four times, Australia three with Canada twice, Argentina, Samoa and the USA making up the number but there remain some glaring omissions; he is yet to make his bow in the Six Nations where France, Ireland, Italy, Scotland and Wales all await him.

There are some big names amongst those clubs looking to emulate Worcester, striving to go that one step further. Exeter, Launceston,

Penzance Newlyn and Plymouth from the South West; Doncaster, Rotherham and Sedgley Park represent the challenge from the north; Esher, London Welsh and Newbury provide competition from along the M4 corridor with Bedford and Nottingham striving for promotion from the east Midlands. In the west Midlands, the comparatively new Birmingham and Solihull amalgamation vies for the top spot with two clubs which have a much longer history—Coventry and Moseley.

As the nineteenth century was being laid to rest, English rugby experienced its worst season to date. In 1899, England lost all three Championship matches, the first time this had happened. It was a case of out with the old in with the new when the selectors met to choose a team to take England into the new century. For the opening match in 1900 the team included 13 new caps to face Wales at Gloucester only full-back Bert Gamlin and Moseley's **Richard Cattell** at half-back with any previous experience of international rugby and it was Cattell who the selectors chose as captain—a choice that is difficult to understand.

Richard Cattell was born in Birmingham in 1871 and, after attending Trinity College in Stratford-on-Avon, went up to Oxford University winning a Blue in 1893. He had already established himself at Moseley and represented the Midland Counties before becoming a first team player at Oxford and it was during this period that he was invited to take part in an England trial. This led to a first cap in 1895. Cattell played throughout the 1895 and 1896 Championships which preceded and immediately followed the breakaway by the Northern Union. These were difficult times, particularly the 1896 season when many players became ineligible for selection after accepting payment in lieu of loss of earnings. It was also the time when Cattell relocated to London. His name is among the records at Blackheath where he continued to play while completing his studies prior to becoming ordained as a member of the clergy in 1897.

Then things changed. Apparently tired of rugby, in 1898 Rev. Richard Cattell joined Welwyn AFC in north London and played for the club until 1903 when he moved to Tring FC. Despite his apparent preference for the round ball, after a three year absence the selectors invited him to play for England again. The game ended in defeat and four of those winning first caps joined Cattell on the unwanted list, never to be asked back.

Everything points to the fact that at the time of his recall Cattell was a

Moseley player although there is some doubt about this if the details concerning his conversion to association football are correct. Until the record books are rewritten and a different connection made, Moseley will continue to claim Cattell as one of its own whenever his outing as England captain is appraised.

A year after Richard Cattell joined the list of England captains another player from the Moseley club received the honour. **William Bunting's** short period in office sees him linked with two clubs and as with John Kendall-Carpenter, the time scale was marginal; on 9 February 1901 Bunting led the team in Dublin and four weeks later he captained England for a second time, Scotland the visitors to Blackheath. In Dublin, Bunting was listed as a Moseley player but come the following month he had transferred his allegiance back to Richmond, the club from which he was first capped in 1897.

William Bunting was born in Bromsgrove where he attended the local school before going up to Cambridge. For a man who a few years later would be hailed by the *Sporting Life* as '…the best centre in England…' His appearance in two Varsity Matches can be taken for granted. When he left university to take up a teaching post at the RNC Eltham, those at nearby Blackheath could have been forgiven if they assumed he would play for the club. Bunting had other ideas, preferring to join Richmond where he remained until his old school in Bromsgrove offered him a teaching post and the link with Moseley was established. Evidence suggests that although he was working in the Midlands, Bunting made every effort to continue playing his club rugby in south-west London winning six caps between 1897 and 1899 as a Richmond player. However, it would appear that common sense finally prevailed because when he next appeared in an England jersey Bunting was playing for Moseley as he was in 1901 when he accepted the captaincy or had he already returned to Richmond?

Life would be much simpler if players remained in one place; played all their rugby at one club rather than adopting something akin to a nomadic existence. **James Byrne** was born in Birmingham in 1871 and 83 years later he died in Birmingham. An industrialist, he was a well known figure in the Midlands long after his successful rugby career had ended but it was as a rugby footballer that he is best remembered and for many years he was considered the finest full-back England had produced.

Five full-backs played for England in the 1891–93 seasons none of whom made the grade. Men from Blackheath, Richmond, Leigh, Runcorn and Middlesex Wanderers were all found wanting. Finally, the selectors gave James Byrne his chance and they came up trumps. Byrne won 13 caps over six seasons in which he missed four matches, the selectors looking at another three players with only Herbert Gamlin making an impression that would see him regularly included in the team after Byrne's dominance at full-back came to an end.

In 1896, a British team toured South Africa. The term 'British' is misleading as the 20 man squad only included players from England and Ireland; nine players with previous international experience and 11 university students. South Africa was still finding its feet as a rugby nation and the British team won many of the games with ease but the tour ended on an historic note with the home side winning the final Test and from that day on the balance of power would gradually swing towards the southern hemisphere. For James Byrne the tour was a personal triumph. He played in all 21 matches scoring 127 points but what is of particular interest is that after the first three matches that saw him in his customary role of full-back he played the remaining 18 in the centre but regardless of where he lined up his ability as a goal kicker ensured his inclusion.

Successful in the centre he may well have been but England needed Byrne at full-back and it was from that most isolated of positions that he led the team in the 1898 Championship. England ended the season at the top of the table but only because an ongoing argument between the Scottish and Welsh unions forced the cancellation of that fixture; another issue concerning money, this time the infamous case of Arthur Gould who was the beneficiary of a house paid for out of funds raised by an adoring public. Whatever result the cancelled fixture may have thrown up England would have been relegated to second place but in 1898, a win and a draw proved sufficient for the team to head the final table with a hard-earned three points.

For 120 years Moseley's home ground was The Reddings, a name once synonymous with Midlands' rugby but no longer. On leaving its traditional home and after deliberating long and hard whether or not to move lock, stock and barrel to Oxford—surely a recipe for disaster—the club took up a short-term residence on the nearby Birmingham University campus before moving to Billesley, also within a stone's throw of The Reddings. The reason for this brief geography lesson on the southern suburbs of Birmingham is that overlooking all three locations is the edifice that is Edgbaston, the home of Warwickshire CCC to which James Byrne headed once the final whistle had been blown on the rugby season.

Byrne was an accomplished cricketer playing for the county between 1897 and 1907. This decade included five seasons as captain. Thirty years later another player who excelled with bat and ball began a long association with Warwickshire spanning the years 1934–54. This also included a lengthy term as captain that began in 1938, encompassed the war years and ended in 1947 and, like James Byrne, **Peter Cranmer** also played his club rugby at nearby Moseley.

After attending St Edward's School, Oxford, Peter Cranmer remained in the city continuing his studies at Christ Church College. His impact on the rugby field was immediate and he was included at centre in the victorious Oxford team in the 1933 Varsity Match. That was in December and after two England trial matches that saw him play for the junior teams, when the side to face Wales was announced Cranmer was included for his first cap. He was 19 years and four months young.

England won the Triple Crown in Cranmer's first season, the young centre playing in all three matches, and the *Rugby Football Annual 1934–35* summed up his performances thus, '...young Cranmer's splendid balance and penetrating run...Cranmer stood out as one of the great players of tomorrow...' This proved to be the case with the centre winning 16 consecutive caps between 1934 and 1938 that included another Triple Crown in 1937 and two appearances as England captain in his final season. His career so nearly ended on 15 caps when he was surprisingly dropped after leading England to a record victory against Ireland but Basil Nicholson was forced to withdraw from the team to play Scotland and Cranmer recalled in his place. He declined an invitation to tour South Africa with the 1938 British Lions and, selection as England captain aside, the highlight of his international career came at Twickenham on 4 January 1936 when England beat New Zealand 13–0 in a match forever associated with one man—Prince Alexander Obolensky.

On his international debut, the Russian émigré scored two outstanding tries but it was the second that brought him the greater acclaim. It began with a strong mid-field break by Cranmer and was finished by the right wing who had ventured in-field in support of the centre and on receiving the ball from outside-half Peter Candler continued in an arcing run to touch down in the left hand corner, his great pace enabling him to leave the covering defence in his wake. In the second half Cranmer dropped a goal and created an opening to put left wing Hal Sever over for a try on his debut to bring to an end a particularly good day at the office but Cranmer's significant contribution towards overcoming the tourists had to play second fiddle to the flying wing outside him.

Peter Cranmer worked in the Stock Exchange and played for Richmond until 1937 before joining Moseley. The outbreak of the Second World War effectively brought an end to his playing days but he did appear in two Red Cross Internationals and the Four-Country Match (fund raising ventures played during the 1939–40 season) and he also represented the British Army team when it played its French counterpart in Paris. Cranmer served in Egypt and Burma with the Royal Warwickshire and Second West Yorkshire Regiments and on his return to civvy street he became a respected journalist also working as a commentator on the game for the BBC.

The international stars who played some or all of their club rugby at Moseley are mostly associated with two periods in the club's history—the years 1895–1910 and 1965–1975. Peter Cranmer played outside these windows and despite the presence of James Byrne, William Bunting and Richard Cattell in the earlier era it is during the 1960s and 1970s that Moseley could finally lay claim to being one of the best clubs in England. Martin Cooper, Barrie Corless, Mike Coulman, Sam Doble, Keith Fielding, John Finlan, Nigel Horton and Jan Webster were among those who played international rugby during the period but it was still a major upset when Staffordshire, including a large number of Moseley players, won the County Championship for the first time in 1970—six seasons after joining the competition.

One name is missing from the above list about whom the *Playfair Rugby Football Annual 1966–67* wrote in its review of the Midlands' 1965–66 season, 'The two most improved sides without doubt were Leicester and Moseley. The latter went from 42 per cent to 60 per cent (as a measurement of games won) and many people believe this was entirely due to the emergence of **Colin McFadyean**. There is no doubt that he had a great deal to do with it…' written by Peter Cranmer who had been beating a drum for Moseley in previous publications. The timing of the article marks the start of the club's rise to the top of the percentages, peaking in the 1968–69 season on 79 per cent when the club won 30 of the 38 matches played.

A product of Loughborough Colleges, Colin McFadyean also had strong associations with Bristol and represented Somerset but he is best remembered as a Moseley player. First capped against Ireland in 1966, McFadyean went on to make 11 consecutive appearances but only enjoyed victory twice—against Ireland and Scotland in 1967, scoring a try in Dublin and two tries against the Scots at Twickenham.

My mother married a Scotsman who was a captain in the Army. He died at Anzio in 1944, a few days before my first birthday, but because of him, I had a dual qualification; I always considered myself to be English but things could have turned out very differently. I received an invitation to play for an Anglo-Scots team against a Scottish team in London which I accepted. At this stage I hadn't played for England. A selector watched a game at Moseley and after the match he took me to one side and questioned me about my involvement in the Anglo-Scots team; did I really want to play in it and was I aware that it was an unofficial Scottish trial which I wasn't. He advised that if I took part I would forfeit any chance I may have of playing for England; the message was fairly clear. I wrote a letter withdrawing from the game and added that I had never thought of myself as a Scotsman which was a big mistake, the consequence of which I didn't learn for some years.

A lot of the Barbarians' committee at the time were Scots and I was later told that Herbert Waddell, a distinguished rugby administrator and senior committee man commented to the effect that, '…this man's father died fighting for Scotland and he says he's English. He'll never play for the Barbarians…' In 1974 it was Moseley's centenary and a fixture was arranged with the Baabaas as part of the celebrations. We were in the changing rooms almost ready to go out when Geoff Windsor-Lewis, another Barbarian committee member knocked and asked if I would play on the wing for them as David Duckham hadn't turned up. My immediate reaction was yes but I thought about it and decided as they hadn't wanted me previously I wouldn't play for them now. Of my era Peter Jackson, Keith Savage and I were the only England internationals that I can remember not playing for the Barbarians; Peter turned them down once and was never invited again, I don't know what happened with Keith and then there was me. The Moseley committee kicked up a bit of a fuss and there was a suggestion that I would be invited on the Easter tour but they never got back to me. Who knows?

Colin McFadyean's first experience of international rugby ended in a draw before both France and Scotland beat a disappointing England and the team finished the Championship propping up the table. Not the best place to be when the British Lions are about to go on tour with selection very much influenced by performances in the Five Nations, confirmed when only five English players were included in the 30 strong party to tour Australia and New Zealand in 1966. McFadyean was one of the quintet and more than justified his selection playing in 23 of the 35 matches including all four Tests in New Zealand. Against Canterbury he suffered a broken nose which sparked off some controversial comment from the Lions management and equally contentious ripostes from the hosts; poor refereeing and the strong arm tactics generally adopted by the New Zealanders top of the agenda. Unfortunately, when it came to the Tests the 1966 Lions were out muscled up front and the series ended with a whitewash. The All Blacks secured a 4–0 clean sweep leaving the home nations to lick their wounds and a true reflection on the state of English rugby in the mid 1960s is the fact that Colin McFadyean was the only Englishman to play Test rugby in New Zealand in 1966.

In the autumn of 1967, England undertook a five-match tour of Canada returning undefeated and in good fettle for the next challenge that would see the All Blacks at Twickenham in November. This time there would be 15 Englishmen lining up against many of the players who had helped defeat the Lions, each with a point to prove.

We came back from the tour in great spirit expecting the bulk of the team that had bonded so well to play against New Zealand. The opposition wasn't that great in Canada but we'd played well and scored a lot of points however there were some off the field issues that may not have helped the cause on our return. We were given a curfew, had to be back at the hotel by midnight. I was out with John Finlan and Dave Watt making the necessary arrangements for the weekend and we arrived back at the hotel 10 or 20 minutes late. John and I decided to find a way in around the back but Dave insisted on going in the front. Next morning Mickey Steele-

Bodger called a meeting and told us he was sending a man home because he had broken the curfew. Finlan and I looked at each other a bit sheepishly wondering if we should own up. We said nothing but the players got together and tour captain Phil Judd ended up telling the management that if Dave went home we were all going and that was the end of it. Dave played very little on tour after that incident, if he played at all, and he certainly didn't win any more caps which was terribly wrong because he was the outstanding lineout forward of that era. When the Midland, London and Home Counties put up a good display against the All Blacks, 11 of the team were selected to play for England the following week which was incredibly naïve; the camaraderie and team work that had been built up in Canada was ignored and New Zealand beat us quite comfortably.

This was familiar territory; a convincing defeat followed by a series of trial matches and a team selection that bore little resemblance to that which had been chosen on merit two months earlier.

I was driving back to Bristol on the Monday following the final trial at Twickenham in which I have to say I hadn't played particularly well. I was motoring along the old A4 listening to the news on the radio when it was announced that the England team to play Wales included eight new caps and a new captain. That threw me and I feared the worst then the presenter added—Colin McFadyean. I felt total elation mixed with fear; why hadn't anybody told me? I had to tell someone so I pulled into a garage forecourt and ran into the café shouting, '...I'm captain of England, I'm captain of England...' People just sat there looking at this madman but I had nobody else to tell. There was no communication from the RFU at all, it wouldn't have occurred to them to ring me up.

Wales were playing England at Twickenham. When the half time break arrived, the outlook looked good with England holding an 8–3 lead. Bob Hiller improved the situation shortly after the interval but England let Wales off the hook; a converted try came from a failed penalty attempt after the ball was knocked on and a late drop goal tied the match at 11–11 with England left pondering what might have been. Ireland were next up, again at Twickenham, and this time it was England that got out of jail. Reduced to 14 men in the first half after losing scrum-half Brian Redwood, the home team survived a typical Irish onslaught to hang on for a 9–9 draw. This must have taken a mighty effort from the forwards and the pack remained intact throughout the Championship. But the backs were found wanting and after leading the team in two drawn matches, Colin McFadyean was replaced as captain and dropped from the team.

Both my games as captain were at home. I was given a suite in the hotel and allowed to entertain the team after the match; players and their wives or girlfriends. Unwittingly I decided to ask the Welsh lads to join us and we had a hell of a good time, drank whatever we wanted, sent out for packs of 200 cigarettes and so on. Later I was officially called in front of Mickey Steele-Bodger and warned that no captain in the history of English rugby had spent as much money as I had and that it musn't happen again. The next game was against Ireland with Willie John, Mike Gibson, Ken Kennedy and the rest so I invited them up and we did the same again. From that day to this nobody has been able to give me any reason for being dropped other than that I spent too much money. I told that story to Nigel Horton a couple of years ago and he said the privilege was taken away after I finished but to me that was the epitome of what rugby was all about; you don't celebrate on your own. Hell, the committee men did well enough out of it, they were having a good enough time. Why couldn't we? Anyway I've made that the reason for my demise!

I was teaching in Cheshire at the time and it was the first XV captain who told me I had been dropped. I had regular meetings with him and as he was walking towards me, I could tell that something was wrong. I went completely icy inside. I knew what was coming. I can't remember what I said or did but I actually went into a sanatorium for two weeks. When I was studying psychology a few years later I realised that I had experienced a Freudian death wish; it was so shattering that I hid myself away for two weeks, I just couldn't handle it. The anger and bitterness went on for 20 years; I felt I was still worth my place, felt I was the best centre around at the time.

I loved being captain. I first had a taste of it with Somerset when I was 22 or 23. Peter Colston was the Bristol and Gloucestershire full-back but for reasons I can't remember he later played for Somerset by which time he must have been in his early thirties. Peter was a great help to me on the field and I learnt a lot from him. He had a good attitude and wasn't the slightest bit miffed that this young upstart was captain which gave me a lot of confidence. That said, having survived Loughborough confidence wasn't something I was lacking because you just wouldn't make it at the college if you weren't sure of your ability. You were surrounded by some great sportsmen and you either survived or went under.

Perhaps I was even over confident, a bit obnoxious at times. I wasn't averse to telling the forwards how to scrummage, something I knew absolutely nothing about but to me it was simple mechanics, if you keep your arse low and your back straight how can you possibly go up in the air? I am still reminded of that. But if you don't believe in yourself don't take it on. Really there wasn't that much to it; being organised and making sure all the players knew what was going on, being a bit flexible, have a plan B. It wasn't that complicated but I found the key was in preparation and I never went in cold.

Colin McFadyean won nine caps in the centre and two on the wing, a position he had been introduced to on the Lions tour when injuries to key players necessitated a restructured three-quarter line but how did he feel about playing outside-half?

Two years after my last cap I played in the final trial for the Rest but at fly-half. I knew I wasn't an international fly-half because I was so right footed, I might have got away with it at club or even county level but not for England. The Rest nearly won the match in which a lot went right for me; I set up a try for Mike Bulpitt, narrowly missed a drop at goal and was almost on the threshold of being England fly-half—it would have been a disaster! I didn't have the left sidedness. Maybe the opposition would not have picked up on that but I knew; today they'd have you sussed out right away.

Talking of kicking, after my England career had finished every time I saw my name in a book or article I was referred to as the player who kicked the ball to Keith Jarrett, the young Welsh full-back who made a dream debut against England scoring 19 points. The match ended with a try which saw him run 60 yards up the touchline after collecting a ball I had kicked up field. We played the match in April on a rock hard ground. Late in the game we had a lineout on our 25 which the forwards won and I was convinced that John Finlan was going to kick for touch but he passed the ball to me leaving little option other than to shoe it. Keith Savage gave chase and Jarrett was out of position but the ball landed on the point and bounced high giving him time to get underneath it and off he went. A normal bounce and Savage may have got his hands on it but for many years, I was only remembered as the man who kicked the ball to Keith Jarrett in what was once billed as the greatest match of all time. Whenever I was introduced to someone it was always the same, 'You're the guy who kicked the ball to Jarrett.'

In Colin McFadyean's first season England won the wooden spoon, a 'trophy' last 'won' outright in 1950 and just as they would in 1966 so too did the British Lions tour 'down under' in 1950. Colin McFadyean was one of five Englishmen included among the 30 strong party in 1966 but in 1950 the number was embarrassingly low; Penryn's Vic Roberts the sole representative among the forwards joined by half-backs Gordon Rimmer from Waterloo and Coventry's **Ivor Preece**. It was outside-half Preece who led England during the 1950 Championship, continuing on from the previous season when the team claimed victories over France and Scotland under his stewardship, now the stakes were higher and competition for places in the Tests would be fierce.

Barring injury, Ivor Preece was always going to be the second or even third choice outside-half. Ireland's mercurial Jackie Kyle was certain to be included in the Test team and Wales' Billy Cleaver was sure to be in contention if Kyle became unavailable. But when injury ruled Welsh centre Bleddyn Williams out of the reckoning for the first Test, Preece replaced him. As the teams lined up in Dunedin, a casual glance around would have confirmed to Preece what he already knew; he was the only Englishman on parade pre-empting McFadyean's solitary contribution 16 years later. It was Preece's only Test appearance and it is somewhat ironic that the match was drawn, the Lions denied by a late try, whereas the other three all ended in defeat.

When the tourists returned home the 1950–51 season was well under way. Ivor Preece had captained Coventry in the 1948–50 seasons however his absence for the first part of the new term necessitated a change but he was re-elected in 1951 for what would be his last season of competitive rugby. In his time as captain, Coventry won 76 of the 111 matches played. This equates to 68 per cent using the measurement favoured at the time; an impressive figure and with a further eight matches ending with the teams tied the stats make even better reading. At the time of his retirement

Ivor Preece's 12 appearances for England were a club record but records are there to be broken and Peter Jackson increased the figure to 20 before a prop who appeared in 10 England trials before finally gaining selection, moved the goalposts a little bit further.

On 5 January 1957, 22 year old **Phil Judd** played for the Rest against England in the final trial at Twickenham but that was as far as it went. The pattern continued over the next five years, Judd playing in another nine trials with the ultimate prize still out of reach. The problem for much of the time was found in the various shapes of George Hastings, Ron Jacobs and Peter Wright; three immovable objects Judd found blocking his way to the top. Props are meant to be immovable objects and are not normally blessed with much patience but Phil Judd had to bide his time during those five years until the day finally came when he was given his chance and in due course he too became an immovable object.

Ivor Preece walked the corridors of Broad Street School, Coventry in the 1930s. Twenty years later the same educational establishment nurtured the rugby career of Phil Judd, introducing him to the game and pointing him in the general direction of Coundon Road when his days in the classroom ended. He remained at Coventry until he retired from the game in 1968 by which time he had played 442 games in the famous blue and white hooped jersey.

Teams still contest the County Championship but the position it once held in the rugby calendar has diminished. The counties are unable to acquire the services of the big names in the game unlike in years gone by. In the past, senior players were eager to represent their county and place themselves in what was most certainly a shop window when the search for international players began.

At no time in its long history has the Championship been more dominated by one county than it was by Warwickshire at the end of the 1950s and the early 1960s. Warwickshire were crowned champions seven times between 1958 and 1965 and it is not too wide of the mark to suggest that for Warwickshire we should read Coventry. During the period the club's representation in the county side varied between nine players to as many as 13 but no matter what number of Coventry players there were, Phil Judd was always included; he played in the seven finals and at one stage enjoyed an uninterrupted run of 70 games before injury took its toll. Appearances for Warwickshire didn't stop at rugby. Judd was equally at home in the water where he represented the county at water polo. If further evidence of his athletic prowess is needed he was also a county squash player.

Despite this great versatility, rugby prevailed and after the five year wait Phil Judd joined the England front row. Ron Jacobs was the player replaced meaning Judd had to pack down on the loose head. Fortunately, he was equally at home on either side of the scrum winning caps in both positions. After playing throughout the 1962 Championship, a year later he was only included against Scotland. But he did win selection for England's summer tour to New Zealand and Australia playing in all six matches. He must have returned home a better player for the experience but other than renewing acquaintances with the All Blacks' front row on their arrival at Twickenham in January he was left out of the team for the remainder of the season. His return against Ireland a year later marked the start of 13 consecutive appearances which included five appearances as captain. This was in 1967 and a Championship that saw England involved in three high scoring matches. France claimed the spoils winning 16–12 at Twickenham. England then gained a 27–14 home victory over Scotland followed by the 34–21 defeat in Cardiff when young Jarrett stole the show.

The Sixth All Blacks toured Britain in 1967–68 and after leading the Midlands, London and Home Counties to a respectable 15–3 defeat against a team that would return home unbeaten, Phil Judd captained England for the final time against the New Zealanders at Twickenham. This was Judd's sixth experience of All Black rugby and he was on the losing side on each occasion, something many fine players can relate to but then there are those who can tell a very different story.

The Ellis Sports Ground, Workington is not a name that immediately springs to mind—it is not a Welford Road or a Kingsholm, a Franklin's Gardens or a Recreation Ground. But for one day in 1972 the Ellis Sports Ground became the centre of English rugby. It was a fine afternoon, the pitch was in good nick and there were 15,000 people crammed into the stands and terraces. The reason? The Seventh All Blacks were in town to play the North-Western Counties and local expectation was high. Ian Kirkpatrick led the visitors out followed by Grant Batty, Bob Burgess, Andy Haden and many other familiar names followed by the North-Western Counties led by a student from Loughborough Colleges, a player who already had three England caps to his name—prop forward **Francis 'Fran' Cotton**. The All Blacks would get used to the rugged Desperate Dan-like features in the coming years and much of the nation would one day walk around with his name on their chest but on 22 November 1972 the only thing on Cotton's mind was beating the tourists which the North-Western Counties did, winning a close encounter 16–14. This was the stuff of legend; the Counties were the first English representative team to defeat New Zealand since Obolensky ran riot in 1936 but how different things could have been for the young captain if a piece of paper produced in 1958 had been marked 'Failed'.

I was born just outside Wigan, very much in the middle of rugby league country. My father was a professional rugby league player, a hooker who played for St Helens and Warrington between 1930 and 1948. He had a long career and my brother also became a professional playing for Leigh and Warrington. I've often been asked how I came to play rugby union. The only reason is that I happened to pass my Eleven-plus Exam and went to a grammar school that played the game. I started off as a hooker but soon became too tall and moved to prop where I stayed, hidden away in the depths of the scrum.

I joined Liverpool from school and stayed a couple of seasons before going to Loughborough College. I'd been vice-captain at Liverpool and captained the college in the 1971–72 season but hadn't led Lancashire when I was invited to captain the counties. I won my first caps in 1971 but it was in the following season that I became an established international. I should have played for England against the All Blacks but I had a problem with my back and missed out fully expecting Mickey Burton to take my place but he broke his leg in a training session and Frank Anderson played his only game for England. Those events really opened the field up and enabled me to establish myself in the team.

When I finished college I taught at Coventry Prep School. I wanted to join Coventry because it was one of the leading clubs in England at that time. A great mate of mine, John Gray, was first team hooker and one of the favourites to take over from John Pullin in the England team but within a month of me arriving at the club he signed for Wigan and went on to play for Great Britain. So much for friendship! I stayed at Coventry for two seasons but didn't play many games for the club. I doubt if I played 20 games before deciding to move back north with the intention of rejoining Liverpool. Smithy [Steve Smith, see *Chapter 7*] was at Sale and great recruiter that he is he had got four or five of his Loughborough mates on board and it just seemed a natural progression to follow suit.

I took a job at Leigh Tertiary College, an amalgamation of the Technical College and the Grammar School which I don't think worked; neither establishment was as strong as they were individually, certainly not in a sporting context, but I taught there for two years. Steve was employed by the Distributive Industries Training Board which put training programmes into retail outlets and he advised me of an opportunity there that took me out of teaching. A spell with Coldshield Windows as Regional Sales Manager for the north-west followed before Steve, now the National Account Manager with Bukta, got me involved and when that went wrong we decided to have a go ourselves and started Cotton Traders.

Lots going on off the field then but comfortably matched by events on it. After leading the North-Western Counties and establishing himself in the England front row Cotton went on the summer tour to New Zealand and had his second encounter with the All Blacks, this time at Test level. In front of a capacity crowd of disbelieving Kiwis in Auckland, Fran Cotton once more enjoyed the sweet taste of victory against the most formidable of opponents. It was his eighth appearance for England and the first as a Coventry player winning six more caps in his time at the club that included his three outings as captain.

When the player you are chosen to succeed ends a long run with a win and the one selected to take over from you gets his tenure under way with a victory and all there is to show for your period of captaincy are three defeats then you know the dice were loaded against you. John Pullin led England to victory against Wales, Tony Neary's team won the Calcutta Cup but sandwiched between these results were the three defeats experienced by Cotton. Other than Bill Beaumont and Peter Wheeler winning first caps there was little else for Fran to get excited about but with his time as captain now over he could get on with life at the coal face without the added burden of worrying about what was going on behind.

I can understand why prop is not seen as a suitable position to lead from – normally you would say back row or the inside backs would be ideal positions. In the front row you are so involved in the physical battle it's not easy to see what is happening elsewhere but there have been massive exceptions. Wilson Whineray was an all-time great New Zealand captain, but I can understand why props are not generally regarded as ideal captaincy material and it isn't because the front row are not seen as the smartest guys, the sharpest knives in the drawer – there are a lot of exceptions to that as well!

Not many players avoid injury and Fran Cotton was no exception. The back injury that cost him his place against the New Zealand tourists in 1973 was the first of many injuries to interrupt his career particularly in later years and which would ultimately bring it to an end.

The serious injuries started in 1978 with a ruptured Achilles tendon. That sidelined me for six months and I don't think I ever really got back to full fitness but I managed to play my way back into contention before dislocating my shoulder. That was at the start of the 1979–80 season. I was determined to play for the Northern Division against the All Blacks at Otley in November which I did but I'm sure that today they would say I was crazy and wouldn't allow it. Anyway, I played in the game but couldn't use the arm properly which isn't very good at tight head and to this day it isn't right. I lasted the season but in hindsight should never have gone on the 1980 Lions tour because I wasn't at the physical level I'd been at previously and of course it was on that tour that I had the problem in Stellenbosch. I'd picked up a leg infection but came back to play in the game against the South African Rugby Federation because it was the last one before the first Test which I was desperate to play in. It turned out to be a viral infection but everyone thought I'd had a heart attack on the field and I never psychologically really recovered from that; it was such a shock to the system I kind of fell out of love with playing. I returned at the start of the 1980–81 season but it all came to an end against Wales in Cardiff in what turned out to be my last game. I pulled my hamstring and that was it. I didn't take my kit out of the boot of my car for three months and never put it on again.

Fran Cotton enjoyed victories against the All Blacks playing for the North-West Counties, the Northern Division and England and in 1977 there was another win to celebrate when the British Lions won the second Test in Christchurch. This was Cotton's second Lions tour following the heroics of the unbeaten team that visited South Africa in 1974. Cotton played in the four Tests against the Springboks and added three more Lions caps to his total in New Zealand but the health problems experienced in 1980 ended his tour before the Tests got underway. Three Lions tours is as good an indication of a player's standing in the international game as is possible to get and for Fran Cotton there would be a fourth. That would take him back to South Africa and again he wouldn't be playing any Test rugby.

When I retired I wrote an autobiography which effectively banned me from taking part in any rugby activities. I think it was in 1994 the ban was finally lifted so for 13 years I had nothing whatsoever to do with the game; the ban covered coaching, refereeing, any administrative function, everything. When it was lifted, I got involved with the North of England and became chairman in 1996 and it was then that Syd Millar rang and asked if I would like to become involved with the Lions; I was absolutely thrilled to be considered for that.

In between there was the advent of professionalism. I had some strong views on what was happening, particularly in England where, typical of the RFU, there was no plan. We had a moratorium but everyone ignored it; Rob Andrew went to Newcastle and started signing up players and there was panic among the clubs. It was a disaster and it was suggested that as I obviously had a lot to say about it perhaps I should get on board and try to do something. Lancashire asked me to be their representative on the RFU which was very interesting with so much going on. The RFU's main problem was that they didn't have a united position. There was a lot of infighting, a big power struggle between Brittle and Jeavons-Fellows that allowed people like Sir John Hall to fill the vacuum. It ended with what we have now, a situation where the RFU don't really run league rugby in England, that is down to the 12 Premiership clubs.

I particularly enjoyed my time as chairman of Club England which was responsible for all the international teams within the RFU. It was then that we looked to reorganise ourselves and a lot of good things happened; massive changes in the way England were coached and managed; the introduction of academies; elite refereeing structures; elite coaching structures. I like to think I had an important voice in those decisions. After the 1999 World Cup people were saying that England was the best prepared team in the game and a lot of countries copied what we were doing. Since the 2003 tournament we have almost become the worst prepared of the elite nations; never really had any strong leadership and hopefully Martin Johnson will fill the void. I think there is an exciting period coming up for English rugby. The players are there and as always it is about good selection, consistent selection, the team being properly prepared and well coached.

The 1997 British and Irish Lions benefited from all the above criteria. Under manager, Fran Cotton together with coaches Ian McGeechan and Jim Telfer the Lions recorded an unexpected series win in South Africa. Critics effectively wrote the squad off before leaving home but the Lions surprised the Springboks and won the first two Tests and the series in what are now three match rubbers. A gratifying experience for all concerned and for Cotton and McGeechan, who had toured as players in 1974 there must have been a feeling of déjà vu when the team won the first Test in Cape Town which had also played host to the first Test 23 years earlier. On that day Cotton and McGeechan played, now they were spectators and watching them sitting in the stands going through the full gamut of emotions during the 80 minutes, there was no doubt where they would have preferred to be.

7

THE NORTH-WEST

Birkenhead Park, Broughton Park, Fylde RFC, Liverpool,
Manchester, Sale, Waterloo

When Ian Kirkpatrick led the All Blacks out at Workington in November 1972 he was followed by Fran Cotton and the North-Western Counties team which included a scrum-half later described by New Zealand journalist Terry McLean in his review of the tour, 'They Missed the Bus', as '…quite the best half-back to be seen in England…' This was Sales' **Steve Smith**, latterly of Loughborough Colleges and it was as students that he and Cotton first joined forces on the rugby field and the friendship that would eventually take them into business together was forged.

The seventies was not England's most memorable decade but there were some memorable matches and great players unearthed between 1970 and 1979. The 1970s saw first away victories in New Zealand and South Africa and Australia defeated twice at Twickenham. Forwards Bill Beaumont, Fran Cotton, Peter Dixon, Tony Neary, Chris Ralston, Andy Ripley, John Scott, Roger Uttley and Peter Wheeler first appeared while in the backs there were debuts for Paul Dodge, Dusty Hare, Alastair Hignell, Alan Old, Mike Slemen, Peter Squires and Steve Smith. These were big names and no sooner had the 1970s ended than the arrival of the new decade saw England deliver a Grand Slam in 1980, the first for 23 years. So what went wrong in the 1970s?

I once worked out that I played with seven different fly-halves; it was a shambles. England was a shambles, there was no structure. If you had played for England there was a good chance of becoming involved in selection, the chairman of selectors bringing in his mates. The current players never had any communication with them; we didn't have anything in common, they didn't speak to you. I was teaching in Chester when I first played for England and got home one afternoon to find a parcel blown into the hedge; it was my cap. The Welsh players had their caps presented to them at the after match dinner but we were just treated like shit really. The whole RFU was awful. I didn't like them as people, they weren't my cup of tea at all and I fell out with them very early on. It was totally different in the north. We had a very successful North of England team and were treated very well; there was good selection, good coaching and the North beat everybody and then you'd get involved with England and it was a shambles.

Opinions will vary on the whys and wherefores but the record books show that of the 51 matches played in the 1970s England only won 15 and that for much of the time propped up the Five Nations table. As Smith suggests, there was rarely any continuity at half-back with nine scrum-halves and 10 outside-halves selected over the period leading to an extraordinarily high number of partnerships numbering 24 in total. Possibly some players were found wanting but for most the ability was surely there, they were just not given enough time to settle. In amongst all this chopping and changing was Steve Smith who hadn't even wanted to play rugby.

I'm a soccer man. I come from a working class background and I was brought up on soccer but when I went to King's School in Macclesfield they made me play rugby. I was selected for the Under 12s but didn't turn up for the first two games, I went off and played soccer with my mates. So it was detention every week until I played rugby. Because of my build I was a hooker and when I decided enough was enough, as an additional punishment, they put me on the wing. These were the days when as soon as you won the ball you kicked it into touch so I just froze my bollocks off out on the wing and hated it. Luckily, I threw the ball into the lineout. We had this routine whereby when the forwards won the ball they would give it to me and I would throw a dive pass to the outside-half, missing out the scrum-half completely who couldn't pass anyway and it dawned on the teacher to put me at scrum-half and suddenly I started enjoying the game.

That he had impressed playing for the North-West Counties against the

All Blacks counted for nought when the selectors announced the England team to play the tourists. Although England lost, the selectors kept faith with the majority of the team for the opening match of the Championship in Cardiff. Wales won the game well, meaning changes were inevitable. The selectors introduced Steve Smith at scrum-half in the team to face Ireland but his was no fairy tale debut, the Irish continuing where Wales had left off. Victories over France and Scotland followed and maybe Smith thought that his time had arrived. With further caps over the next 12 months, perhaps it had, but between 1975–80 opportunities became scarce with only one appearance in three seasons, that from the bench—decisions had to be made.

Looking back, perhaps my face didn't fit. There was a lot of that, a lot of the old school network, a world I wasn't used to, aware of or liked; it was a strange situation which I fell out with and walked away. Later, I knew I would always regret it if I ended my career with nine caps and, as I was now 27 I decided to give it another go. Fran gave me a talking to, said that it was our last chance, so we trained hard in the summer of 1979. I changed my life style, sorted myself out, lost a bit of weight and got back to full fitness.

It worked. Against New Zealand in November, Smith began a run of 19 consecutive appearances at the end of which he enjoyed his five matches as captain.

Scrum-half is the perfect position for a captain. It's quite funny really having come through the system with Billy [Beaumont] who I captained when he played for the Under 23s at a time when nobody knew much about him but a few years later he became England captain. Even then I'd say, '…you get us the ball and we'll sort the game out…' He wanted to do the lineout calls but I wouldn't have it; as long as I was scrum-half I gave the calls. Only the scrum-half can do that and Billy eventually came around to it but he'll probably deny that!

I've always said that all captaincy can ever be is an extension of yourself; you can't pretend to be something else because you'll be found out. Billy was and still is an all time great guy and that was exactly how he captained the team; led by example and always let players get on with their game. When we played Wales in 1980 we were hanging on to a two point lead and I had a kick charged down by Alan Phillips which led to a try. The television cameras showed Bill with his arm around me and the comment was along the lines of '...Beaumont consoling Smith...' but he actually said something like, 'You stupid little shit,' To which I replied, 'Billy, that's leadership for you.'

That game was a filthy brawl, seven or eight of us needed stitches, there was so much incident, Ringer being sent off and so on but nobody ever mentions that we scored a perfectly good try under the posts which was disallowed. Mike Slemen kicked the ball through and Dusty Hare touched it down but the referee didn't award the try thinking Dusty had bounced the ball. I've seen it since and there was nothing wrong with it. But you have to say the Welsh lads gave their all that day; it was a hell of a battle.

Twelve months later Steve Smith took over as England captain after Beaumont's premature departure.

When Billy left there were big boots to be filled, he had been captain for so long. No one in our era had enjoyed such a lengthy period as captain and taking over wasn't easy. Billy had captained Lancashire, England and the Lions, now he wasn't there and being asked to replace him as England captain was always going to be tough because he was such a popular guy. Peter Wheeler should probably have been made captain, he was the natural choice and we all said he should have got it. To this day I don't know why he didn't but when it's offered you can't say no, you don't want to and it remains one of my proudest achievements. I was so wound up when I led the team against Ireland I came off the pitch thinking we'd drawn the game and it was only when being interviewed by David Coleman for the BBC that it dawned on me we'd lost by a point.

I got myself really wound up that day and realised that in future I was going to have to calm down, be myself. Next up was France in Paris, which is always a tough one, and I knew that if England lost I was out. We played well and won. Then we beat Wales at Twickenham in the last match of the season which was a great day because I also broke Dickie Jeeps' record number of caps for a scrum-half. I led a young team to North America in the summer and against Fiji in the autumn; we won all those matches so when England comfortably beat the Rest in the final trial things were looking good.

Then we came up against a very good French team at Twickenham, a really good French team and they did us; you know when you have been beaten by a better team. We got a draw in Cardiff, the best result there for 20 years but they took the captaincy off me and after the Scotland game decided to kick me out. What upset me most was that I'd told chairman of selectors Budge Rogers and coach Mike Davis that I thought Nigel Melville was going to be a terrific player. As I was over 30, I asked them not to drop me, just to let me know when they wanted me to step aside, making it a natural progression, with which I was perfectly happy. They couldn't even do that. I wasn't actually selected in the team to play Scotland but Nigel got injured as usual [see *Chapter 11*] so they called me up. That was a weird experience going from being captain to watching someone else doing the job—I didn't enjoy it.'

This was not the end of Steve Smith's representative honours. In 1972 he had been called up as a replacement for the England party that toured South Africa and in 1980 answered a similar request from the British Lions to travel to the same country as cover for the final Test in Johannesburg but played no part in the game. He was unlucky not to have made the original party in 1980 and after the disappointments of the Championship his inclusion in the 1983 Lions was unlikely but once again he received the SOS that took him to New Zealand where injuries had ruled out Terry Holmes and Nigel Melville. Steve Smith was rightly rewarded with two appearances in the famous jersey. He was also handed the captaincy against Hawkes Bay, some consolation after missing out in 1980. In his dedication to rugby, between 1972, 1980 and 1983, Steve Smith flew the best part of 50,000 miles to play four hours of rugby. Then there is the 'side line'.

Fran and I run Cotton Traders a bit like a rugby team; everything is team orientated, it's the way we've always done it. We took the rugby background, the captaincy and leadership skills that we both learnt playing the game into business and they are a tremendous help, brilliant. Tony O'Reilly always says that his greatest education was rugby. He had a reasonably good business career and I would say he was bang on. Business is about communication, motivation, leadership and the more involved you get in business the more you come to realise how few leaders there actually are in life. There are very few people who make good managers. You can put them on all the courses, but if they haven't got it they haven't got it.

Steve Smith and Fran Cotton obviously have it. From a standing start in a small unit near Altrincham railway station Cotton Traders has grown into a multi-million pound business run from a splendid suite of offices on the outskirts of the town. They are two larger than life characters who must be a delight to work for having learnt as much from the many things that they both perceived to be wrong with the English game as from those that they deemed good. They are two men who have been there, done it and most definitely have the T-shirt to prove it.

When Steve Smith helped England to a long overdue Grand Slam in 1980, the local press would undoubtedly have reminded him, if he needed any reminding, that the last time England won the Grand Slam, one of Sale's finest captained the team. **Eric Evans** was born in Droylsden and after spending his formative years at nearby Audenshaw Grammar School, was another who continued his education at Loughborough Colleges.

His first year at college began shortly after Britain declared war on Germany and as the months rolled into years it was certain that on completion of his studies, Evans would be drafted into the war effort. From 1942 he served with the Border Regiment rising to the rank of Sergeant before the hostilities ended. On returning to Manchester, he joined Sale (his only club) and at the same time he began a long association with Lancashire representing the county 105 times over the next 10 seasons.

Eric Evans is best remembered as a hooker but he was first selected to play for England at prop against Australia. His performances in the County Championship winning Lancashire team of 1947 and his efforts in helping the combined Lancashire-Cheshire team defeat the Wallabies had not gone unnoticed by a selection committee still trying to identify the best players to represent England after an eight year break. Australia proved too good at Twickenham and Evans was not included in the team to play Wales a fortnight later, the start of a two year wait for a second cap. When he next played for England it was in his preferred position of hooker. However, another England defeat meant it would be 12 months before he was selected again.

When he won his third cap, Eric Evans was 30 years of age. For many players this is a time of life when there are better things to be doing on a Saturday afternoon than spending it in the depths of the front row scrum after scrum. Even more the case when a player was doing it for love not money but Eric Evans was not a normal rugby player. Employed as a physical education teacher he took his personal fitness to levels which would not be out of place today and reportedly spent time with Matt Busby and his young squad of players to help ensure that his stamina would never be found wanting. He was the complete package. An accomplished player, a particularly fit individual and a person who had a great love of the game. So what if he was the wrong side of 30.

Following his recall Eric Evans made the hooking berth his own. He played in 14 of the next 16 matches that saw England win the Championship in 1953 and a Triple Crown in 1954. But come 1955 he was deemed to be past his best, possibly too old for the rigours of international rugby and South African born Nick Labuschagne took his place in the team. The 34 year old Evans appeared to have joined the ranks of ex-internationals but he was far from finished. In fact he had barely started.

In 1955, England managed to hold Ireland to a draw in Dublin and beat Scotland at Twickenham. The defeats inflicted by Wales and France had been neither calamitous nor embarrassing so come the following season imagine the amazement with which the announcement of the England team to play Wales was received. It included 10 new caps and a 35 year old captain who last played for his country two years earlier.

Time would show that the selectors got it right, that they were correct to throw caution to the wind and blood the likes of Peter Jackson, Dickie Jeeps, Ron Jacobs, David Marques, John Currie, 'Ned' Ashcroft and Peter Robbins. Time would also show that by inviting Eric Evans to captain the team they were inspired in their choice. All this sent a clear message out to the followers of the game—the selectors really did know a bit about rugby. This was not a new selection panel, all six had been in the job for some years but in 1956, Brigadier Alfred Aslett, J.T.W. Berry, Carston Catcheside, Tom Kemp, Robin Prescott and Mickey Steele-Bodger got it right. All too often, the selectors take the blame when things go wrong. So it seems only fair that they should get some credit when everything goes to plan, when a team wins Championships, Triple Crowns and Grand Slams.

After being allowed to bed in, Evans' team delivered a first Grand Slam for 29 years in 1957 and in 1958 won the Championship. England was undefeated in the four matches with the added bonus of a victory over Australia against which country Eric Evans was first capped 10 years earlier. The 1956–58 seasons saw England win seven of the nine matches played, only Wales and Scotland preventing a perfect record with hard earned draws and they brought a fitting end to Eric Evans' rugby career during which he won 30 caps falling one short of the England record held by Wavell Wakefield. In 1963, he was invited to join the committee of selectors. No doubt he brought to the table living proof that age should have no bearing on a player's eligibility for selection—if said player is of sound body and mind.

The battle for the County Championship title returned to the fixture list in 1947, eight years after Warwickshire beat Somerset in the 1939 final at Weston. On its resumption, Lancashire dominated the tournament, the county winning three consecutive titles. The forwards were admirably led by lock forward **Joseph Mycock** of Sale and they provided more than enough good possession for the backs to play both entertaining and winning rugby football. Orchestrating proceedings from the centre was **John Heaton** who was captain in 1947 and 1948 but injury forced him to miss the semi-final and final in 1949, Mycock taking over in his absence.

Heaton was a product of the Waterloo club based at Blundellsands, a short distance up the coast from Liverpool. He played for England six times between 1935 and 1939 and following the war, now aged 34, he was pressing for more international honours. In due course he would become one of the few players capped either side of the Second World War, however his services were not immediately required and it was Joseph Mycock who was asked to lead the first post-war England team that included 14 new caps, Mycock among them.

England beat Wales 9–6 in Cardiff and travelled to Dublin three weeks later in high spirits. The team only showed two changes, both in the centre where John Heaton partnered new cap, New Zealand born Martin Donnelly. Norman 'Billy' Bennett and Edward Scott had played against Wales and both would go on to win further caps, no doubt after a few silent words of thanks to whoever had determined they should not face the Irish. For Donnelly there would be no recall after the demolition job exacted by the home side which ran in five tries in a record 22–0 drubbing. His international rugby career over, Martin Donnelly returned home and went on to become one of his country's finest Test cricketers while John Heaton did not only survive the expected cull which was contained at five casualties but he was also named as captain of the team to play Scotland.

England won well at Twickenham, Heaton converting the four tries, and the following month he retained the captaincy against France who proved much stronger opponents before going down 6–3. Joseph Mycock also survived the selectors' scrutiny after England's defeat in Dublin and kept his place throughout the Championship and played against Australia in the New Year but there was no place for John Heaton, despite him leading the combined Lancashire-Cheshire team that defeated the Wallabies. Nine caps spread over 13 years but there would be no more and in his last two seasons it was Lancashire and Waterloo that benefited from his mid-field craft and leadership qualities until his eventual retirement in 1949.

A similar story unfolded at Sale which continued to count Joseph Mycock among its playing staff after his international days ended following the Australian match. Mycock joined the club in 1933 as a raw 17 year old. He quickly established himself and a year later was introduced to the Lancashire team. He played a full part in the championship winning team in 1935, and the following season represented the combined Lancashire-Cheshire team which lost to the third All Blacks. His season ended on a high when Sale were invited by the committee of the Middlesex Sevens to take part in the final stages of the prestigious tournament which traditionally brought the season in England to an end. Mycock found himself lining up alongside Welsh stars Wilfred Wooler and Claude Davey together with Ken Fyfe and George Shaw of Scotland, a strong set of backs which restricted Sale and England's flying wing Hal Sever to running the line. Sale won the tournament in some style and the young second-row forward was clearly destined for great things but the outbreak of war dictated that the first cap was put on hold.

H.B. 'Bert' Toft played his last game for England in 1939, not a result of the eight year break but because that was the way it was planned. Bert Toft was a highly respected player and the RFU had invited him to join the selection panel for the 1939–40 season, a difficult responsibility to take on board if he was still playing in the depths of the scrum. Toft was an exceptionally good hooker who like John Heaton also played his club football at Waterloo.

Toft was raised and educated in Manchester. He attended Manchester Grammar School, continued his studies at Manchester University and on his graduation returned to Manchester Grammar School to begin a career in teaching whereupon he joined the Blundellsands club and as a matter of course played for Lancashire. His international debut was against Scotland in 1936, three months after New Zealand had succumbed to the overtures of Peter Cranmer and the Russian prince. A scoreless draw in Swansea followed by defeat in Dublin saw the selectors carry out some running repairs as the season unfolded. The backs remained intact but up front there were a series of changes which saw Toft introduced as the third hooker in as many matches but he made the position his own, playing in 10 consecutive games which came to an end at Murrayfield three years later when he led England in her 200th international.

He replaced Peter Cranmer as England captain in 1938 and continued during the 1939 Championship. In 1938 England scored a massive 60 points that included 10 tries in three matches, France excluded from tournament since 1931. Despite such prolific scoring, England lost the matches against Wales and Scotland but in a remarkable turnaround, the following season brought victories over the Welsh and Scots but Ireland managed to turn the 36–14 defeat of 12 months earlier into a 5–0 victory. In 1939, England registered a paltry 12 points, including one try but enjoyed greater success than the previous season's 60 points had produced. One wonders how Bert Toft would have viewed things in his new role as selector if he had been given the opportunity. It is likely he would have favoured the inclusion of Joe Mycock and John Heaton and one can only surmise how many caps those two were denied as a result of the Second World War.

While Mycock and Heaton had a chance to make up for the lost years others were not so fortunate; Hubert Freakes, Ronald Gerrard, Bob Marshall and Alexander Obolensky all played for England alongside Bert Toft in the seasons immediately before the outbreak of war but each made the supreme sacrifice. Similarly, the Great War of 1914–18 also claimed the lives of many who either played for their country or were destined to do so and while we are focussed on the north-west there are four names which now need to be discussed. These four men who not only played for England in the years prior to the war but were also appointed captain. Forty-six men had captained England by the start of the First World War.

That five of that number lost their lives is a figure possibly no more or less than a statistician playing the percentages might have expected to see. What a statistician could not possibly have predicted is that four of the five played their rugby for clubs within no more than a couple of miles of each other as the crow flies. They played their rugby for Birkenhead Park and Liverpool, clubs which face each other from opposite banks at the mouth of the Mersey.

Harry Alexander was an all round sportsman; give him a stick of some description and he could hit things with it. He was a county hockey player and also a scratch golfer. If you gave him a pair of ice skates and pointed him in the direction of Switzerland, his skills at bandy would quickly surface. Bandy is a hybrid of field hockey and ice hockey played between teams made up of 11 players on a rink the size of a football pitch. Harry Alexander was apparently very good at it. It is doubtful that he was as good at bandy as he was at rugby union but the suggestion of a forward on ice skates with a stick in his hands coming hell for leather down a rink of football pitch proportions, probably singing, because Alexander was good at that as well, certainly provides ample food for thought.

We can only guess where he learnt the intricacies of bandy but as far as his rugby exploits are concerned it is safe to assume these began at Uppingham School and developed on his arrival at Oxford University where he won Blues in 1897 and 1898. Birkenhead Park was his first club beyond the corridors of academia and it was on the Wirral that he began to attract the attention of the county and more importantly, the England selectors. Brigadier Aslett and his colleagues may have got it right in 1956 but those charged with the responsibility in 1900 got it terribly wrong when they brought in 13 new caps to face Wales. The England team was well beaten and for the Irish game a few old hands earned a recall alongside three players making their debut including Harry Alexander. He made the first of seven consecutive appearances that started and ended with victories over Ireland but lacked much else in between, only a scoreless draw with Scotland giving England supporters something to cheer—if scoreless draws warrant cheering.

Alexander joined the ranks of England captains when he led the team against Wales at Blackheath in the opening match of the 1902 Championship. Two points ahead with the clock counting down the final minutes, England looked like returning to winning ways but the referee awarded the visitors a penalty in front of the posts and with it went any hopes the captain may have had of leading the start of a revival. England lost the game 9–8 and Harry Alexander lost the captaincy but remained in the pack for one final appearance, the game in Dublin that produced the victory English rugby so desperately craved.

Harry Alexander took a teaching position at Stanmore Park Preparatory School in north London and this effectively brought to an end his association with Birkenhead Park. He would have been a welcome recruit at any of the leading London clubs but Richmond secured his services. He remained there for the rest of his playing days captaining the club in the 1905–06 season. Middlesex replaced Cheshire in Alexander's affections and he took his place in the county team that played the 1905 New Zealand tourists. Alexander packed down alongside captain 'Curly' Hammond, but the visitors, these newly christened All Blacks, were in the process of writing a piece of rugby history and there was no quarter given in a 34–0 victory over a Middlesex team which on paper certainly looked more than capable. A month later Richmond entertained the tourists. Harry Alexander and his team may have improved on the Middlesex score, but were still well beaten and it would have been with more than a passing interest that the Richmond captain cast his thoughts northwards when it was the turn of Cheshire to try to stop the black tide.

Cheshire included 10 players from Birkenhead, three from nearby New Brighton and two from Sale. At outside-half and captain was **Percy 'Toggie' Kendall**, a local lad born in Prescot on the Liverpool side of the Mersey but educated at New Brighton. The task awaiting Kendall and his team was huge. Most thought a win was impossible and they were right when the All Blacks ran in 10 tries, recording another emphatic victory. The 34–0 defeat matched that inflicted on Middlesex two months earlier but there was little satisfaction from such comparisons, the only person likely to register the similar score sitting behind a desk in distant Stanmore.

Percy Kendall was four months older than Harry Alexander, they would have been in the same school year and it is not beyond the realms of possibility that when Alexander was at Uppingham School and Kendall at Tonbridge they may well have encountered each other on the rugby field. With Alexander at Oxford and Kendall at Cambridge one would expect them to have opposed each other in the Varsity Match but although playing for the university Percy Kendall didn't win his Blue. However, the pair did play together at Birkenhead Park. Kendall arrived at the club after finishing his Articles with a firm of solicitors in London during which time he played for Blackheath. This was before Alexander made the reverse journey which took him to Richmond. And of course, there was England.

Kendall won his first cap in the final match of the 1901 Championship and was in the team when Alexander assumed the captaincy but when England lost a fourth consecutive match he was one of the four players dropped. He was recalled against Scotland in 1903 and appointed captain but he was unable to turn around a miserable campaign in which Wales and Ireland had already beaten England and the Scots proceeded to do likewise.

Percy Kendall and Frank Hulme, his half-back partner at Birkenhead Park, had drawn a clear line between what constituted a scrum-half and an outside-half, making great strides in introducing the specialisation of each position. It worked at Birkenhead Park and there is no reason to suggest that the partnership would not have flourished on the bigger stage but for some inexplicable reason it was never given a chance.

Reg Schwarz and Ernie Walton were England's half-backs for the opening match in 1901. Later in the season Kendall and Bernard Oughtred replaced them. Oughtred then linked up with Ernie Walton. Frank Hulme became the next player to partner Oughtred before Kendall returned together with new cap Walter Butcher. Butcher continued in the team following Kendall's departure but now with Patrick Hancock to keep him company. Then, in 1905, Butcher was selected alongside Frank Hulme, the season ending with the arrival of Adrian Stoop. All in all, this was a merry-go-round of swapping and changing which never arrived at what commentators of the day suggest was the best half-back partnership in England at the time—Percy Kendall and Frank Hulme. All we can do a century later is wonder why not.

Dave Gallaher's 1905 New Zealand tourists left these shores after winning 31 of the 32 matches played. Only Wales managed to defeat a team that had introduced a new dimension to the game in the country of its origin. Next up were South Africa—what would they bring to the table? Paul Roos led the first Springboks on a 28 match tour and if the results weren't quite as comprehensive as those seen 12 months earlier they remain impressive. The Springboks only lost two matches, Scotland and Cardiff earning memorable victories. The Springboks also drew one match, that against England who dug out a 3–3 result at Crystal Palace. What follows is not the cock and bull story it may at first seem. Alfred Alcock played for England—he shouldn't have but he did. The record books state that Alfred Alcock won his only cap against South Africa at Crystal Palace in December 1906 playing in the forwards alongside the likes of Bob Dibble, Vincent Cartwright, John Green and Basil Hill, men who would all captain England. It must have been some pack of forwards, but what was a medical student doing in such illustrious company?

Nowadays a computer would be blamed for the error. In 1906 there wasn't a computer to blame so when Alfred Alcock received a letter confirming his selection in the England team to play South Africa it had to be put down to good old human error. That the RFU rightly stood by those invited to play is commendable. There is nothing to suggest that Albert Alcock did not take a full part in helping England to a hard-earned draw but the selectors never made the same mistake again. When they announced the team to meet France, included among the forwards was **Lancelot Slocock** of Liverpool and Lancashire.

Lancelot Slocock was born in a small village in Warwickshire on Christmas Day 1886. He attended Marlborough College where in addition to his classroom education he undoubtedly learnt the rudiments of rugby football and when that establishment sent him on his way into the world he headed for Liverpool where employment in the cotton industry and rugby football at the city's oldest club beckoned.

Founded in 1857, Liverpool had been involved with international rugby football from day one. Three of the club's players took part in the first international since when the England selectors had called up several more players. In the early 1900s, it appeared that the well was running dry and there would have been much celebration at the club when Lancelot Slocock got his belated international call up against France, the first of eight consecutive caps. He scored a try on his debut and closed his England career with another try when he led the team against Scotland at the end of the following season. However, the captain's efforts came to nought and Scotland won the match 16–10 to retain the coveted Calcutta Cup.

'Great' is a word used so excessively so that its true meaning has diminished. Now referring to something as great has become so much the norm we have to look elsewhere to find a suitable superlative for someone who really was 'great'.

'In every sphere of effort there is a distinction between genius and talent; geniuses are few. He was one of them. The intuitions of genius, the flashes of inspiration, are match winning qualities…Usually he seemed a man apart. He had great individual gifts—all round powers. He could do brilliantly everything a centre three-quarter was expected to do; but over and above the power and willingness to do the obvious duty was a quality of unexpectedness which played havoc with the defence.' So wrote W.J. Townsend Collins in *Rugby Recollections* in 1948. He was writing about a player he had the good fortune to have seen perform thereby enabling him to discuss his merits with some authority. He was writing about **Ronald Poulton** or **Ronald Poulton-Palmer** as he later become known, England's last captain before the outbreak of the First World War.

Ronnie Poulton first played for England when he was at Oxford University; later he would be capped during his time at Harlequins and finally as a member of the Liverpool club. Rather appropriately for one destined to receive such plaudits his journey began at Rugby School before continuing at Oxford where he won a hockey Blue to add to the three gained playing rugby. In 1909 he scored five tries in the Varsity Match, which remains a record to this day, followed by two in 1910 and another in 1911, the year he was captain and perhaps it is stating the obvious to add that Oxford won all three matches.

Poulton was a seasoned international before he won his first Blue having won three caps earlier in the year. With no shortage of quality three-quarters at their disposal the selectors were spoilt for choice and it was only on coming down from Oxford and joining the Harlequins where he partnered John Birkett in the centre that his international career really took off. Poulton featured in three matches in 1912, scored a try against South Africa in the 9–3 defeat at the start of the following year and kept his place in the team throughout the Championship which produced England's first Grand Slam.

On leaving university, Poulton joined Huntley and Palmers Ltd in Reading, a biscuit manufacturer of some standing in which an uncle was a substantial shareholder. George William Palmer was one of the second generations of Palmers associated with the business and it was his intention that his adopted nephew Ronnie should serve an apprenticeship in

Reading. He also spent time working for Mather and Platt, a large pump manufacturer based in Manchester to acquire some experience in engineering. During his time in Reading he played for the Quins and when in Manchester he travelled to Liverpool to play his rugby and it was as a Liverpool player that he led England to a second successive Grand Slam. Never can it be said that winning the Grand Slam is easy. Poulton had to call on all his team's resources to beat Wales and Scotland by a single point and hold on to a five point lead against Ireland. Only France proved no match for the champions. The last match of the season (and the last match for six years) was played in Paris where Ronnie Poulton scored four of England's nine tries going some way to replicate his extraordinary achievement in the Varsity Match five years earlier.

George Palmer did not live to see his nephew lead England, passing away in October 1913. His will showed that Ronnie Poulton was to be the beneficiary of a large inheritance but there was a proviso that Ronnie had to observe before he could claim it—Ronnie Poulton would have to become Ronnie Poulton-Palmer. Following his international exploits, the necessary paperwork was completed putting him in a position to take up the inheritance but it would have to wait; the storm clouds were gathering over Europe.

Harry Alexander, Percy Kendall, Lancelot Slocock and Ronald Poulton-Palmer were all killed in action during the First World War. They were young, well educated men who, having succeeded on the playing fields, were each looking forward to similar levels of achievement in their chosen professions before fate determined otherwise.

Poulton-Palmer was four months short of his 26th birthday when a sniper's bullet killed him on the battlefields of Belgium; no England captain has lived a shorter life. At the other end of the age spectrum, some captains lived well into their eighties and beyond, one of the oldest on record being **Edward Kewley** who, like Poulton-Palmer and Lancelot Slocock also played his club rugby at Liverpool.

It could be said that where Edward Kewley led some 30 years later Lancelot Slocock followed. Both men were educated at Marlborough College before pursuing careers in the cotton industry, which had long since been a major employer in the north-west of the country, Lancashire recognised worldwide as the major manufacturing area with local mills turning the cotton into articles for onward distribution. The port of Liverpool serviced the ships bringing the raw material into the country and for a businessman such as Kewley who became a cotton broker it was the place to be.

Attending Marlborough College in the 1870s Edward Kewley would have been familiar with a version of the game that leant more toward kicking or dribbling than handling and he excelled at it. All would come together in the fullness of time but initially there were varying interpretations of what was a game very much in its infancy. And it wasn't until the formation of the RFU in 1871 that clubs began to pull in the same direction while at the outset the game was organised and controlled by clubs mostly to be found in London, those in the north of the country would soon come to play a big part in English international rugby.

The first England team may have included three players from Liverpool but for the matches played in 1872 and 1873 the players were all drawn from clubs located in London or the south of the country. Edward Kewley would later become a grand advocate of northern rugby but his first involvement came as a player when he was one of the 14 forwards selected in the team for the fourth match against Scotland. After missing the first encounter with Ireland, he was recalled to the team for another cross border meeting, kept his place and continued to gain favour following the Law change which saw teams reduced to 15 players. Ireland were the visitors to the Oval on 5 February 1877 for the first 15-a-side international and Edward Kewley was appointed captain in the landmark match. His appointment made him the fifth man to lead England and most importantly, the first player from the north of the country.

Kewley never stopped working on behalf of rugby football. His enthusiasm encouraged the formation of new clubs and his efforts on behalf of Liverpool saw him take up the roles of honorary secretary, honorary treasurer and president which extended to the county when he was elected vice-president and later president of Lancashire. Such dedication was rewarded with his election as the fourth vice-president of the RFU, another first he readily accepted on behalf of those clubs found north of the Watford Gap.

Beating the drum of northern rugby in the 1870s was no easy task. The principal public schools were largely to be found in the south and it was the pupils from institutions such as Rugby, Winchester, Harrow, Marlborough and Eton who together with a head full of knowledge took the rudiments of the game with them when they set off in search of fame and fortune. For some this meant further learning at the universities and for others it was a job in commerce or industry which usually took them to London. Natural then that the union game should have a higher profile in the south in the early stages of its development. But it would be wrong to suggest that those clubs based in the north of the country arrived late. Liverpool, Sale, Preston Grasshoppers, Wigan and Manchester were among those founded before the RFU and it would not be long before the northern clubs would gain more than equal representation in England's team selection. Edward Kewley played a big part in promoting rugby in the north. Equally prominent in this crusade was Manchester's **Albert Hornby**, a late arrival to international rugby but a player who nonetheless became one of the best-known sportsmen in England during the latter part of the nineteenth century.

Born in Blackburn in 1877 Albert Hornby was the son of a prominent businessman, the proprietor of a cotton mill who also harboured political aspirations that saw him elected as Member of Parliament for Blackburn. After attending Harrow School where he showed great promise on the cricket field, Albert returned to Lancashire where it is believed he joined the family business but he certainly made his way to Manchester RFC, via Preston Grasshoppers, and Lancashire County Cricket Club.

Hornby is generally described as a back which was suffice in the 1870s. But on his international debut in the first 15 man team captained by Edward Kewley he can be identified as a three-quarter and an old one at that. Despite being 30 years of age, Albert Hornby kept his place in the team, was present again the following year and, but for his great cricketing ability would surely have been included in 1879. England's cricketers spent the winter of 1878–79 in Australia and it was on this tour that Hornby played in his first Test match. Already an established county cricketer with a wealth of runs to his name Hornby failed to carry his Lancashire form with the bat into the Test arena as his average of 3.50 confirms. But in the second of his three Test matches he became indirectly responsible for the emergence of cricket's greatest prize when he led England against Australia in a one off Test played at the Oval in August 1882, the visitors winning by a mere seven runs.

A few days later the *Sporting Times* contained an obituary, which read as follows, 'In affectionate remembrance of English cricket which died at the Oval on 29 August 1882. Deeply lamented by a large circle of friends and acquaintances RIP. NB.—The body will be cremated and the ashes taken to Australia.' Contradictory to the message this sent out those ashes gave birth to cricket's greatest rivalry and since 1882 whenever England and Australia contest a Test series a small urn which history tells us contains the remains of the bails used at the Oval is the trophy presented to the winning country.

Earlier that year Albert Hornby led England against Scotland, the match played at his home ground in Manchester. He now played at full-back after being introduced to the position on his recall to the side in 1880. In his only match as captain, which also proved to be his last for England, the Scots ran out comfortable winners scoring two tries without reply. When he led England at the Oval, Hornby became the first man to captain the country at both rugby and cricket, a feat matched by Andrew Stoddard a few years later but by no other player since. Stoddard was 10 years younger than Albert Hornby when he experienced the joy of leading England to victory in both arenas. But for Hornby the winning or losing becomes something of an irrelevance when weighing up the ability of a man who in his 36th year was good enough to represent and lead his country in the two sports.

Cotton has played a prominent part in this chapter on the north-west. From Steve Smith and his involvement with Fran Cotton and the success story that is Cotton Traders back to the Hornby family and their mill, Edward Kewsey brokering the raw material and Lancelot Slocock working in the industry circa 1905. Lancashire was thriving as the nineteenth century drew to a close but there was more than just raw cotton arriving at the Liverpool dockyards. The port was also the gateway into England for the vast numbers of Irishmen who arrived in search of work.

One who could trace his ancestors back to Ireland was **Harold Greaves Periton**. Born in 1901 he gained his formal education at the Merchant Taylors' School in Crosby and in later life became a member of the Stock Exchange but in between there was a rugby career to get through. This started and ended at Waterloo where he became the club's first England international. For many years, he was its most capped player which was no inconsiderable feat when one considers the odds stacked against him, influences that had nothing whatsoever to do with his Irish roots. English rugby had long since recognised residency as a more important factor than country of birth when considering players for international selection. So the matter of Periton's family line was an irrelevance but for a young wing forward hoping to be selected by England in the 1920s it was the outstanding quality of the other candidates that made the task daunting.

Arthur Blakiston, George Conway, Tom Voyce and Wavell Wakefield were among the star forwards of their day. Pick any three of these players and you had the perfect back row. The selectors were prone to do this and if they wanted to include all four then Wakefield would play in the second-row. Periton gradually worked his way into contention and when the selectors chose Blakiston at lock in the team to play Wales at the start of the 1925 Championship, they gave the Waterloo flanker his opportunity. England beat Wales but Blakiston was at his best playing in the back row and for the Irish game he dropped back to his preferred position at the expense of Periton who had at least got his foot in the door, had age on his side and would just have to be patient. At 33 years of age Blakiston was coming to the end of his career and if Conway, Voyce and Wakefield were still in their 20s, Periton was three or more years younger. His time would come.

A year later Voyce, Wakefield and Periton formed the back row and the unit remained together for the season, the man with Liffey water running through his veins having the dubious pleasure of scoring a try against Ireland at Lansdowne Road; an unnerving experience to be sure! From waiting in the wings Harold Periton was now a regular member of the back row playing in the four matches in 1927. After missing out against New South Wales and Wales in 1928, he played a prominent part in the remaining fixtures scoring a brace of tries against France which helped set England on the way to a Grand Slam.

When Ronald Cove-Smith's long and distinguished international career came to an end the selectors turned to Harold Periton to take over the mantle of captain. His term of office began with a defeat at Murrayfield and then closed the season with a fine victory in Paris, the captain scoring one of his team's four tries. England beat Wales in Cardiff to get the 1930 campaign off to a good start but a 4–3 defeat in Dublin saw the captaincy handed to Sam Tucker for the remaining matches, Periton retained in the back row. The end was near and following a scoreless draw with Scotland the Waterloo player bowed out after winning 21 caps.

Waterloo waited a long time before Harold Periton finally brought the club international honours. Over the next 30 years a steady flow of names extended the list of England players to 18 and then nothing. Production seemed to have come to a standstill following wing forward Alan Ashcroft's last game in 1959 before a graduate from Cambridge University returned to Lancashire, took a teaching position at Stonyhurst College in Clitheroe and, as was common practice for Merchant Taylors' alumni, joined Waterloo and the honours board would soon need updating.

J.R.H. 'Dick' Greenwood later became known as Will Greenwood's father. His son was a gifted centre who won 50 caps more than dad, got a World Cup winners medal and would later entertain television viewers from the touchline with his enthusiastic comment on the game. That was a long way off in 1966 and 50 caps more or not, young Will would not captain his country unlike Dick Greenwood who was a proven captain when his chance eventually arrived. His leadership qualities first reared their head at Merchant Taylors', continued at Cambridge where he was skipper of the Varsity Match winning team in 1963 and progressed to Waterloo and Lancashire, the county winning the County Championship under Greenwood's stewardship in 1969, the year in which he also captained England.

First capped against Ireland in 1966 the debutant marked the occasion with a try and kept his place for the remainder of the season. He led the North-West Counties to victory against the Australians later in the year and won a fourth cap when the visitors played England at Twickenham a few weeks later. The Wallabies surprised the home side winning the game 23–11 which led to a familiar scenario—wholesale changes. Of the team that lost to Australia, two three-quarters, both half-backs, both second-row forwards and the entire back row were dropped and it would be two years before Greenwood played international rugby again.

Some sterling performances for Lancashire could not be ignored and for the opening match of the 1969 Five Nations Dick Greenwood joined Budge Rogers and Dave Rollitt to form an experienced back row replacing en bloc the unit that had played throughout the previous season. Not only was Greenwood about to win a fifth cap but he was also handed the captaincy in what was England's 300th capped match emulating Bert Toft, also of Waterloo, who had captained England in the 200th. The team included five new caps and it is worth recording that future stars Keith Fielding, David Duckham, John Spencer, Keith Fairbrother and Nigel

Horton all debuted at Lansdowne Road but despite such an influx of talent England lost a close match and for the new captain it marked the end of the road. The only change in the team to play France was in the back row, Greenwood replaced by Bob Taylor with Budge Rogers reunited with the captaincy after a two year break. For once the selectors could not be held responsible, the villain of the piece a squash racquet which found its way into the captain's eye, a nasty injury that forced him to withdraw and brought an end, albeit a temporary one, to his involvement with England.

Long gone are the days when the only coach a rugby team became familiar with was the one that took them to away matches. The 1960s was the decade during which another type of coach arrived at clubs up and down the land. In 1969 the RFU took the plunge and made its first official coaching appointment, the task falling on the broad shoulders of Northampton's Don White, a no nonsense, uncompromising back row forward who won 14 caps in the seasons immediately following the Second World War.

In January 1983, Dick Greenwood became the sixth man to coach England in 14 years suggesting the position was not one that held any long term prospects. Greenwood's earliest coaching experience was at Stonyhurst where he helped prepare the first XV but more recently Preston Grasshoppers had gained the benefit of this thinking man's philosophies. Now it was England's turn. As a player, Greenwood had never been part of a winning England team but in his first match as coach, he enjoyed a notable victory. The All Blacks were the visitors to Twickenham, a ground on which they had beaten England on their last six visits but under Greenwood's guidance England found a fresh impetus and ran out 15–9 winners to get the new coach off to the best of starts. Dick Greenwood's tenure lasted little more than 18 months, victory over New Zealand proving to be the high point after which only Scotland, Romania and Ireland were defeated before Martin Green took over in 1985.

We live in a world well attuned to the great technological advances that have made some of the most sophisticated instruments available for domestic use. Home entertainment systems mean viewers can watch what they want, when they want; rugby from the other side of the world is beamed into homes live and if an early morning slot is not suitable, then the DVD recorder will help overcome the problem allowing the match to be viewed at convenience. We take it all for granted and with so much on offer it is easy to overdose. In the 1960s, BBC television brought the big matches to screens but there was no recording facility available and if kick off time was inconvenient then tough, someone could always tell you about it down the pub later. Consequently there is relatively little footage of rugby available before 1970 but there always was, still is and always will be the team photograph to fall back on. If ever we need reminding of how times have changed then the team photograph is the place to look; jerseys and boots, hair styles and the preferred facial attachments of the day are all reflected by the players who to a man would quite clearly prefer to be elsewhere.

The photograph of the Lancashire team that won the County Championship in 1969 shows Dick Greenwood and his men in solemn mood. Something right of camera has attracted the attention of most players, only lock forward Mike Leadbetter more interested in events taking place in the opposite direction but for the player standing to his immediate left there are no such distractions, he is totally focussed on what is going on in front of him. That was how he played his rugby; totally focussed on what was going on in front of him.

Tony Neary was 19 when that photograph was taken, a student in his first year at Liverpool University who had immediately broken into the first XV and who also played for Manchester club Broughton Park at every given opportunity. At 19 he was a seasoned international having represented England at Under 15 and Under 19 level and such was his meteoric rise to fame he was already being touted as a senior international. In November 1970, 11 days short of his 21st birthday, Neary played for an England Under 25 team against the Fijian tourists at Twickenham and two months later he was selected for his first full cap against Wales in Cardiff. This proved to be a tough baptism. A magnificent Welsh team which would sweep all before it in a Grand Slam winning season produced a forward display hailed as one of the best ever seen, and the 22–6 victory was even more emphatic than the score suggests.

Realising that an outstanding team had beaten England, the selectors didn't panic and Neary was included in the side that ground out a hard fought 9–6 victory in Dublin. Two home matches followed; a draw with France and a close encounter with Scotland that ended 16–15 in favour of the visitors but it was a memorable occasion for the young wing forward who scored one of England's two tries—Tony Neary had arrived. He played in the next 23 matches that included the away victories in New Zealand and South Africa under John Pullin and 12 matches that saw him in unison with Peter Dixon and Andy Ripley in the back row. The run also included his winning debut as England captain, Scotland beaten in the last match of the 1975 Championship. Neary continued as captain in Australia during the summer, an eight match tour that included two Tests. Unfortunately a back injury forced him to leave the field in the first, played at Sydney Cricket Ground, ending his involvement in what was a disappointing tour, England losing four matches including both Tests. The following season Australia toured Britain and Ireland giving England the chance to exact revenge for the recent defeats. Under Neary's captaincy, the impressive home pack won the forward battle that in turn laid the foundation for the backs to score three second half tries. In winning 23–6 England registered her biggest score in the fixture which would not be improved until 1988 and equalled a winning margin that stands to this day.

Two weeks later the Five Nations Championship got under way and English rugby was immediately brought back down to earth. This was a desperately disappointing year in which England lost all four matches for only the second time; in 1972, captains Peter Dixon and Bob Hiller shared the responsibility but in 1976, Tony Neary led the team throughout the campaign and is the only England captain to have this albatross around his neck. Now, with an expanded tournament in place, his dubious achievement cannot be equalled but there is the possibility that one day in the future it may actually be 'bettered'.

Not surprisingly the captaincy was passed on but Neary featured in the team over the next four seasons winning another 11 caps taking his final tally to 43 to which one other international appearance can be added. The British Lions selectors recognised his qualities in 1974 when they included him in the party that toured South Africa. A year after he was replaced as England captain it was the Lions selectors who again found reason enough to include him in the squad of players chosen to tour New Zealand in 1977. It was on this second tour that he won his Lions cap in the fourth Test.

The British and Irish Lions is an institution, an amalgam of the best players from the four home unions which rears its head every fourth year. The cycle now in place began in 1989 when for the first time in the modern era

Australia was the sole destination; then followed New Zealand in 1993, South Africa in 1997 and a return to Australia in 2001—the cycle now well established. For many years, a manager and assistant manager led the players, a coach first introduced in 1966. Subsequent tours saw various permutations of the administrative roles which threatened to get out of control in 2005 when Clive Woodward, now referred to as chief coach took 27 support staff that included experts in media relations, the law, diet and nutrition and a chef. With the playing personnel increased to 45, the logistics of moving such a huge body of people and the accompanying baggage around the country could not have been easily organised. Overseeing what had become something akin to an expeditionary force was manager Bill Beaumont who as a player had visited New Zealand in 1977 and South Africa in 1980 on which tour he become the first Englishman to captain the British Lions in 50 years.

Fylde RFC is located in Lytham St Annes, a town better known for its association with small white balls rather than large oval ones. Founded in 1919 the club had no international representation until a centre named Malcolm Phillips came down from Oxford University having won 12 caps then went on to gain another 13 as a Fylde player. At last the club was on the international map but after Phillips' retirement it was another 10 years before the second man to represent Fylde in an England jersey arrived.

William Blackledge Beaumont was always going to play for Fylde. Family tradition all but dictated this would happen, his father and grandfather had both played for the club which automatically ruled out the prospect of looking elsewhere. Difficult to believe it may well be but Bill Beaumont was a schoolboy outside-half who later reverted to full-back from which position he played his first game for one of the lower sides at Fylde which also happened to be his last—at full-back. Within a year he had moved up the ranks and into the second-row and the process of creating a rugby legend had begun. Beaumont made his first team debut in 1970 and soon after got the call to play for Lancashire. Then things started to happen quite quickly; he was included in the North of England team which defeated Tonga at Birkenhead on 1 October 1974 and four days later came on as a replacement for the England Under 23s at Twickenham against the same opponents.

In 1975 John Burgess succeeded John Elders to become England's third national coach. Burgess had a fine track record at Lancashire and the first team under his charge saw Beaumont introduced as Chris Ralston's second-row partner. Ralston was a seasoned international who won his 19th consecutive cap in Dublin but the 12–9 defeat meant that while he would win a 20th cap against France a fortnight later there would be no second cap for Bill Beaumont. This would come on the summer tour to Australia when he replaced the injured captain Tony Neary in the first Test before starting the second. Following this he was never out of the team until forced into early retirement seven years later.

Bob Wilkinson, Nigel Horton, the late Maurice Colclough, John Scott and John Fidler could lay claim to having partnered Bill Beaumont in his run of 32 consecutive matches which included 21 as captain, breaking the previous record of 13 set by Wavell Wakefield in the 1920s. English rugby had unearthed an extraordinary player and after leading the team for the first time in Paris in 1978, two years of hard graft followed during which he built up a wonderful rapport with players and spectators alike. When the 1980 Championship got under way with victories over Ireland at Twickenham and France in Paris there was more cause for optimism than had been seen for many years.

England then beat Wales 9–8 in one of the most controversial matches ever witnessed at Twickenham with Wales' wing forward Paul Ringer given his marching orders early in the game following a late tackle on England outside-half John Horton. The Grand Slam, Triple Crown, Championship and Calcutta Cup all rested on the outcome at Murrayfield but Beaumont's men were never going to fail at the final hurdle and ended the season in style scoring five tries in a convincing 30–18 victory. The year 1980 proved to be Bill Beaumont's annus mirabilis. In addition to England's great triumph, Lancashire were crowned County Champions when they defeated Gloucestershire in the final at the Vale of Lune and to cap it all he was selected to lead the British Lions in South Africa.

Beaumont was not in the original party selected to tour New Zealand in 1977 and didn't make his first appearance until midway through the tour but played in nine matches including three Tests. In 1980, his appointment as captain meant there would be additional demands on his time that would extend beyond the field of play. This didn't impact on his appearances that saw him lead the team in the 10 Saturday fixtures; six provincial matches and four Tests. When considering the provincial matches were against Eastern Province, Natal, Orange Free State, Transvaal, Northern Transvaal and Western Province, all of which the Lions won, the rugby Beaumont played on 10 consecutive Saturdays was of the highest intensity. After narrowly losing the first three Tests victory in the fourth was nothing less than the Lions deserved—Bill Beaumont had led his men well.

Two years and eight caps later it all ended. The County Championship final played at Moseley in January 1982 saw Lancashire defeat the North Midlands but the result paled into insignificance after the sight of Lancashire captain Bill Beaumont being led from the field clearly suffering from concussion. Following medical advice Beaumont decided to retire from all levels of rugby immediately leaving a huge gap in the Fylde, Lancashire and England second-rows and the national selectors with the dilemma as to who should take over the captaincy from one of rugby's most charismatic characters.

Life went on and the demands on his time were even greater than he had experienced as captain of the Lions. Beaumont had a thriving family business to help run; media work whenever he wanted it; and the chance to emulate Derby winners Troy and Henbit when he gave jockey Willie Carson a piggy back to the *Question of Sport* studio. His decision to write an autobiography meant that like Fran Cotton, he too was barred from any involvement in the game but time passes and attitudes change and in due course Bill Beaumont became a fine ambassador for English rugby which in turn led to his appointment as manager of the 2005 British and Irish Lions.

In 1995 rugby union became a professional sport. Where once, union players would be lured by the financial deals offered by the northern based league clubs now the opposite prevailed. Ex-union players could return to their roots and were immediately eligible to play and in time, some familiar faces would appear once more on the international stage. The 1997 Lions managed by Fran Cotton included six players who had 'Gone North' but were now back in the fold; Alan Bateman, John Bentley, Scott Gibbs, Scott Quinnell, Alan Tait and David Young. All enjoyed great success on their return to rugby union but it was a game they were familiar with making the transition a fairly comfortable one and it could even be argued that they were better players for their experiences in the 13 man game.

Once the initial spate of transfers and relocations was over movement of players from league to union all but dried up. For any club to take on an ex-league player with no experience of rugby union was a gamble few were prepared to take but on occasion one would stand out from the rest; look as if he had the necessary attributes to adapt to the different code. After all, the pitch did not vary in size; the ball was the same shape; the ability to give and take a pass was essential to both sports; and players had to be able to tackle—and those rugby league lads could certainly tackle. But there was one important difference, one that particularly applied to the backs; rugby union involves more kicking from open play, a skill that regularly exposes the inadequacies of many players but if a player was the fastest guy on the pitch—why would he want to kick the ball?

In his seven years as a rugby union player **Jason Robinson** achieved more than most could hope for in a career lasting twice as long. This, after leaving a sport at which he had already reached the heights playing for Great Britain and England and winning Challenge Cup, Super League and World Club Challenge winners medals with Wigan together with numerous individual awards. In October 2000 Robinson signed for Sale and five months later he was an England player after being introduced from the bench against Italy at Twickenham. On 12 June 2001 he made his debut for the British Lions playing on the left wing against a Queensland President's XV at the Dairy Farmers Stadium in Townsville and celebrated by scoring five tries. It had all happened very quickly proving once and for all that there really is no substitute for pace. Robinson added to his try count scoring in the first and third Tests of a series that saw Australia come back from the grave. There was an early opportunity to exact some revenge when the Wallabies arrived at Twickenham later in the year and Robinson was selected for his first start at full-back. Revenge was sweet even if it was down to the boot of Jonny Wilkinson who scored all 21 points but for England, this match began the countdown to the 2003 World Cup with only France able to contain the juggernaut pack, Wilkinson's boot and Robinson's pace over the next two years.

Jason Robinson scored England's try against Australia in the World Cup final, a turn of blistering speed leaving the defence stranded, but throughout his career this most self effacing individual would insist that he was the scorer of tries grafted for and created by others. In two years Robinson had done much to enhance his reputation as a rugby union player and clubs hoping to add similar talent to the pay roll scrutinised their league counterparts in the hope of unearthing players who could offer the

W. J. A. DAVIES.

W. W. WAKEFIELD.

R. COVE-SMITH.

England have won the Grand Slam 12 times, more than any other country and no decade has been more productive than the 1920s during which four Grand Slams were claimed. Leading the team in 1921 and 1923 was W.J.A. Davies (top left), the United Services outside-half who boasts an impressive 10 victories and a draw in his 11 matches as captain.

Wavell Wakefield (top right) was England's 50th captain. Although he is mainly associated with the Harlequins Wakefield was a Leicester player when he led England to Grand Slam glory in 1924.

Four years later Ronald Cove-Smith of Old Merchant Taylors' (bottom left) became the fifth player to achieve the accolade of Grand Slam winning captain when England won a fourth in eight seasons.

There are several instances of brothers playing for England but only Fred and Lennard Stokes of Blackheath and Richmond's Charles and E. Temple Gurdon both went on to captain the team. Charles Gurdon (left) was handed the honour first but his term was limited to one match which saw England draw with Ireland in Dublin. However, he won 14 caps and appeared in 10 internationals alongside his elder brother.

E. Temple Gurdon upstaged Charles by winning 16 caps and leading his country nine times. After a run of eight consecutive victories he missed the opening matches of the 1896 championship but returned to lead the team in Edinburgh. The match was drawn and marked the end of the brothers' international careers. Temple Gurdon led Richmond for 10 seasons and in 1890 he became the 11th president of the Rugby Football Union.

During the late 1970s and early 1980s Bill Beaumont was the face of English rugby. The Lancastrian first captained England in 1978 and was at the helm for all but one of the next 21 matches. His tenure included a Grand Slam in 1980 following which he was the automatic choice to lead the British Lions in South Africa during the summer. Beaumont was forced to retire from the game on medical advice in 1982, two months short of his 30th birthday, but by then he had become England's longest serving captain.

When Bill Beaumont won his first cap he was introduced into a team led by fellow Lancastrian Fran Cotton although the record books will advise that Cotton was playing for Coventry at the time. That was against Ireland in 1975 and over the next six years the pair played in the England pack on 18 occasions before injury also brought an end to Cotton's playing days, forcing him to leave the field when playing against Wales in 1981.

©PA Photos

©PA Photos

©PA Photos

Rugby union in the 1950s was a game much removed from that played in the twenty first century and the question that can never be answered is how the stars of that particular era would have fared in the modern game. However there is every reason to believe that Northampton's Jeff Butterfield, a sublime centre with a reputation as a solid tackler who graced every stage he played on would have coped with the physicality today's centres have to prepare for. And if mid-field breaks are now few and far between, a player with Butterfield's craft would have undoubtedly provided some additional options.

A familiar sight to many defenders in the 1960s—the back of one of England's finest outside-halves here seen leaving the field after his match winning try against Scotland in 1963. Like Butterfield, Richard Sharp could ghost through a defence without a hand being laid upon him, skills which the paying public greatly appreciated at a time when the game often became a forward orientated affair.

Chosen to lead England against France in February 1969 Dick Greenwood was forced to withdraw from the team after an accident on the squash court when he was hit in the eye by a racquet. The ultimate beneficiary of this was Budge Rogers who took over the captaincy and in doing so became England's most capped player having equalled Wavell Wakefield's record of 31 caps against Ireland two weeks earlier, a record which had stood for over 40 years.

Mike Weston led England on a first tour to the southern hemisphere when New Zealand and Australia were visited in 1963. A hectic schedule saw three Test matches played in the space of 11 days and, not surprisingly, an under strength England lost all three but there was much to applaud, several players returning home with their reputations enhanced.

Records are made to be broken and it was Bristol hooker John Pullin who improved on Budge Roger's 34 caps in winning 42. Seen above leading the team out against France at Twickenham in 1973, Pullin had the distinction of becoming the first England captain to lead his team to victories over Australia, New Zealand and South Africa. Of particular relevance is the fact that New Zealand and South Africa were both beaten away from home, results that continue to be hard earned.

In 1927 Leonard Corbett (below left) became the first player from the Bristol club to captain England. He was followed by fellow Bristolian J.S. 'Sam' Tucker in 1931.

Apart from Pullin, Corbett and Tucker, Richard Sharp and scrum-half Richard Harding are the only players from the famous West Country club to have received the captaincy.

CHURCHMAN'S CIGARETTES

B. C. GADNEY

D. A. KENDREW

©PA Photos

For the three seasons 1933–36 two Leicester players shared the captaincy of England. Scrum-half Bernard Gadney (top left) led the team in eight matches which sandwiched prop forward Doug Kendrew's two outings as captain. Only two of the matches were lost and under Gadney England gained a first victory over New Zealand, the game played at Twickenham in January 1936.

England had to wait 47 years before registering a second home victory over the All Blacks. Ironically it was the next Leicester player to captain his country who led the team in what was his first match as leader. Peter Wheeler won the first of his 41 caps in 1975 and at the time of his retirement was England's most capped hooker. As Chief Executive of Leicester Tigers Wheeler continues to be actively involved in the game and is one of English club rugby's leading administrators.

Steve Smith was handed the unenviable task of taking over the captaincy after the premature retirement of Bill Beaumont. Here Smith gets the ball away in what proved to be his last match as captain, a 13–13 draw with Wales in Cardiff. He was replaced for the Scotland match by Cardiff's John Scott who can be seen at the tail of the lineout.

Richard Hill became England's 101st captain but surprisingly he was the first Bath player appointed to the role. His short tenure of three matches all ended in defeat and no little amount of controversy but Hill bounced back to be a permanent fixture in the team in 1990 and again in 1991. Richard Hill is now Director of Rugby at Bristol.

An essential component of any team is the goal kicker and here we have two of England's finest. Bob Hiller (above) scored in each of his 19 appearances often saving English blushes with his reliable place kicking and the occasional try. Against France in 1971 he scored all his side's 14 points in a drawn match at Twickenham. Hiller had the distinction of leading England in the first victory against South Africa.

Rob Andrew (below) was another player blessed with a reliable boot. In addition to the place kicking duties which helped him score 396 points in 71 appearances, Andrew converted 21 drop goals including a last gasp effort against Australia in the quarter-final of the 1995 Rugby World Cup which saw England win 25–22.

Fred Alderson (left) was a product of Hartlepool Rovers. He played for England in the early 1890s, the years leading up to the breakaway of the clubs which saw the formation of the Northern Union and ultimately rugby league. Alderson was a centre who reportedly stood over six feet tall and he is one of only four players chosen to lead England when winning their first cap.

Alderson was a founder member of the Barbarians and took part in the famous club's first match which took place at Hartlepool on 27 December 1890. Despite his involvement in the invitation side he nevertheless remained true to his club and played for Hartlepool Rovers.

E.W. 'Little Billy' Taylor was another player who represented England during the last decade of the nineteenth century. Taylor was a half-back and played his club rugby at Rockcliff, a Northumberland club particularly strong in its day but which no longer exists. He played before and after the formation of the Northern Union but was not tempted to join one of the breakaway clubs. Taylor became a professional golfer when his rugby days were over.

©PA Photos

Will Carling (above) holds the record number of appearances as England captain with 59 matches, a world record shared with Australia's George Gregan. Under Carling's leadership English rugby enjoyed great success winning three Grand Slams in 1991, 1992 and 1994. Carling led the team to the 1991 Rugby World Cup final played at Twickenham which ended in disappointment when Australia claimed the spoils in a match many believed England should have won. Despite this, Carling's inclusion as one of England's finest captains is assured and it is unlikely that his record number of appearances in the role will be broken.

When Will Carling stood down as England captain there were some big boots to be filled. It needed someone of the highest calibre to step up to the plate particularly as Carling continued in the centre. Alongside him was Phil de Glanville who had proven himself as a capable leader at Bath and it was to de Glanville that the selectors now turned. The second player from the famous club to lead England, de Glanville's team narrowly missed out on another Grand Slam when losing 23–20 to France but there was some consolation when Wales were beaten in Cardiff, England winning the Triple Crown.

©PA Photos

For some 27 years the captaincy was handed to players attached to clubs based either in the north or south of England. At the turn of the nineteenth century two players from the Midlands helped to correct the disparity when firstly full-back John Byrne (top left) and then half-back Richard Cattell (top right), both from Moseley, were invited to captain the team. Byrne played in all 21 matches on the British tour of South Africa in 1896 while Cattell turned his attention to football before making his one appearance as England captain against Wales in 1900.

Captain Eric Evans introducing the Duke of Edinburgh to Northampton scrum-half and future captain, Dickie Jeeps before the England-Wales match played at Twickenham in 1956. To Jeeps' right is prop Ron Jacobs, another from Northampton, who also went on to lead his country. The match was Evans' first of 13 as England captain and it also heralded the debuts of both Jeeps and Jacobs.

Roger Uttley played for Gosforth during the heady years in the 1970s when the club won the domestic cup competition in back to back seasons. In 1974 on the British Lions tour to South Africa Uttley was introduced to the back row and made an immediate impact on the blind side of the scrum. However England selectors preferred him in the second-row and it wasn't until 1977 that he was selected at number 8 which coincided with his introduction as England captain. But for injury Roger Uttley would certainly have won more than his 23 caps but he played a significant part in England's Grand Slam winning team in 1980 and in 1991 was part of the coaching team when England next collected Grand Slam honours.

Part of the reason Roger Uttley played his early international rugby in the second-row was the wealth of back row talent available to the selectors. In particular, the back row unit of Peter Dixon, Andy Ripley and Tony Neary provided a perfect balance and the trio played together 12 times. Neary, seen below playing against France in 1979, won 43 caps and on his retirement from international rugby in 1980 was England's record cap holder, a position he held until 1991 when Rory Underwood took over the mantle.

Martin Johnson (right) was unquestionably one of England's finest leaders. His record of 39 matches as captain included only five defeats with only one at Twickenham. Australia, New Zealand and South Africa were all beaten both at home and away and in the Six Nations only France in 2002 were successful against a team destined for greatness. That of course arrived in 2003 when Johnson led England to victory in the Rugby World Cup thereby setting a standard which those who followed found difficult to match.

Martin Corry played his club rugby with Johnson at Leicester and he was one of those chosen to lead England during the period between world cup tournaments. These were difficult times and Corry, seen below playing against Italy in his first match as captain, could do nothing to prevent the value of England's stock plummeting despite his most courageous individual performances.

Matt Dawson, seen above scoring against Ireland in 2004, is England's most capped scrum-half. His 77 appearances for his country include nine as captain. In 2000, but for an extraordinarily bad day at the office by all team members and an uplifting performance by Scotland, he could have joined the comparatively short list of Grand Slam winning captains. A year later, Dawson was also England captain in Johnson's absence when another tilt at the elusive Slam went awry in Dublin, the match held over from the previous season and played in October.

Lawrence Dallaglio (left) is another who knows all about Grand Slam disappointment at the final hurdle. In 1999 it was Wales who upset the odds with a dramatic victory in a 'home' match played at Wembley Stadium. This match marked the end of Dallaglio's second period of captaincy for reasons well distanced from the game but he was reunited with the role five years later. Dallaglio's 22 matches as England captain see him in third position behind Will Carling and Martin Johnson.

A distinguished front row triumvirate (above) includes from left to right: Phil Vickery, England's captain in the 2007 Rugby World Cup; Dorian West, one of many players to have led his country once; and Jason Leonard with a record 114 appearances for his country.

With Phil Vickery injured Bath second-row Steve Borthwick (below) was invited to lead England against Italy in Rome during the 2008 Six Nations Championship. It was a close but important victory at 23–19 and when the team to travelled to New Zealand in the summer, Borthwick led the party.

same but with relatively few exceptions this has proved to be a fruitless exercise.

No Premiership club was better located to capitalise on any league talent found west of the Pennines than Sale. If anyone doubted Robinson's ability to adapt to rugby union, the player soon confirmed his signing had been a wise one. Sale appointed Jason Robinson captain in 2003 and he led the club for three seasons which ended with Sale winning the Premiership in 2006. In November 2004, he became the 118th player to captain England and with this final accolade, he had ticked all the relevant boxes.

There was a second tour with the Lions in 2005 and two more Test appearances and after overcoming a series of injury scares he was able to take his place at full-back in the 2007 World Cup final, his last appearance in an England jersey. Jason Robinson ended his career at Twickenham in December 2007 playing for the Barbarians against the newly crowned world champions. South Africa were defeated for the first time since they lifted the trophy in Paris bringing a fitting climax to the rugby union career of a one-time rugby league player who had adapted well to the 15 man game—his was a great talent. In a game which comes to resemble its league counterpart more with each passing season Robinson could break the well organised defences which now dominate; could show a clean pair of heels given the smallest space in which to manoeuvre; could get crowds on their feet—a rare gift.

Jason Robinson was born in Leeds but made his name as one of the great rugby league players on the other side of the Pennines at Wigan. The rift that tore rugby apart in 1895 created repercussions for many northern based clubs. In visiting the north-west there have been no examples of England captains whose loyalties to club and country were put to the test, led them to change codes and turn their back on the amateur game. A different story waits in the north-east which is where the road now takes us: to Leeds and Sheffield, Durham, Newcastle and much else besides.

8

THE NORTH-EAST

Bradford, Durham City, Gosforth, Hartlepool Rovers, Headingley,
Heckmondwike, Huddersfield, Newcastle Falcons, Rockcliffe,
Skipton, Wakefield, West Hartlepool

As a geographical entity, the north-east of England comprises three principal counties—Northumberland, Durham and Yorkshire. At the time of writing, it is Leeds Carnegie and Newcastle Falcons who carry the flag in the Guinness Premiership while Doncaster and Rotherham endeavour to join them from National Division One. Many familiar names are found in the lower divisions but not Heckmondwike, Rockcliff or Wakefield, clubs that no longer exist, nor Gosforth and Headingley which have been absorbed into Newcastle and Leeds respectively. Despite the names no longer appearing in the leagues these five clubs can all lay claim to an England captain as can Bradford which since joining forces with Bingley in 1982, now plays under the joint names of the two old clubs. Durham City, Hartlepool Rovers, Skipton and West Hartlepool, can also be included.

The north-east is also the region where we will come across the first man to lead the team at the Rugby World Cup; the one given the honour of leading England in the centenary matches; the first captain against an overseas touring side; and the man chosen to take England on a first visit to the southern hemisphere. And, lest we forget, the list includes possibly the biggest name ever to grace the English game.

A Norman cathedral dominates the city of Durham which took the best part of 200 years to build. Home to the remains of St Cuthbert and the Venerable Bede the magnificent edifice is strategically positioned in the middle of a city all but enclosed by an extreme meander of the River Wear. Hills surround the scene which offer panoramic views of the city and its environs with none better than that offered from the home of **Mike Weston**.

A product of Durham School, his early involvement with rugby saw the young Weston at fly-half and it was in this position that he first appeared for Richmond Fourths following a move to London to study at the College of Estate Management. A successful afternoon saw the newcomer score most of his team's 40 plus points and the following week he appeared for the first XV. It wasn't long before the England selectors, alerted to the potential, wanted to take a closer look at Richmond's find but there was a surprise in store.

My international story began when I was selected to play at fly-half for the Possibles in an England trial held at Exeter in December 1959. It was pouring with rain and I was playing opposite Bev Risman who had just come back from the Lions tour. At half-time I was replaced by Richard Sharp, fresh from playing for Oxford in the Varsity Match. I was fairly upset because I didn't think I had done too badly. I was sitting in the dressing room, head in hands, when in walked Mickey Steele-Bodger, one of the selectors, to tell me that I was playing the second-half for the Probables but in the centre. I pointed out that I had never played centre before but he just asked if I wanted to play for England or not. I was included in the Rest in the final trial at Twickenham but there were some late withdrawals which meant promotion to the England team, again in the centre alongside Malcolm Phillips. A few days later I was walking along Kensington High Street and picked up a copy of the *Evening Standard* which had the England team to face Wales in it and that was how I heard about my first cap.

Expectations weren't high. England included seven new caps and there were seven British Lions in the Welsh team. It was 10 minutes before I touched the ball. Wales were camped in our half and Malcolm Price put a grubber kick through which I caught on the bounce, and suddenly found myself in space with only full-back Terry Davies to beat. He was committed to the tackle but I was able to get the ball to Jim Roberts who scored under the posts, the first of two tries on his debut and the first try England had scored in two years. We went on to win the Triple Crown and but for a draw in Paris it would have been a Grand Slam. Dickie Jeeps was captain as he was for my first 12 caps and I must add that without any doubt he was the best I played under.

Richard Sharp was England captain for the 1962–63 season when another draw, this time at Lansdowne Road, cost England the Triple Crown and Grand Slam. Many leading players were unavailable for the summer tour to New Zealand and Australia, Sharp among them, and the selectors invited Mike Weston to lead the party. A lot had happened since that first cap; 15 more had been added and Weston toured South Africa with the British Lions in 1962 playing in the four Tests making him something of a veteran and a sensible choice as captain.

Scotland were the first home nation to undertake a tour to the southern hemisphere visiting South Africa in 1960 followed by Ireland a year later. Both countries played one Test, strangely the first match of each tour, and both lost but remained unbeaten thereafter, Scotland winning two matches and Ireland three. A long journey even by today's standards but the major advantage of a short visit to South Africa is the minimal time difference which eliminates the onset of jet lag. Contrast travelling to New Zealand and Australia where a 12-hour time differential throws the body clock markedly out of tune which means several days of irregular waking and sleeping hours before the traveller acclimatises. Even allowing for the great advances made in long haul travel over the past 45 years no home union would agree to the fixture list arranged for England in 1963. Between 18 May and 4 June the tourists played six matches including three Tests in 11 days, all but the first game against Wellington ending in defeat.

It was madness. After three days travelling we played Wellington almost immediately and then it was Otago, New Zealand, Hawke's Bay, New Zealand and Australia, the last two Tests taking place on a Saturday and the following Tuesday. We were certainly up against it but despite losing five games I felt we gave a good account of ourselves particularly in the second Test against the All Blacks when some refereeing decisions denied us what should have been at the very least a draw. We spent much of the second period in their half and one decision in particular with the score at 6–6 probably cost us the match. I think it was Phil Judd propping on the loose head who shouted to Vic Marriott in the back row, something along the lines of 'For f**k sake Marriott, shove...' and the referee gave a penalty against him for swearing. Don Clarke put them back up field and that was it. Shortly after he kicked a long range goal from a mark and we lost 9–6.

Four days later England were well beaten by a young Australian side in Sydney. In atrocious conditions, the Wallabies threw caution to the wind, flung the ball about from the start and raced into an 18–0 lead scoring four tries in the process. Late in the half England adopted similar tactics and scored two tries. But despite having the better of the second period could only add one more, Australia failing to improve on the early points' spree winning by 18–9—a disappointing finale to a most demanding journey into the unknown; such bad planning wouldn't happen again.

Weston's assertion that England were the better team in the second Test in New Zealand is substantiated by that country's *Rugby Almanac* of 1964 which reported, 'England, back and forward, exerted a great effort in the second Test and could be counted rather unfortunate to suffer defeat…when a draw at worst seemed likely. Indeed, so dominant was England that on several occasions late in the game a score seemed imminent, as when the New Zealand pack was twice pushed back on its own goal line.'

I played throughout the following season but injuries began to take their toll and I was restricted to five appearances between 1964 and 1968, all at fly-half. I did play against Scotland in 1965, a game best remembered for Andy Hancock's late try, in fact it was me who passed the ball to him—he only had 85 yards to run! I had one game in 1966 but wasn't included again until the trip to Paris two years later when I was also asked to captain the team. France won a first Grand Slam that season but England could so easily have denied them. We were leading 9–3 when Keith Savage crossed just to the right of the posts for what appeared to be a perfectly good try but which the referee, H.B. Laidlaw of Scotland, disallowed claiming to be unsighted. There was nothing to do about it and France went on to win 14–9 but the story doesn't end there. A couple of years later I was chairman of the North of England and there was a match at Gateshead Stadium which was an athletics venue not often used for rugby matches. It was a bit chaotic after the game and I was queuing to get a drink at one of the temporary bars when this chap came up and tapped me on the shoulder. He asked if I was Mike Weston and introduced himself as H.B. Laidlaw, the referee in Paris in 1968; he wanted to shake me by the hand and offer an apology. Apparently, when he saw the television replays after the match he realised he had disallowed a perfectly good try. Laidlaw particularly wanted to thank me for the way the players had reacted to his decision by just getting on with the game, not disputing it or making a fuss after the event. I told him if he really wanted to make amends he could buy me a drink and that was it.

Three weeks after losing in Paris the same 15 went to Murrayfield with little to play for other than the Calcutta Cup. We travelled up on the Thursday and stayed at Peebles in the Scottish Borders, a short distance south of Edinburgh. On Friday we held a training session at the local rugby ground where there must have been a thousand or more people who turned out to watch us. I'd wanted to practise a few moves but wasn't prepared to do this in front of a crowd so when we returned to the hotel I told the players we were going back in the afternoon when hopefully we would have the place to ourselves.

The main problem I anticipated was a chap called Peter Stagg who stood at about 6 feet 10 inches and I wanted to look at ways of nullifying his obvious advantage at the lineout. I'd played against him a few times at county level and knew we had to come up with something or he would dominate that area of play. The plan was quite simple really but it depended on a high level of accuracy. On our throw in at a lineout 10 or 15 yards from the Scottish line we would withdraw four forwards. Three of them would stand by me a bit further in field and the fourth, Mike Coulman, would position himself 20 yards back, for all intents and purposes hidden from the opposition. Now Coulman was built like the proverbial brick shit house and on a given signal the wing would throw the ball long and the three forwards and myself would stand aside to let Coulman through. By this time he was flat out and if everything went to plan he'd collect the ball and with the three forwards in support charge on towards the line.

We practised the move several times before one of the players, I think it was Bob Hiller, pointed to a man sitting in a tree watching us through a pair of binoculars; we'd gone to a lot of trouble to have this extra session in private and were being watched. Anyway, a few of us went over to speak to him, find out what he was doing. It turned out he was due to commentate on the game the following day and was using this training session to familiarise himself with the players, get to know our body language and so on which he said would help him out. We doubted that and I think we actually accused him of spying on behalf of Scotland which was strongly denied. He commented that the move we were practising looked good and promised not to tell anybody what he had seen and with that, he offered around a bag of Hawick mint balls and was on his way. That was the first time I met Bill McLaren.

Come Saturday we were six points behind early in the second-half when the opportunity to use the ploy presented itself. It worked like a dream, Coulman crossed for a try, which Hiller converted, and a little later Bob kicked what proved to be the winning penalty. After the game Coulman and myself were taken to the BBC's temporary studio to be interviewed by David Coleman and there sitting in the corner was McLaren who smiled at us and said, 'See, I did'nae tell.' He was a lovely man. I got to know Bill quite well over the years but I don't believe I've seen Mike Coulman since that day.

That game at Murrayfield proved to be the last of Mike Weston's 29 appearances in an England jersey. Five years separated his two spells as captain and rather unfairly all five matches were played away denying him the opportunity to lead the team out at Twickenham. A British Lion in 1962 and again in 1966 he played a total of 31 games including the four Tests in 1962 but having already ruled himself out of selection for the 1968 tour to South Africa he stood by his decision when asked by the selectors to reconsider following the victory at Murrayfield.

Mike Weston is right in his assessment of the 1963 tour; there wasn't sufficient time for preparation neither were there enough days between the Tests but consider this—on 23 June 1888 a New Zealand native team began a tour which would come to an end some 14 months later, on 24 August 1889 to be exact. It began and ended with short internal sectors and included matches in Australia on both the outward and return journeys. Of the 107 matches played, 74 were in the British Isles beginning with Surrey at Richmond and ending against the Southern Counties at Leyton. There was much else in between including matches against Bradford and Yorkshire, both of which were lost, so when the England team to play the tourists at Blackheath was announced as expected, the man who had inspired his club and county to victory was chosen to captain England—the first Yorkshireman to do so.

Fred Bonsor won his first cap against Wales in 1886. He partnered Alan Rotherham at half-back throughout the season and again in two of the three games played the following year. Five matches in which Bonsor was not on a losing side, England only slipping up on the visit to Dublin in a match in which Bonsor didn't play. Then followed England's self imposed two year period of exclusion from the Championship meaning that come the match against the tourists there were 12 new caps in the team. But even that couldn't prevent Bonsor achieving a unique hat-trick of victories as captain—club, county and country all defeated the tourists under his leadership.

During the two year break from international rugby the committee members at the RFU took time to consider the future of county rugby which resulted in the first official County Championship being played in the 1889–90 season. Yorkshire secured the title and as a result were invited to play a game against the Rest of England that took place at Bradford between the Wales and Scotland matches. Yorkshire won in emphatic style and the selectors, very much influenced by what they had seen and bearing in mind the recent defeat by the Welsh, included six of the team for the trip to Edinburgh including Fred Bonsor at half-back. Bonsor had not played against Wales or for Yorkshire in the match with the Rest of England and neither would he play against the Scots but as to the reason why, reports of the day differ. On the one hand, we are led to believe that the player was carrying a knee injury while on the other there is the suggestion that he declined the invitation preferring to play for Bradford in a Yorkshire Cup game against Dewsbury. Whatever the reason, and the latter seems the more plausible, the selectors never chose Fred Bonsor to play for his country again.

John Hickson did play against the Rest of England at Bradford and he also played against Scotland enjoying two victories as captain of Yorkshire and England. Now the county could claim two England captains, as could Bradford. Fred Bonsor played all his club rugby at Bradford whereas Hickson was introduced to the game at nearby Bingley but for the best part of a decade the two players' rugby careers ran parallel courses. They helped Bradford to success in the Yorkshire Challenge Cup in 1884, both eventually going on to captain the club and Bonsor and Hickson led Yorkshire to the County Championship in the first two seasons of a structured tournament. On the international stage, each won six caps and led winning England teams on their sole appearance as captain. The players differed in their field positions—Bonsor a wily half-back, Hickson a gritty forward—but there is nothing to suggest that either player represented Bradford after the formation of the Northern Union in 1895 by which time they would have been in their mid-thirties.

Fred Bonsor and John Hickson featured prominently in the early history of a club that has become one of the biggest names in rugby league football leaving the now combined Bradford and Bingley as the standard bearers for the union game in what is a rugby league stronghold. Bradford Bulls and near neighbours Leeds Rhinos are Yorkshire's big guns in the Super League and as the professional era in the union game approached there seemed little likelihood of a Yorkshire presence at the highest level. This would eventually change following the merger of the Headingley and Roundhay clubs which introduced the newly formed Leeds to National Division 3 in the 1992–93 season.

Take the Leeds-Carlisle train and within a few miles of leaving Leeds city centre, the old Headingley ground can be seen. Clarence Field, Kirkstall is now a training facility used by both Leeds Rhinos and Leeds Carnegie, clubs that also ground share at Headingley Stadium which is adjacent to the home of Yorkshire CCC. Headingley bought Clarence Field in 1920 as a memorial to those members who had lost their lives in the Great War and for many years it played host to English club rugby of the highest level. Included among an impressive list of international representatives are Carl Aarvold, Joseph Auty, David Caplan, Michael Lampowski, Ian McGeechan, Chris Rea, John Spencer and Peter Winterbottom.

Any alphabetical record of England rugby internationals has the name **Carl Aarvold** at the top (more formally referred to as His Honour Sir Carl Douglas Aarvold OBE, TD). Born in 1907, Aarvold attended Durham School where he was introduced to the game before heading to Emmanuel College, Cambridge with no plans other than to, '…learn what life was about…' as he was once quoted as saying. The lure of rugby football never failed to attract the better players on their arrival at Cambridge and Aarvold was soon identified as a three-quarter of some ability. Over four seasons he appeared at full-back, on the wing and in the centre confirming his versatility and he was the only freshman in the Cambridge team which won the 1925 Varsity Match. He eventually appeared in four of the annual encounters all won by Cambridge, a record yet to be equalled. But it wasn't that straightforward as Rowe Harding relates when discussing the 1926 match in *Rugby: Reminiscences and Opinions*. 'It is interesting to note that Aarvold played full-back in this match, having failed completely to find his form at centre, and it is an ironical commentary upon the frailty of Rugby (sic) players and the vagaries of form, had Witham not broken his leg, Aarvold would probably not have got into the side…'. Fine, but for someone with nothing more on the agenda than, '…to learn what life was about…' Aarvold's rugby days at Cambridge can be viewed as an outstanding triumph.

In 1927 a British team toured Argentina, very much a missionary expedition but one which was received by an enthusiastic public who turned out in numbers to watch the nine matches including four uncapped meetings with the host nation. Carl Aarvold was one of six current Cambridge players included in the 23 strong party and it was on this tour that he confirmed he was ready to play international rugby and won his first cap against New South Wales the following year. Six more followed during his time at Cambridge then against France in 1929, he made his first England appearance as a Headingley player. A year later he became the club's first British Lion, touring New Zealand and Australia with F.D. Prentice's team. With the captain not certain of his Test place and vice-captain Wilf Sobey ruled out by injury Aarvold led the Lions in three of the four Tests played in New Zealand once again proving himself under the most exacting circumstances. He was in his final season with Headingley when he was selected England captain for the games with Scotland and France in 1931 before work commitments took him to London. He then joined Blackheath continuing to lead England throughout 1932 and against Wales in 1933 in what was his final appearance, rugby finally having to give way to a distinguished legal career.

Called to the Bar in 1932 Aarvold held a variety of high profile positions including Deputy Chairman of Surrey Quarter Sessions, Judge of the Mayor's and City of London Court, Recorder of London and he was the last Chairman of the City and London Quarter Sessions before it fell under the jurisdiction of the Crown Court in 1971. Outside rugby and the law Carl Aarvold's other great love was tennis and he became president of the Lawn Tennis Association in 1962 continuing in office for 18 years. In 1968 he received a knighthood, the culmination of a life dedicated to the legal profession but during which he also found time to achieve recognition on the rugby field and become the figurehead of one of England's most famous sporting institutions. There has been much written about Carl Aarvold extolling his fine qualities and sporting prowess with all correspondents arriving at the same conclusion—first and foremost Carl Aarvold was a gentleman which is praise enough.

After continuing its journey through Shipley and Keighley the Leeds-

Carlisle train stops at Skipton. John Spencer was born in Skipton. Whether he played rugby football is unknown but what is certain is that he met a chap called Marks somewhere along the way and their names appear together along most high streets in the land. But it is the other **John Spencer** we have come to meet, the one who did play rugby and even though he probably supports his namesake's retail empire that is where any common ground between the two surely ends. So, for high street retailer read high street solicitor, the chosen career of the rugby playing Spencer who elected to follow his father into the legal profession.

My first club was Wharfedale. I was away at school but played fairly regularly for the club and it wasn't unusual for me to creep out of prep to get a lift home—some 30 miles or so—play club rugby at the weekend and then sneak back in via the fire escape at night. I played for England schools and continued my association with Wharfedale but once that stage of my education was over, Headingley poached me—'Come and play for us...' I took advice from my father and being a sensible man he told me that I had to go if I wanted a future in the game. So within a matter of weeks I'd joined Headingley.

After leaving Sedbergh I took a gap year, which allowed me a season with Headingley, before going to Cambridge University in the autumn of 1967. At that time, there was concern that students coming up were not as mature in terms of rugby physique and playing experience as earlier intakes attributing this as a direct result of the end of National Service. The same fixture list was in place and the then president, Geoff Windsor-Lewis, was getting worried that it couldn't be maintained, the younger students not being able to compete with the major clubs, but looking at the teams during my time at Cambridge I'm not sure that was actually so. Behind the scrum we had Jacko Page at scrum-half, Ian Robertson and then Roger Shackleton at stand-off, Gerald Davies alongside me in the centre with Keith Hughes on the wing and Tony Jordan at full-back. The only uncapped player among the backs in 1968 and 1969 was Chris Saville who went on to play for Blackheath with Tony and also represented the Barbarians but not England.

Spencer won three Blues and was captain in his final year. By this time he had four caps to his name having first caught the selector's eye in the

1968 Varsity Match. He was called up to play for the Whites in the first trial
at Falmouth in December that year and was then included in the Probables
at the second trial held a fortnight later at Hartlepool. So far so good, but
when an enthusiastic Rest defeated the England team at Twickenham it
was a case of hoping for the best come selection time. Throughout the trials
Spencer had been opposed by a tall, fair haired player from Coventry.
When the team to travel to Lansdowne Road was announced both were
selected to win first caps. John Spencer and David Duckham played nine
consecutive games together in the centre before Duckham was moved to
the wing after which the partnership was only renewed on one occasion;
the centenary match against an RFU President's XV with Spencer as
captain in what proved to be his final international appearance.

I still see quite a lot of David. He's very well—overweight, but very well.
He retired from the game pretty much when his international career came
to an end but we still see each other quite a lot, our families are very close.
I chose to end my playing days where I had started, at Wharfedale and I
think I was 44 when I called it a day having moved down the teams to
finally playing at outside-half for the sixths. I probably played too long
because I started getting arthritis in the knee and had to have a
replacement.

John Spencer won 14 caps and captained England four times. In addition
to the President's XV, England also celebrated the centenary season by
playing an additional fixture against Scotland 100 years to the day from the
first international rugby match. The game was played at Murrayfield and
Spencer led out a team showing two changes from that which seven days
earlier had lost to the Scots by a point at Twickenham. One hundred years
earlier Scotland won; seven days earlier Scotland won; and on 27 March
1971 Scotland won again. But the importance of that first fixture at Raeburn
Place was recognised in the best possible way. His England career may have
ended at Murrayfield but there was one more level to reach that remains an
exclusive club for the relatively small number of players allowed through the
door—the British Lions.

The Lions are very important. There were only five English players in the
original selection for the 1971 tour but it gave us a great opportunity to play

with guys we'd been knocking lumps out of over the years and through that an enormous respect evolved. Gordon Brown became one of my biggest mates only because we had been on a Lions tour together and Gerald and I went back to our university days but I'm still in touch with so many of them. Unfortunately a lot of the Premiership clubs don't like the Lions because it tends to take the players away for too long; they don't understand the spirit and character it engenders but if you talk to any player who has been on a Lions tour they will defend it with their lives.

John Spencer played in 10 matches for the 1971 Lions and had the distinction of leading the team against a South Canterbury, Mid Canterbury, North Otago combination, the game played at Timaru and won by the tourists 25–6. He also touched down for the first of the 95 tries scored, this against Queensland in the opening fixture which the Lions rather surprisingly lost. Twenty years would pass between the heady heights of being a member of arguably the greatest ever British Lions party to leave these shores and a final run out with Wharfdale sixths but the story doesn't stop there. The game of rugby union does not run itself and it is in his capacity as a leading administrator that John Spencer now thrives.

I've been president of Wharfedale for 30 years, I was still playing when I accepted the position, and when in 1995 Yorkshire were looking for somebody to represent them on the RFU council they asked if I would be interested. The timing was right and I readily accepted. A year earlier Fran Cotton had invited me to become a selector for the Northern Division so within a couple of years of retiring I found myself fully involved again.

Now I'm on the management board of the RFU and chairman of Club England, the committee for elite rugby made up of Rob Andrew, Brian Ashton, Bill Beaumont, Kevin Bowring, Simon Halliday, Damien Hopley, Jason Leonard, Conor O'Shea and myself. We deal with all aspects of English rugby—coaching appointments, World Cup schedules, tour itineraries, accommodation etc. There is no involvement with team selection but we are quite close to the players.

Martin Corry has just announced his retirement from international rugby. There is a guy who demands immense respect because, like Martin Johnson and Bill Beaumont, he always put his body on the line in what were some extremely difficult games. He always took the flak even though he was playing well but that is captaincy; when you take the appointment I think you have to be prepared to put your career on the line. When it goes wrong the captain and the coach have to take the blame even if it is not their fault. There are many examples of coaches who have lost their jobs but didn't have the raw material with which to work and similarly there have been poor captains who were saved by the quality of the players around them

England have been criticised over the last four years for a lack of succession planning. There was a lot of succession planning in place following the 2003 World Cup but we had a mediocrity of players at our disposal. There were a lot of very, very good club players available but you need more than that to be a good international footballer and the results reflected it. Obviously there were exceptions but generally speaking since 2003 there have been a lot of players selected who in a different era would not have gained international status. This meant that when we arrived at the 2007 tournament we were looking at maybe two or three positions where players were certain to be selected whereas Australia, New Zealand and South Africa could put 12 or 13 names on the team sheet immediately. Consequently we were still looking at players during the pool stages which was far from ideal; throw in a couple of injuries and the whole thing becomes even more difficult. It wasn't until the semi-final and final that we were able to reproduce anything resembling a stable side which was a direct result of finding out that too many players were not up to international standard and having to start again. In the end we opted for experience which turned out to be the right choice. Now we have to start to bring in new faces but at the same time retain a level of experience within the team which is why I think that captaincy is of such great importance in the aftermath of a World Cup. I doubt that Phil Vickery will lead England into the next one but he can do an important job in the immediate future.

International captaincy is a fine art. The captain has to be able to express himself in a way that commands people's attention. He has to know the players, what each of them reacts to and be able to light the touch paper of each individual to make sure he gets the best out of them. Some players respond to praise, others to criticism and it is these little individual quirks that the captain has to be aware of. Some will respond to a general team talk but others have to be addressed individually. Some you shout at, some you talk to—it's very interesting.

I thought Dick Greenwood was the best captain I played under. He led the trial teams I was involved in and when I made my debut against Ireland. Dick got the best out of me by addressing me individually; he certainly knew how to get me fired up. He'd praise the backs, tell me how the forwards were going to give us a lot of ball and then he would outline what we were going to do with it. He was very good. Off the field, away from the demands on him as a player, the captain still has the media to contend with and the social responsibilities that have always gone with the job. Then there is the after match dinner, still a big part of international day at Twickenham, where both captains have to say a few words; traditions which are still valued by a lot of people.

John Spencer's involvement with rugby continues and is likely to do so for a while yet. Similarly, his legal career also took a new direction a few years ago when he went into partnership with Andrew Davies. In the hi-tech twenty first century when everything seems to be run by mobile phones there was an opportunity here which Spencer and his new partner found much too inviting to ignore.

I've always been a fan of Steve Winwood; through *Traffic, Blind Faith* with Eric Clapton and his solo career. But it was the early days with Spencer Davis which I recall particularly well and when Andrew and I set up the partnership it had to be called Spencer Davies. We even set the ring tones on our mobile phones to play 'Keep On Running', a minor classic. Great stuff.

For over 40 years John Spencer has been a stalwart of English rugby on and off the field. His little black book contains the numbers of all the great players of his era, players with whom he has established friendships that will last a lifetime. Such a list of contacts will ensure that come what may, up on the Yorkshire Dales Steve Winwood and Spencer Davis will continue to get regular plays.

Skipton is a typical North Yorkshire town. There is a castle, a canal, old mills converted into upmarket residential space and a champion purveyor of pork pies. The town also hosts a weekly market, lays claim to be the home of the

Craven heifer—the largest cow ever bred—has a fair smattering of public houses, many with a cow on the sign above the door in reverence to said heifer, and Skipton also has a rugby club.

John Green was first capped against Ireland in 1905. He was a forward who came into a side that had been humiliated by the Welsh in the season's opening match, Wales scoring seven tries in a 25–0 victory. The Irish game played in Cork produced another comprehensive defeat, England conceding five more tries and John Green was one of eight players summarily dropped by the selectors. But nothing changed. England lost the final game of the season and ended the year losing to New Zealand before two further defeats to Wales and Ireland saw Green reinstated for the first of seven consecutive appearances that included his one outing as captain. In the six Championship matches played during 1906 and 1907 John Green was one of six captains experimented with. Captain at Skipton and the current Yorkshire captain he was well accustomed to what the role entailed but wasn't able to alter England's fortunes and following defeat in Ireland the selectors looked elsewhere for a man to lead the team. They retained Green's services in the pack for the final game of the season—another defeat.

Of all England's captains, perhaps the least is known about John Green, certainly from that which is in the public domain. His associations with Skipton and Yorkshire are well documented and he is known to have served as president of Ilkley RUFC for many years but there the trail ends. What can be confirmed however is that he lived to the ripe old age of 87 making him one of the longest living captains and John Green also provides us with some rugby trivia; in winning his eight caps he played at eight different grounds.

In 1963, Mike Weston was chosen North Sportsman of the Year. This is no mean feat when one considers the dominance of association football in a region where Newcastle United has always enjoyed fanatical support despite rarely living up to the high expectations of its followers. What chance does rugby union have in such a soccer stronghold?

North of Newcastle the presence of rugby posts on the landscape takes a marked downward turn before the Scottish Borders introduce a semblance of normality. This is a statement the good folk of Alnwick, Blyth and Morpeth, among others, would undoubtedly contest. But it is a fact that there are very few clubs playing in the national leagues found north of Newcastle. Of course, in and around the city the story is very different with several providing aspiring young players the opportunity to develop their game in the hope that one day someone from the Newcastle Falcons will come calling with a contract.

The Falcons can trace a history back to 1877, albeit one that has seen the club play under various guises—Gosforth and then Newcastle Gosforth before the rebranding as Newcastle Falcons in 1996. Prior to the formation of Gosforth, at the instigation of a group of ex-pupils from Durham School, the biggest union clubs in the area were Northern and Percy Park, both still to be found competing in the Northumberland and Durham leagues, and Rockcliff, which may no longer exist, but in 1892 produced a half-back good enough to play for England and good enough to captain the team.

The 1890s can be viewed as one of the most significant decades in the history of English rugby. From being a game which had its origins in the public schools, rugby union had moved away from such elitism and a look through the England team sheets of the period will confirm the strength of the game in the north. However, the great social divide between north and south meant many players in the north of the country were financially penalised as a direct consequence of their involvement in the game. Moves had been taken to introduce a system of payment to compensate for any loss of earnings. It was widely known within the corridors of power that northern clubs had been making 'broken time' payments for some time. It was also recognised that this state of affairs was prominent in Yorkshire. Strange, or perhaps not, that it should fall to a member of the Yorkshire RFU to become the governing body's 'witchfinder general' in an attempt to bring an end to the obvious breach of the amateur code on which the union game placed such value. The Reverend Frank W. Marshall set about his mission with great vigour spreading the gospel and damning the insurgents at every opportunity but to no avail. In August 1895 representatives of 21 clubs met at a hotel in Huddersfield and the Northern Union, later to become the Rugby League was formed.

The contribution of the Rockcliff club during this period of upheaval was **Ernest William Taylor**. One of four captains from the north-east to lead England in the last decade of the nineteenth century, Ernest Taylor was known as 'Little Billy' and is not to be confused with J.T. 'Long John' Taylor of which more later. 'Little Billy' won 14 caps between 1892 and 1899 and led England six times including the first game following the formation of the Northern Union. This upheaval was expected to have a damaging effect on the national side but it has to be noted that in the previous season England defeated Wales and Ireland with only three players from northern clubs included in the team; H. Ward and T.H. Dobson from Bradford and Taylor. For the visit of Wales to Blackheath in 1896 England included 10 players from northern clubs and in scoring seven tries for a comfortable 25–0 victory, one could be forgiven for thinking the disruption was minimal. But that Wales played much of the game reduced to 14 men and England went on to lose the next four games it was clear that it would be some time before the loss of so many players was accommodated.

W.J. Townsend Collins wrote of Taylor, '...To say that he combined in himself individual ability and exceptional judgement—that he was a fast, dodgy and clever runner who got away himself or fed his three-quarters with judgement, kicked cleverly and tackled well—gives but a poor idea of a brilliant footballer and a likeable personality.' Words which suggest he was the complete footballer. In the same publication Collins is less enthusiastic about a player whose record as England captain was significantly better than Taylor's. Fred Alderson had relinquished the captaincy when described in his last game, against Wales in Cardiff as, '...altogether too cool; a man with obvious gifts who was not making the most of himself. Yet he had the stamp of distinction...'

On 7 March 1891, all roads led to Richmond where England met Scotland on the final weekend of the Championship. England were hoping for a third Triple Crown, Scotland desperate for a first. A month earlier the England selectors had introduced nine new caps for the game against Wales at Rodney Parade, Newport, among them an exciting three-quarter from Hartlepool Rovers who was also handed the captaincy, the second man to achieve this accolade 20 years after the first international when circumstances dictated the double honour being handed to Fred Stokes.

Fred Alderson represented Northumberland but it was at Durham that he is credited with the introduction of the four three-quarter system before England eventually adopted it. He played in two Cambridge winning teams in the Varsity Match and was also a founder member of the Barbarians appearing in that grand institution's first ever fixture in 1890—not for the invitation 15 but his club, Hartlepool Rovers. Come 1891 here was an experienced footballer at all but international level and that would change over the next two seasons during which he won six caps and captained England five times. The first game could not have gone better, Alderson converting two of the three tries in a comfortable victory and five weeks later in Dublin, England were rampant scoring five tries in registering what now seems a ridiculously small 9–0 victory but early scoring values awarded a point for a try with conversions worth two. The Scots also had similar victories to their credit hence the winner takes all showdown at Richmond.

England were appalling. Observers rated the performance the worst in the 20 years since the start of international fixtures and it was clear where the selectors placed the blame. The half-backs would never represent their country again neither would seven of the nine forwards, only Tom Kent and Sam Woods given further opportunities. Fred Alderson did remain in favour and the following season continued as captain. Though forced to stand down for the Irish game he returned against Scotland and the new look England regained their much damaged pride by winning that third Triple Crown.

Hartlepool Rovers was formed in 1879 and three years later West Hartlepool set up store. Unlike Fred Alderson, **J.T. 'Long John' Taylor** elected to join West Hartlepool on arriving in the area from South Yorkshire where he had played for Castleford and represented Yorkshire captaining both club and county. Before upping roots it is probable that Taylor led Yorkshire against a Durham County team captained by Fred Alderson and a Northumberland team led by Ernest Taylor. So it is with some certainty that we can say that the two Taylors had come across each other before joining forces in Dublin in 1897 when 'Little Billy' led out an England team that included 'Long John' in the centre.

John Taylor must have grown to loathe Lansdowne Road. Following his debut there in 1897 he was in the teams which crossed the Irish Sea in 1899, 1901 and 1903 all of which returned home defeated. In 1901 Taylor captained England against Wales sent to Cardiff with a team including 10 new caps to take on a side full of seasoned international stars at the start of a decade when Welsh rugby would reach the heights. England were beaten 13–0 and Taylor is another player who led his country once but unlike many others the defeat in Cardiff didn't mark the end of his international days.

Reports inform us of a complete centre three-quarter who could bring his co-centre and wings into play with great effect. Defensively sound Taylor was a good kicker of the ball and could show a clean pair of heels when the opportunity presented itself but after 10 caps John Taylor disappeared from the international arena and but for a national team which was stumbling from bad to worse that is where he would have stayed. The heavy defeat suffered in Cardiff in 1905 left the selectors scratching their heads—who should they to take to Dublin? They must have consulted the record books, seen Taylor's miserable record across the Irish Sea and decided to look elsewhere. England lost and 'Long John' was well away from it but he did win that final cap at full-back against Scotland and yes—England lost that game as well. It would be remiss to let the reader continue thinking that John Taylor didn't experience success in an England jersey, not so. Against Ireland, twice and Scotland there was some compensation for the other eight games in which defeat reared its ugly head but despite those four fruitless visits to Dublin things could have been much worse—in 1903 he could have died!

John Taylor's final visit to Lansdowne Road was in an England team captained by **Bernard Oughtred**, a scrum-half from local rivals Hartlepool Rovers. Oughtred took over the captaincy for the first match in 1903, a visit to Swansea that saw a Welsh team reduced to 14 players for most of the game run out comfortable winners. Wales' captain Tom Pearson left the field midway through the first half and was replaced on the wing by loose forward Jehoida Hodges who scored an improbable hat-trick of tries. The team that travelled to Ireland for the next match showed five changes including a recall on the right wing for Reginald Forrest in place of John Miles, the first player to be capped from the Leicester club and who appears to have shouldered the responsibility for the tries scored by a forward replacement he was expected to contain. The party also included ex-president Robert Whalley who had made his mark as an administrator with both the RFU and the International Board, was instrumental in the restructuring of the County Championship and a staunch opponent of 'broken time' payments. Two months later Forrest and Whalley were both dead and Bernard Oughtred was recovering following a serious bout of illness. All three were diagnosed as having typhoid and it was suggested they had in all probability contracted the infectious bacterial fever during the visit to Dublin.

Durham were the dominant force in the County Championship during the first decade of the twentieth century featuring in 10 consecutive finals, winning six. Bernard Oughtred captained the team during the start of this period of dominance but a move to Hull meant he had to sever relationships with both club and county. All was not lost however and despite never being selected for England again he continued playing for Hull and East Riding and eventually returned to county rugby with Yorkshire but with nothing like the success previously enjoyed. A naval architect, it was work that had necessitated the move south and it was work which ultimately took him across the Pennines to Barrow-in-Furness where he supervised proceedings at the Vickers yard while ending his rugby days at the local club and again sampling county rugby, this time with Westmoreland. When war broke out in 1914, Bernard Oughtred was attached to the Royal Navy with the rank of acting Captain which was quite appropriate for a man who had led two clubs, two counties and his country.

Which brings us to Gosforth, Newcastle Gosforth and the Newcastle Falcons; three names that illustrate the development of a club founded in 1877. Gosforth RFC survived in name for 113 years but on moving to a new ground in 1990 the club became known as Newcastle Gosforth and on the advent of professionalism in 1995 it finally evolved into the Newcastle Falcons; the northernmost club in the Guinness Premiership.

For the best part of 100 years, Gosforth had not made any waves beyond the boundaries of Northumberland. Scotland and British Lions captain Arthur Smith played for the club in the mid 1950s as did Ireland's Ray McLoughlin in the early 1960s but the only connection with England was through George Robinson in the 1890s and Alistair Smallwood in the 1920s. Both men played for Gosforth but were elsewhere when called up for international duty. This was small return for a club approaching its centenary but as if aware there would be something to celebrate in 1977 a team of some stature began to assemble; one which would ensure that the celebrations would not pass by unnoticed.

One of those involved was **Roger Uttley**. When he arrived at the club, there were already signs that Gosforth was ready to reach out beyond the county boundaries and put its stamp on the English game. The team he joined was full of talented players waiting for their moment to arrive; hooker Duncan Madsen who was destined to play for Scotland; scrum-half Malcolm Young who would win 10 England caps; wing forward David Robinson was only denied international honours by the presence of Tony Neary; and the arrival of Peter Dixon brought more experience to a team full of unsung heroes. Overseeing proceedings was captain Jack Rowell, later to make his name as one of England's leading club and international coaches. But how did Blackpool born Roger Uttley end up in Gosforth?

I wasn't particularly studious and much to my mother's chagrin I failed the Eleven-plus Exam which meant I went to Montgomery Secondary Modern School. I wasn't much good at football, played a bit of rugby and a lot of basketball but I really took to cycling; 30 mile time trials which were pretty demanding for a young lad. At that early stage of my adolescence all that hard physical exercise meant I had a big engine, good lungs and a decent pair of legs. Of the team sports, I much preferred basketball; it was a much more skilful game and in rugby you tended to be knocked around—I think I was a bit on the soft side—but as I grew into my size and gained in confidence rugby began to take over.

On the back of a rather weak set of O levels I got into the sixth form at the local grammar school. After being well looked after by Bryn Jones, the PE master at Montgomery and a good scrum-half for Halifax RLFC, I now came under the influence of Jack Cornby. Jack had played full-back for Fylde and Lancashire and it was during my two years at Blackpool Grammar that I finally decided I wanted to concentrate on rugby. I was selected for England Schools and invited to play for Fylde Falcons—the colts—and later Fylde Saracens which was the old lags team; they couldn't run about a lot but had good rugby brains. That was a fantastic education which a lot of lads miss out on these days.

Through the examples shown by Bryn Jones and Jack Cornby I realised that PE teaching was a good vocation. If I wanted to be a half decent rugby player, and by this time people were telling me that I could be, then teaching would allow me to train and work at the same time which was a big attraction. I applied for teacher training college and my first choice was Cardiff. I went down to Cyncoed and had an interview with Bill Samuel, Gareth Edwards' great mentor, and Lynn Davies the Olympic long jump gold medallist—but I didn't get in, wasn't good enough. That was a bit of a worry because I'd also applied to Loughborough, St Luke's, St John's, York and St Pauls, Cheltenham but having been turned down by Cardiff I wasn't going to be accepted at any of them. Fortunately the headmaster at Blackpool Grammar had a contact at Northumberland College, arranged an interview for me and I was accepted. This was a defining moment because if I had got in at Cardiff there is no doubt I would have found it tough being a small fish in a big pond but it was very different at Northumberland, the place was a bit of a sleeping giant. Fylde had given me a letter of introduction and that was how I came to join Gosforth.

Roger Uttley became Gosforth's first international when he was selected against Ireland in 1973; joint first actually because Peter Dixon who had joined the club from the Harlequins won his first cap as a Gosforth player in the same match. Uttley was chosen in the second-row alongside Chris Ralston and he retained his place playing in five matches during the year which included England's win in New Zealand and the victory over Australia at Twickenham. He appeared in three Championship matches in 1974 following which he was selected to tour South Africa with the British Lions. In a repeat of events in New Zealand three years earlier which saw Peter Dixon find his true position it was on this tour that Uttley developed into an outstanding back row forward playing in 16 of the 22 matches including the four Tests. Unlike Dixon who England selected on the blind side after his conversion 'down under' when Uttley returned to England duty it was in the second-row with only the occasional appearances on the flank or at number 8.

I only played in the back row on the Lions tour because Tommy David got injured. I was asked to play on the blind side against the Proteas in the week before the first Test and was then selected in the same position against South Africa. 'Are you sure?' I asked and Syd Millar said yes, we'd give it a go—all I had to do was stop them coming around the short side. Fortunately they never tested me out; I don't think I was ever exposed. Working with people like Syd and Willie John was a great experience and I came back from that tour a much harder player with a much clearer idea of what was expected.

In 1976 Gosforth reached the final of the John Player Cup but club captain Roger Uttley had to watch from the stands, a broken leg ruling him out for the second half of the season. Gosforth defeated Rosslyn Park and a year later were back to defend their title against Waterloo. This time Uttley was able to lead the team in the end of season showpiece and Gosforth didn't let him down. Coventry, Gloucester and London Welsh were all beaten on the road to Twickenham and Waterloo had to settle for the runners-up medals in the final; the pride of the Midlands, the South West, London and the north-west each had to play second fiddle to the pride of the north-east—Gosforth could celebrate its centenary in style.

It was during the 1976–77 season that Roger Uttley led England for the first time. Scotland and Ireland were beaten before France gained a narrow victory at Twickenham but it was against Wales in Cardiff that the injury problems which disrupted the rest of his career began. A broken leg is certainly a bad injury though rarely a recurring one unlike back problems which are a different thing altogether and very often they just won't go away.

We played our worst game of the season in Cardiff and Wales played their best. I attempted to tackle JPR which shook me up a bit and I was ready to go off but Peter Dixon persuaded me to stay on. It was a bad day for me and I didn't play again for a while. I made it to the cup final, took a bit of a shoeing, then decided to have a month off before going to New Zealand with the Lions—that was a mistake. The squad met up a few days before flying out and after the first training session I couldn't sit down, couldn't stand up, couldn't do anything—I was in bits. I didn't say anything, just took myself off to bed and watched the rugby league cup final but the next morning I had to ring John Dawes and tell him I didn't think I'd be able to last 30 hours on a plane—I was in a dreadful state for the next six months. All the sensible people told me I should forget about rugby and lead a sedentary life which isn't very good if you are a PE teacher.

Roger Uttley left his teaching post at Cramlington for a job working in sales when a chance meeting with an osteopath brought with it a glimmer of hope that he could get his back repaired and maybe resurrect his rugby career. After 12 months' treatment not only was he able to consider returning to the game but the chance meeting had developed into a business partnership which took him to the Home Counties. His involvement in a clinic specialising in sports injuries run in conjunction with an executive health club was the reason he left the north-east. If that didn't turn out to be what he was ultimately looking for it did mean he was in the right place when the job that would dominate most of his working life presented itself.

Uttley returned to the England team against the All Blacks in 1978 and two months later was appointed captain for the start or the Five Nations, the last cap he would win as a Gosforth player. Forced to leave the field against Scotland with yet another injury one wondered how much longer he could carry on. After moving south and joining Wasps for his final seasons in the game he defied the odds and returned to England duty ending his career on a high, an integral part of the 1980 Grand Slam winning team. For the first time he was selected on the blind side for England and it is worth mentioning that in arguably the most important eight matches of his international career neither the British Lions in 1974 nor England in the 1980 Championship were beaten.

I was selected to carry on as captain after the Scotland game in 1979 but on the eve of the Irish match I fell terribly ill and John Scott was called in to take my place with the captaincy passing back to Bill Beaumont; the next season we won the Grand Slam with Billy as captain. There was a really horrible, nasty atmosphere before the Welsh match, which was all so unnecessary, and I sometimes think the media have to take a look at how they get involved in some of these games; they have to remember that sport is sport not war. Anyway, we got to the game and Paul Ringer did one silly thing and then he did another silly thing and David Burnett sent him off. Then a scrum erupted, Terry Holmes and John Scott were having a good old ding dong and I thought someone's going to be carried off here. Lo and behold, the ball popped over the top, I went down on it and the next thing I remember was thinking my head is flying between the posts. I had to go off. I was in a terrible mess and needed a lot of stitches to repair the damage. When I arrived home the following morning the look of horror on my two lads' faces said it all—who was this deformed character?

After the match we were sitting in the old tea room under the west stand; my wife was there and my mother and father who had come down for the match. Dear old Geoff Wheel comes up behind me 'Oh Roger...how are you? Sorry about that. Didn't see you—accident see boy...' But that match just highlighted the very ugly side of rugby. Paul was just stupid but he had been wound up, something had got to him and he just had to go and get in Johnny Horton's face so when Dusty Hare kicked the winning penalty late on I was sitting in the stands and just felt that justice was done. It was all very silly, a great pity.

My last game for England was against Scotland when we won the Grand Slam, I was lucky because it was four weeks after the Welsh game which gave me ample time to recover properly. My last club game was for the Wasps against Rosslyn Park on a nice, sunny November afternoon. I'd been injured again and was looking to test out my fitness to see if I was ready for another England trial where I would probably come up against John Scott. Andy Ripley was in the Rosslyn Park back row, a fantastic athlete but a player I would normally expect to get the better of but on this occasion he was all over me. I was playing number 8 and Nigel Melville was having one of his first games for the club at scrum-half. It was a shambles; I was leaning on at the back of the scrum making a mess of getting the ball to Nigel—a complete shambles. I told Andy in the showers after the match that was it—I'd had enough.

It is a long way from Montgomery Secondary Modern School to Harrow, one of England's finest educational establishments, but that is exactly where Uttley found himself in 1982 after leaving the world of sports injuries and health spas accepting a golden opportunity to become sports master at the famous public school. The rugby team were under performing and a new headmaster wanted someone to take over who could arrest the fall in standards and 26 years on it is clear that in Roger Uttley the right appointment was made.

The standard of rugby here is generally very good and every two or three years we find one or two boys who if they were a bit lucky and had the necessary desire could possibly play Premiership rugby. I believe that all schoolboys should be physically literate but unfortunately that is no longer the case. I was very fortunate; in my schooldays PE played a part throughout every school year and while boys may have lots of games periods here it doesn't necessarily mean they are taught how to run, jump and throw. They are taught the basic game but not the basic skills which is one of the problems I've had in recent years. It wasn't always like that but because of academic pressures PE has been squeezed in the Lower School to allow more time for other subjects. We do PE as an academic subject in the Upper School the result of which is that you have boys coming up from the Lower School who I have had nothing to do with and all of a sudden we meet in the Lower Sixth. Some may think they are very good players but I take a look at them and very often disagree and they often find that very difficult to take.

In 1988, Geoff Cooke was appointed England manager following the resignation of Mike Weston after a disappointing World Cup and Roger Uttley replaced Martin Green as coach. The new regime began with defeats by France and Wales but a dour struggle in Edinburgh did secure the

Calcutta Cup which the players of both teams redesigned with some unorthodox football as the night unfolded. A devastating demolition of Ireland brought the Championship to a satisfactory close and the new management team could reflect on a season during which England had turned the corner.

The British Lions toured Australia in 1989 and this time Roger Uttley was on the plane as assistant coach to Ian McGeechan. The Lions won the three match series after Australia won the first Test adding further kudos to Uttley's growing reputation as an international coach. He confirmed this with a good Championship in 1990 that saw England denied a Grand Slam at the final hurdle by Scotland. In 1991 there were to be no such hiccups and it was the leadership of Will Carling and the driving force of Geoff Cook and Roger Uttley which helped England go through the tournament unbeaten, ideal preparation for the second World Cup to be played in England later in the year.

England were beaten by Australia in the final at Twickenham and for Roger Uttley it was time to move on. He remained in coaching taking over at Richmond while his teaching post allowed him to continue to search for the stars of tomorrow on the playing fields at Harrow. Unquestionably, there have been some fine players unearthed in north-west London but it was the playing fields at Lord Wandsworth College in Hook, Hampshire that would see the emergence of one of the biggest names in English rugby.

England won a Grand Slam in 1997. On 12 April, Wales were beaten 18–17 at Narbeth, a small town in Pembrokeshire and not one normally mentioned in the same breath as Grand Slams but this was the Under 18 competition and 1997 proved to be England's year. Leading his country for the first time was the Lord Wandsworth College outside-half a talented player and accurate goal kicker who had converted one of centre Mike Tindall's two tries to add to an earlier penalty but as the game entered the final minutes England trailed 17–15. Cometh the hour, cometh the man and the skipper saw his team home with a last gasp drop goal, an indication of things to come but events that would be played out on a much bigger stage than the west Wales town could provide.

Jonny Wilkinson had been introduced to rugby at Farnham but it was at Wandsworth that he began to attract the attention of the England selectors playing for the Under 16s before moving up to the Under 18s. With rugby union now a professional sport there was a career waiting for those considered good enough to get a club contract and Wilkinson deferred a place at Durham University but still made the move north when Newcastle offered him the chance to see if he could cut it at the highest level.

The 1997–98 season saw the newly promoted Newcastle take the Allied Dunbar Premiership by storm. Rob Andrew, Gary Armstrong, Tim Stimpson, Alan Tait, Va'aiga Tuigamala and Tony Underwood were included in a star studded back division which the likes of Gareth Archer, Pat Lam, Nick Popplewell, Dean Ryan, Peter Walton and Doddie Weir up front ensured had enough ball to weave their magic. It is difficult to imagine a better place for Wilkinson to begin his rugby education in earnest and with Andrew taking him under his wing he was in more than capable hands. Time would look after the rest.

Wilkinson spent the afternoon of Sunday 22 March 1998 in Edinburgh sitting on England's replacement bench watching the team run up a record score at Murrayfield and outside-half Paul Grayson rack up 19 points with a try, four conversions, a penalty and a drop goal—rugby's full house. Two weeks later England won a fourth successive Triple Crown beating Ireland at Twickenham. Wilkinson replaced Mike Catt on the wing for the final two minutes. He was on his way.

England's summer tour in 1998 makes Mike Weston's experiences 35 years earlier seem a stroll in the park. Wilkinson began his international career for real at Brisbane, selected at outside-half in the team depleted of many first choice players that suffered a record 76–0 defeat. Two weeks later in Dunedin the All Blacks continued the demolition winning 64–22 and finished the job in Auckland seven days later with a 40–10 victory while in between the Tests, New Zealand A, New Zealand Academy and the New Zealand Maoris picked at the carcass of English rugby. Wilkinson only featured against Australia and in the first Test in New Zealand missing out at Newlands, Cape Town when the final act of this disastrous tour was played out. South Africa added to the misery winning 18–0.

Never mind the body there was much mental damage to repair before the players could once more take to the field with confidence. Fortunately, making sure that mind always gets the better of matter and possessing the ability to focus totally on the job in hand are areas Wilkinson thrives on. In 1999 he showed his value to the team when he was included in the centre and handed the kicking responsibilities scoring 60 points in the Five

Nations. Wilkinson and Grayson were included in England's World Cup later in the year and both enjoyed some game time on that balmy autumn day in Paris when South Africa's Janie de Beer showed that he could kick a bit as well.

It was against Italy in the 2003 Championship that Jonny led England for the first time since that day in Narbeth six years earlier. Then his late drop goal had saved the team when all seemed lost and a similar effort saw England home in extra time against Australia in the World Cup final later in the year. Wilkinson returned home a hero, feted wherever he went and the sponsors were after him with more intent than any back row forward had ever shown—then there were the injuries.

That Jonny Wilkinson still plays rugby is a tribute to his own attitude and the constant presence of his mentor and confidante Steve Black. The succession of injuries which were heaped on Wilkinson in the years following England's triumph would have seen lesser minded individuals call it a day; suffice to say that he did not turn out for England again until 2007 when he took the field against Scotland in the opening game of the Six Nations. By scoring a try, two conversions, five penalties and a drop goal in this come back match of epic proportions Wilkinson announced to the rugby world that it was business as usual. This was World Cup year and England as defending champions were not expected to make much of a defence of their title but with Jonny back in the fold the bookies' odds took a sudden tumble.

His second tilt as England captain came on the 2007 summer tour to South Africa when he stood in for the injured Jason Robinson, following which all roads led to France and hopefully a packed Stade de France on 20 October, the date of the final. England's World Cup story is told elsewhere but defeat in the final was hard to accept and even Wilkinson, a player who pretty much excluded alcohol from his strict regime, admitted to taking the odd glass or two with the squad after the formalities were done with. One can only wonder what would have happened if they had won!

Jonny Wilkinson scored England's six points in the final to add to a total which was getting close to the world record of 1090 held by Wales' Neil Jenkins. The 'Ginger Monster' scored 1049 for his country and another 41 for the British and Irish Lions; at the start of the 2008 Six Nations Wilkinson had scored 982 points for England added to which were the 47 scored for the Lions in his five Test appearances in 2001 and 2005. Then there were the 20 points scored for the Lions in the pre-tour match against Argentina in 2005 which had recently been granted international status by the IRB leaving Wilkinson needing another 42 points to beat the record.

He kicked 14 points in England's Twickenham debacle against Wales and by the Scotland match, the 27 points registered against France and Italy saw him tied with Jenkins at 1090. Any points gained at Murrayfield would secure the record. England produced another abject performance but in kicking three penalties in the 15–9 defeat Wilkinson became international rugby's top points scorer which counted for nought when he was dropped to the bench for the final match against Ireland. Wasps' Danny Cipriani had long been touted as Wilkinson's natural successor. He didn't disappoint when given his chance and only time will tell how Jonny responds to this latest challenge but whatever the outcome, he can always look back with some pride on that late drop goal in Narberth—neither will he ever be allowed to forget the other one!

The 2003 Rugby World Cup was the fifth. What began in New Zealand and Australia in 1987 has grown into a global event to rival the Olympic Games and the Football World Cup but those attending the inaugural event would have doubted that in 16 years rugby union would undergo such a dramatic transformation.

Sheffield boasts two football teams. Sheffield Wednesday and Sheffield United both currently play in the Coca-Cola Championship, one division below the Premiership and all the kudos that goes with competing against the game's big boys week in week out. Gain promotion and Manchester United, Liverpool, Arsenal, Chelsea etc will ensure full houses. Which is how it once was for two teams that have won first division titles and FA cups in their respective histories. But ask sports minded folk distanced from the city what its sporting claim to fame is and an educated guess suggests that rather than football it would be a much quieter sport which would provide the popular answer. For three weeks in early spring television schedules are dominated by wall to wall coverage of snooker, the action transmitted from the Crucible Theatre, Sheffield. Steve Davis, Stephen Hendry, Alex Higgins, Jimmy White, Ronnie O'Sullivan and many more besides have helped put this most unlikely of sporting venues on the map. And it is not much more than a good long pot from the entrance to this citadel of the green baize that we find a man with a unique position in the annals of English rugby.

Mike Harrison is Yorkshire through and through. Wakefield's only

England captain he remained loyal to the club which had helped him become established as an international rugby footballer, ignoring all efforts to entice him into playing his rugby at some of the more fashionable names. Told he would never play for England while he remained at Wakefield— moves to Headingley, Leicester or Nottingham were suggested—Harrison ignored the advice and stayed true to his roots relying on the proven county system to highlight his undoubted talent.

I played rugby at Queen Elizabeth's School in Wakefield because they didn't play football. I was a scrum-half at that time and played for the first XV and the county at the age of 16. The plan was to go to Loughborough College to continue in a sports based education, to play rugby really, which was probably the wrong reason, but in my final year at school I was in a car accident. My head went through the windscreen and I had to have part of my eye taken out and was told I couldn't play any sport again.

This brought an end to my proposed years at college and on leaving school I ended up joining a local bank. Soon afterwards, I sought out the advice of another specialist and he was happy for me to play football but definitely ruled out rugby. It was all sport to me so I joined the bank team which played to a good standard; Sheffield United and Sheffield Wednesday reserves were on the fixture list as were Nottingham Forest reserves and Cloughie would often appear on the touchline. The bank then asked if I would consider playing a game of rugby for them and I decided to give it a go and quickly realised what I'd been missing. I met my old schoolmaster for a chat and he took me along to Wakefield who gave me a game in the thirds at scrum-half. Then it was in the centre for the seconds and I finished the season on the wing for the firsts displacing someone who had been there forever.

Wakefield grew in stature during the latter part of the 1970s and into the 1980s with a young back division that upset many teams with their open, exciting brand of running rugby, wings Harrison and Neil Bennett scoring record numbers of tries. Inside them was Bryan Barley, by now an England international, and the club won various northern league titles in addition to supplying several county players.

I represented Yorkshire and played for the North against the Australians

191

in 1984. There were some England trials but it was probably the Barbarians Easter tour to Wales that got me noticed by the selectors. I was chosen in the England party to tour New Zealand, probably as third choice behind John Goodwin and Simon Smith—Rory Underwood was unavailable. I picked up my nickname on that tour. The try I scored in the first Test came from an interception, Warwick Taylor floated a pass out to John Kirwan which I was in a position to catch leaving me 50 yards to run. The same happened in the second Test, Steve Pokere looking for Kirwan with a long pass which I grabbed this time with 70 yards between me and the try line. I've got a New Zealand radio recording of the Tests and it was the commentator who first called me 'Burglar Bill' and it has stayed with me ever since.

The following season Rory Underwood reclaimed his left wing berth, Simon Smith included on the right for the opening match against Wales. Injury ruled Underwood out against Scotland so Harrison was brought in on the left, Smith keeping his place. A devastating 33–6 defeat saw a rethink and for the Irish visit to Twickenham, Underwood returned on the left wing with Harrison moved across to the right and that was how it remained for 11 of the next 12 matches, Underwood rested once during the 1987 World Cup. 'Burglar Bill' had made it but there was more to come.

The game against Wales in 1987 was a nightmare, all hell broke loose and some players including captain Richard Hill were disciplined and dropped. I don't believe anything was premeditated it just happened which it often did in those days. Some games it was always going to be like that, in others it wasn't but that was a passionate encounter and it happened; now of course there are citing commissioners and you have to be a bit more careful. I'd had some experience of captaincy with Wakefield and Yorkshire and I got a call inviting me to be captain. I don't know whether someone had gone down the list and was still looking when he got to number 14 but it was great. We beat Scotland and then it was off to the first World Cup.

Nobody knew if it was going to work, if it was going to make any money; it was quite low key really but exciting for the players. From an England point of view 1987 was the first year when a professional approach to the game was properly implemented. We all had individual fitness programmes and were shown how to use weights properly and Tom McNabb from UK Athletics came in to teach the props how to run. The southern hemisphere countries were well ahead in these areas but at least by implementing a fully structured training plan we were addressing the issues.

Everything was very different to what we see today. I think we took a squad of 28 players plus the manager, coach, physio and doctor and were away for a month. All our matches were played in Australia and I think we acquitted ourselves well except in the quarter-final when all 15 players had a poor game; I believe we should have beaten Wales but it was just a bad day at the office. Elsewhere the tournament was clearly a success and I think it actually did make some money. Obviously there were teething troubles but they were ironed out and whereas it had a dusting of amateurism about it with the advent of professionalism it has become big business. I enjoyed it—playing and captaining the side, getting everybody pulling in the right direction. I was mainly there as a motivator, something which I believe I do well, and there were key decision makers in the team who I allowed to control their particular areas of expertise.

I don't have any issue with the captain being on the wing. You are close enough to the action to appreciate fully what is going on and there are plenty of breaks in play which give you the chance to talk things through. Provided the right person is chosen, somebody who is going to be certain of selection, then I don't think any position should be viewed as being unsuitable. I was 31 when I was chosen to captain England and I viewed it as a great show of confidence in me, not just as a captain but as a player. Taking over after the Welsh game my first focus was to sort out any cliques that may have developed and try to get everybody focussed on the job. I wasn't expecting to be there for any great length of time, not at 31 years of age. But if I'd fallen on a loose ball in Paris instead of trying to pick it up, gifting France a try in the process, I might have seen out the Championship in 1988. That mistake and the Welsh game which followed saw the writing on the wall. I was hired and then I was fired, that's the way it is. I never had any issue with that, disappointed of course, but nothing more.

I enjoyed it. Enjoyed being with the lads. I still meet up with them in the ERIC bar at Twickenham for a beer before the match and within minutes you are talking about things that happened years ago but the stories are always as funny, they may get slightly embellished on each telling but that's what it's all about really. I think that is reflected in the way the game has changed. I don't see as many characters about now but it's a job and we have to accept that. The game itself has come on, the players are all athletes, they're all much fitter. Even at club level, they come off the pitch, take time to rehydrate, have an ice bath, maybe go into the hospitality areas because the contracts say they must and then they go home. All of which is fine, I know I wouldn't want to talk about banking 24 hours a day.

We are in the professional era and while it's finally getting there I do think a lot of things could have been handled differently when professionalism was first introduced. If you are running a business and you make a big strategic decision you usually have a plan to put it into action but that didn't happen and it's taken years to find a balance; the club-country issue in particular has taken some resolving. The number of games played is still an issue; we still play far too many in the northern hemisphere. It was probably 40 or more in my day and it's certainly not that number now but there are still far too many.

In April 2006 when Sandal Veterans took the field for the last game of the season there was a familiar face in the team who was about to play his final game 30 years after making his debut at Wakefield. Mike Harrison was now 51 and had decided to call it a day. He had remained at Wakefield for several seasons following the end of his international career and was quite happy to continue serving the club at the lower levels when no longer required by the first XV. A casualty of the professional era Wakefield was finally disbanded but Harrison and several other stalwarts of the club had already joined nearby Sandal and it was there that a long and successful rugby career finally ended.

I was back at scrum-half where I had started and although there was always somebody looking to have a pop at me because of who I was and what I had done I think that overall players respected me and the fact that I was still out there playing—I do miss it.

Mike Harrison believes there should be an elite level of rugby beneath which amateur principles are observed. While he readily accepts that now the game is open no matter what attitude toward payment of players individual clubs adopt there will always be one in any league that because of individual backers or sponsors will be prepared to pay that little bit more. This is far from unique to Yorkshire. It is a problem wherever the game is played but perhaps the county can relate to the effect money has had on the game more than most as it was here that the introduction of 'broken time' payments and the eventual formation of a profession sport had a major impact.

Huddersfield was one of the founder members of the Northern Rugby Football Union which meant that the town had no involvement in the strictly amateur game. This became more of an issue as firstly lineouts were removed by the breakaway group of clubs and later teams would be made up of 13 players by which time rugby league was a very different game. This absence of a union club in the town was addressed in 1909 when one was founded with the intent of playing the game as prescribed by the RFU, hence the second coming of Huddersfield RUFC.

Norman Hall was born in Huddersfield on 2 August 1925. He attended Worksop College before setting his sights on a career in medicine that took him to St Mary's College, London where he met future England stars Norman Bennett and Edward Scott. The trio formed a potent mid-field unit for the Hospital first XV and an exciting trio of backs in the seven-a-side teams which won the Middlesex Sevens in 1944 and 1946. Hall was a fine exponent of the reduced game and was in three more winning teams in the 1950s but as a Richmond player.

'Nim' Hall completed his studies at St Mary's in 1947 but rather than pursue the career in medicine he had worked for took up a two year commission in the Royal Signals, Northern Command during which time he represented the Army and Combined Services as required. But he played most of his rugby for Huddersfield and it was while at the club that he led England against Wales and Ireland in 1949 before losing his place after two disappointing defeats.

Later that year he left the Army and returned to London where he made the career change that introduced him to the world of insurance where he remained until 1965. The move also marked the start of his long association with Richmond and after three years in the international wilderness he resurrected his England career against South Africa in 1952, the first of nine consecutive appearances, five at outside-half and four at full-back, all as captain. England fared rather well during this phase of Hall's captaincy.

South Africa and Wales both won at Twickenham but none of the seven matches that followed were lost, only Ireland preventing a Grand Slam in 1953 with a 9–9 draw at Lansdowne Road. And there his international career would have ended had the selectors found a suitable replacement but in deciding that neither Harrogate's Ian King or Nigel Gibbs of the Harlequins were the answer to their prayers at full-back they reverted to the experienced Hall for the opening two matches in 1955 with the added sweetener of another spell as captain. It all ended in Dublin by which time Hall had won 17 caps including 13 as captain.

After a long illness, Norman Hall died at St Mary's Hospital on 26 June 1972. The high regard with which he was held among the rugby fraternity was reflected in the number of distinguished names who attended his funeral. His had been a varied career that had seen him represent St Mary's, the Army and Combined Services, Richmond, Yorkshire, Middlesex, the Barbarians and England but it is for his time at Huddersfield that he is best remembered in the north. His two games as England captain while a member of the club ensures it will always be associated with the best job in English rugby.

Before leaving the north-east there is one more tale to tell; one which perhaps best summarises what the decisions made at the George Hotel, Huddersfield in August 1895 meant to the union game in the north of England. One of only two players to feature in all six of the Championship matches during the 1890–92 seasons was wing three-quarter **Richard Lockwood**, a player whose career went full circle over a 20 year period but finished in different circumstances to how it had begun.

In 1839 Charles Dickens introduced the literary world to a myriad of characters through the pages of one of his most popular novels, *Nicholas Nickleby*. The daughter of showman Vincent Crummles and Mrs Crummles unashamedly and with no hint of embarrassment appeared on stage as 'The Infant Phenomenon' a more immodest or less self effacing handle it is difficult to imagine, that is until we get to Dewsbury circa 1885 where 'Little Dicky, The World's Wonder' first began to acquire some sporting prominence.

Richard Lockwood was 17 years of age when he made his debut for the West Yorkshire club from which he won a first cap in 1887. England took no part in the 1888 and 1889 Championships and Lockwood did not improve his tally until 1891 by which time he was playing for Heckmondwike. Eight consecutive appearances followed before he missed the game at nearby Leeds against Scotland at the end of the 1893 Championship. Perhaps his omission was because he hadn't scored enough tries, hadn't lived up to his billing or possibly he was injured but 'The World's Wonder' did return the following year and led England to a convincing 24–3 victory over Wales followed by a 7–5 home defeat by Ireland. Although scoring tries in both matches, his short spell as captain was over as indeed was his international career.

Richard Lockwood's story perfectly illustrates the dilemma which faced so many of the northern based players of the day, particularly those in Yorkshire. A poorly paid worker in the wool industry it is not surprising that he was one of the leading players to benefit from the introduction of 'broken time' payments and even less surprising, that he was one of the first high profile international players to join a Northern Union club. Talk of extra payment and appearance money was rife and it was only a matter of time before one of the breakaway clubs would acquire his services once the rift with the RFU was confirmed. Wakefield Trinity got their man and he represented them with distinction for eight years before returning to Dewsbury in 1903 thereby completing the circle started 20 years earlier.

Many players would follow Richard Lockwood—nobody could blame them. The impact rugby league had on its sibling sport in the north of the country can never be accurately measured. It was certainly significant and rugby league continues to thrive despite the union game joining sport's professional ranks. Many devotees would argue that it continues to go from strength to strength which makes it all the more important that Leeds Carnegie and Newcastle Falcons continue playing rugby union at the highest level, continue producing players for England and by doing so ensure that the game remains prominent in an area where it played second fiddle for 100 years.

9

MIDDLE MEN—PART TWO

Bedford, Northampton, Nottingham

The last region to be addressed before returning to the metropolis is the east Midlands, in particular a larger stretch of land found between the A1, the original north-south link road, and its big brother the M1. East of Sheffield the two roads are linked by a small stretch of the newer M18 and to the south they all but converge on their arrival in north London. In the area bordered by these major arteries is to be found a wealth of rugby history. Bedford, Leicester, Northampton and Nottingham are the clubs we need to focus our attention on and as was found with Blackheath, Harlequins and Richmond, the number of England captains associated with Leicester determines that club should be looked at in isolation.

The town of Nottingham is home to a couple of football teams, a racecourse where Lester Piggott rode his first ever winner, a county and Test cricket venue, a famous goose fair, a castle, university and the legend that is Robin Hood. It also has a rugby club which battles away in National Division One together with its west Midlands rivals Coventry and Moseley in the hope that at the end of a season's hard graft the reward will be promotion to the Guinness Premiership.

In recent years Rob Andrew, Dusty Hare, Simon Hodgkinson, Brian Moore, Chris Oti and Gary Rees have played for the club. Way back in time when Dave Gallaher and his 1905 New Zealand tourists were on their destructive dismantling of English rugby the man selected to lead the national team was Nottingham's **Vincent Cartwright**, a forward who had captained the Midland Counties against Gallaher's men earlier in the tour.

Like so many others it was at Rugby School and Oxford University that Vincent Cartwright was knocked into shape, had the rough edges taken away and made ready for the legal profession that awaited and the game that would knock him out of shape again and restore the rough edges. He won four Blues from 1901 to 1904 during which time he also won his first cap, against Wales in 1903. In fact 'Lump' Cartwright won eight caps while at Oxford and what an education those eight games were; seven were lost with only a 14–14 draw with Wales bringing any comfort.

Born in Nottingham in 1882, on graduating Cartwright returned home, took up employment with a local firm of solicitors and joined Nottingham RFC. His first season coincided with the New Zealand tour and when he led England out to meet the tourists at Crystal Palace he not only became his club's first England captain but its first international player. England came second but Cartwright was asked to continue in the role of captain only for defeats by Wales and Ireland to add to the misery—the record now read 10 defeats in 11 appearances.

Then—joy of joy! On 17 March at Inverleith, Scotland rolled over and at the 12th time of asking Vincent Cartwright found out what it was like to be part of a winning England team. The visitors outscored the Scots by three tries to one in the 9–3 victory and five days later in Paris England scored nine tries against France on the occasion of the first meeting between the two countries—'Lump' was on a roll! The following season the first South Africa tourists arrived and after leading the Midlands against the Springboks on another mission impossible, Cartwright was once again asked to captain England in what would be his last international appearance. Crystal Palace was again the venue and witnessed a much improved England performance which earned the home team a 3–3 draw in a game that created a little piece of rugby miscellany—in the space of 12 months Vincent Cartwright captained England in the first matches played against France, New Zealand and South Africa.

Following the First World War, in which he was awarded the Distinguished Service Order for outstanding bravery, Cartwright returned to the game in an administrative capacity and was elected the 30th President of the RFU in 1928. This was the culmination of his long association with the game which saw him play and administer it at the highest level added to which he also gained recognition as an arbitrator, not of the law of the land but of the Laws of rugby union—as a referee.

The second match of the Springboks tour was played at Leicester against the Midlands team captained by Cartwright. Two days earlier it had got under way at Northampton where an East Midlands team provided the opposition and the referee in charge of proceedings was Mr V.H. Cartwright. Playing in the centre for the Counties that day was a young man whose name would become synonymous with rugby union and the Great War—**Edgar Robert Mobbs**.

Five former England captains lost their lives in the First World War; Harry Alexander and Percy Kendall of Birkenhead Park; Liverpool's Ronnie Poulton-Palmer and Lancelot Slocock; and Edgar Mobbs from Northampton where he is remembered in two very contrasting ways. Firstly, there is a permanent memorial found in the Gardens of Remembrance, a large statue with the appropriate dedication inscribed and secondly rugby football remembers Mobbs in an annual fixture that dates back to 1921. Played in February or March, usually at Franklin's Gardens the home of Northampton RFC, the match sees an East Midlands team play the Barbarians in what is known throughout the rugby playing world as the Mobbs Memorial Match.

Though born in Northampton, Edgar Mobbs attended Bedford Modern School but there is no record of his having played for the first XV and there was no further education, no Oxford or Cambridge, Mobbs content just to venture into the outside world and see where the road led. He worked for a local motor company and found his way to Northampton where he spent most of his time out on the wing waiting for the ball and the opportunity to demonstrate his great pace. Mobbs proved to be a popular recruit with players and spectators alike and there must have been plenty of passes because he scored plenty of tries, something he continued to do when invited to play for England.

Mobbs won his first cap against Australia in 1909, scored a try to celebrate and added to his tally against France, Ireland and Scotland ending the season with five caps and four tries to his credit. In 1910 he only played in two matches of what was the first Five Nations Championship and after leading the team against France he departed from the international game. It had all happened in little more than a year and although now 28, Mobbs did continue to play for Northampton, captaining the club between 1907 and 1913, and also the East Midlands which he led for an even longer period, 1906–13.

When war broke out Edgar Mobbs immediately applied for (and was refused) a commission. Not to be denied he quickly raised a company of men similarly denied that eventually rose to over 250 in number and

'Mobbs' Own' was integrated under the auspices of the Northamptonshire Regiment. No new regiments were formed during the war but battalions such as that assembled by Mobbs appeared in numbers and were allowed to use the standard ranking system which saw him begin his years of service as a Sergeant and end as a Lieutenant-Colonel three years later.

Seriously injured on more than one occasion he always returned to the front line and was awarded the Distinguished Service Order in the New Year Honours List of 1917. On 31 July Lieutenant-Colonel Edgar Mobbs and his battalion were part of the offensive at Passchendaele, one of the Great War's bloodiest campaigns. Attempting to take enemy trenches, he was killed in action at Zillebeke, struck down by machine gun fire as he led his men over the top. It is not known whether or not on this particular occasion he kicked a rugby ball into the breach ahead of his men. This was something he had done previously, but once a year 30 men do kick and chase a rugby ball for 80 minutes with no purpose in mind other than to ensure that the name of Edgar Mobbs is not forgotten and since 1921, they have succeeded in their mission.

Heckmondwike appeared in chapter eight thanks to the exploits of 'Little Dicky, the World's Wonder' but Richard Lockwood aside, the West Yorkshire town would still have made these pages. It was at Heckmondwike that **Jeffrey Butterfield** announced his arrival to the world on 9 August 1929 and 30 years later he would retire from rugby hailed as the finest centre three-quarter of his generation and one of the best ever to play for England. He may have attended school in nearby Cleckheaton but the local club would never benefit from his silky skills when, armed with the necessary qualifications attained from Loughborough College, he took a job teaching PE at Wellingborough Grammar School and joined Northampton; all his playing career would be spent at Franklin's Gardens. What a glittering career it was.

Jeff Butterfield played in the Mobbs Memorial Match staged at Northampton in 1952. As a proud Yorkshireman he was committed to that county which explains his presence in the star studded Barbarians team that defeated the East Midlands 9–3, Butterfield scoring two tries. Performances such as this gained him international recognition in 1953 winning his first cap against France at Twickenham. He made an immediate impact scoring one try and creating another of England's three tries. In the mid 1950s the selectors were embarrassed by the surfeit of riches at their disposal when it came to selecting players in the centre. On his debut, Butterfield was partnered with Lewis Cannell of St Mary's Hospital and in his second match he was alongside Phil Davies of the Harlequins. James Quinn from New Brighton was another player who attracted the selectors' attention and later Fylde's Malcolm Phillips came knocking at the door. Between them these four players would win 60 caps but they were effectively competing for one place because following his introduction to the team Jeff Butterfield won 27 caps playing in every match until his retirement in 1959.

Butterfield was appointed England captain in his final season which saw England lose the opening match in Cardiff, beat Ireland and then draw with both France and Scotland. These are acceptable results but one is left wondering how the skipper felt on reflection because in four matches, his team was unsuccessful in its quest for a try. This was a glaring contradiction to how Butterfield played the game. His approach was to move the ball; straighten the line and get it to the quick men out wide. Equally, he was also capable of shoring up a defence, all of which made him the complete centre three-quarter, one seen at his finest in South Africa with the 1955 British Lions.

In 1974 Willie John McBride and his men remained undefeated and in 1997 Martin Johnson's captaincy led to a surprise Tests series triumph but ask any followers of the game in that rugby mad country which Lions team was the finest of them all and those of a certain age will unhesitatingly confirm the 1955 side. If young South African men familiar with the game today paid any heed to the words of wisdom proffered by their fathers and grandfathers the chances are that they too will talk about the 1955 Lions as if they were old friends. Bryn Meredith, Rhys Williams, Russell Robins and Jim Greenwood; a few of the superlative forwards who made their mark securing the ball which enabled the backs to cut loose, outstanding backs that included Cliff Morgan, Tony O'Reilly, Phil Davies and Jeff Butterfield among their number. The Test series ended all square but it was the manner in which they played the game that would be the 1955 Lions' lasting legacy and four years later Butterfield was included in the party which travelled to Australia and New Zealand with similar intent. He played in four Tests in South Africa scoring tries in the first and third in which he was also successful with what he later claimed was a first ever attempt at a drop goal. 'Down under' injury disrupted his tour restricting him to appearances in nine provincial matches.

A fitness enthusiast who prided himself on his physical condition, Jeff Butterfield knew better than anyone when it was time to call it a day. His retirement from the game following the 1959 Lions tour left a big gap in the England mid-field but rugby had not seen the back of him. In the 1980s he opened the Rugby Club in central London, a venue that attracted visitors from all over the world and one where the exploits of those 1955 Lions and much else besides could be remembered and discussed by likeminded folk.

The 1955 Lions party comprised 10 Welshman, nine players from England, six Scots with Ireland's contribution of five reflecting that country's poor performance in the recent Five Nations. Of the English representatives seven had played during the Championship with centre Jim Quinn chosen on previous form, the selectors accepting that although Butterfield and Davies were first choice for England, Quinn was still one of the best players in his position. Making up the number was an uncapped scrum-half considered good enough to warrant selection alongside the England incumbent Johnny Williams and Wales' Trevor Lloyd.

Dickie Jeeps belies his 76 years. He arrives in a room with a spring in his heels looking as if he could still throw out a stream of unerringly accurate passes from the base of the scrum—once a scrum-half always a scrum-half. This is pretty much as it was for Jeeps who could cajole his pack of forwards, commit the opposition back row and free the backs at his disposal with seemingly consummate ease.

I started playing rugby at Bedford Modern captaining the Under 14s and Under 15s from full-back; I wasn't particularly quick but I could tackle so full-back was fine. One afternoon I was watching the firsts play the seconds and the master in charge of rugby told me to go and get some boots, he wanted me to play. I had no idea what he had in mind but I got changed and he put me on at scrum-half. Within a couple of weeks I played for the firsts at Haberdashers and never looked back. It was always scrum-half after that.

On leaving school I joined Cambridge City which had a really good team. I started in the seconds playing my first game at Norwich. We didn't have a full side and went searching for players which meant arriving late for the match but I remember the circumstances quite well because it was the only time I ever played for a second team—ever! A week later I was in the firsts where I found myself partnering a chap called Spray, a brilliant fly-half who won a couple of Blues at Cambridge and, as I remember, only ever had one stud in two boots but that never stopped him. During the summer I played Minor Counties cricket for Cambridgeshire. There was a match which clashed with a trial at Northampton that I had been invited to take part in so I withdrew from the team which was all a bit of a waste really because I only played for about six minutes before being taken off.

Despite such an inauspicious start Jeeps eventually joined the club but living 55 miles from the ground made attending training sessions on a regular basis nigh on impossible, even more so for a self-employed fruit farmer and he had to rely on his physical labours to keep him fit. The planting of hundreds of small trees and their maintenance proved good exercise for a scrum-half, the task involving lots of bending, stretching and stamping down of the soil—great for the thighs!

Jeeps is embarrassed by how little training he did at Northampton but this would not appear to have detracted from his performances on the field. In January 1954 he took part in his first England trial and was included in the Rest for the final trial at Twickenham. The form book was upset when the underdogs beat the supposed superior England selection but this counted for nothing when the team to play Wales was announced; the Lancashire half-backs Martin Regan and Gordon Rimmer finding favour with the selectors. It was the same the following season with Doug Baker and Johnny Williams getting the nod following the series of trial matches. When it came to selecting the Lions party the bold decision to include a player yet to be tested at the highest level was about to pay off and a future English rugby legend would win his first international honours in a red jersey 6,000 miles from home.

It came as a bit of a shock being chosen for the Lions. I later learnt that one of the selectors heard I'd had a brilliant game playing for Northampton against Cardiff. We won the match 22–9 beating a side that included Rex Willis, Cliff Morgan, Bleddyn Williams and Jack Matthews. Northampton were also a strong team at the time and I know I played very well that day but had no idea where it would lead.

It was a brilliant tour. We met up at Eastbourne and gelled as a group right from the start. Jack Siggins was the manager and Danny Davies his assistant. Jack always struck me as being a bit aloof but neither he nor Danny were there to help in any team preparation so we did all the training ourselves and determined how we were going to play. It was clear there was plenty of pace out wide, O'Reilly and Pedlow etc so we decided to run the ball as best we could.

When the Lions arrived at Johannesburg for the first Test they had already lost two matches but injuries and illness had played a big part in disrupting selection. When it came to selecting the Test side most of the squad were available meaning the Lions would be at almost full strength and included for his first cap was the man yet to play for his country; scrum-half Dickie Jeeps.

They said there were 80,000 there that day but there were many more, maybe 100,000. There was scaffolding all around the ground and those without tickets were pouring in from all parts; it was a huge crowd. We played really well and even without Reg Higgins who went off early in the second half we won the match 23–22. The ligaments in Reg's knee went and it was if somebody had fired a shot, what a noise. Poor Reg didn't play again on tour. I partnered Cliff Morgan who always liked a flat ball placed where he could run onto it and on one occasion deep in their half I put one on the tips of his fingers which he collected on the run and he was around the wing forward and under the posts like lightening. I can see it now...a great player. They scored a late try and Jack van der Schyff had the conversion to win the game. I was standing under the posts looking into the non-white stand where everyone had been cheering us on. I was next to Billy Williams, the Welsh prop who kept on repeating, '...the Lord will keep this out. The Lord will keep this out...' It worked.

We were well beaten in the second Test. They took Tom Reid out straight from the kick off and he was a passenger for the whole match. The Springboks ran in seven tries including three by left wing Tom van Vollenhoven moved from the centre where he featured in the first Test. Tony O'Reilly was a fantastic player and it was all too easy to forget how young he was but it was his job to mark van Vollenhoven and he came off

second best that day. But he was a cute one. After the match he went up
to Jack Siggins and tried to explain to him how he wasn't really a right wing
much preferring to play on the left and perhaps the manager would like to
consider him there in future. The cheek of it…he was 18!

Jeeps and Morgan played throughout the series establishing a
formidable partnership. Some suggest that Jeeps was the preferred choice
of his outside-half and that may well be so. Regardless of preferences, the
team was always picked on merit and there is little evidence to suggest
anything other than that in South Africa in 1955 it was the uncapped
England scrum-half who was best suited to the conditions and the physical
presence of the Springboks. Now all Dickie Jeeps had to do was convince
the England selectors that he was their man.

After playing in the three trial matches Dickie Jeeps was finally selected
for his first cap, won against Wales on 21 January 1956. Jeeps and outside-
half M.J.K. Smith were among 10 players making their debut but a less
promising start in an England jersey is difficult to imagine. It seems that
the more ball the half-backs received so did their deficiencies become
more apparent and with no shortage of ball at their disposal it was not
surprising that the pair would be dropped following the home defeat. For
Smith it was his only cap and for Jeeps the unusual off day meant it would
be another 12 months before he had the chance to make amends.

Dickie Jeeps won his second cap at the start of the 1957 Championship
and played throughout the Grand Slam season. With Australia touring
there were five more appearances the following year. In 1959, he lost his
place to Cambridge University's Steve Smith and only played against
Ireland when Smith was ruled out with flu. This was not a year to be out of
the limelight as the Lions were touring Australia and New Zealand in the
summer but when the squad was announced his absence for most of the
Championship was ignored. Dickie Jeeps was off on another long trip.

That was a frustrating tour. We lost the first Test 18–17; six Don Clarke
penalties to four tries. We were convinced one of the kicks was wide of the
posts but the referee didn't agree. Some of us went to the cinema a few
days later and the newsreel footage of the match showed every score
except that disputed penalty which makes you wonder. I'd played the two
Tests in Australia and was selected for the first three in New Zealand but

I had a knock on the hip and missed the last which the Lions won. A big lump appeared which was diagnosed as fluid and Andy Mulligan ended up playing but my career was relatively injury free. I've no complaints really. I had a few problems with ligaments but nothing too serious and there was the time I played against France when I probably should have stood down. I cut my eye the week before which needed some stitches and the only way I could protect it was to use some clear nail varnish, a bit of bandage, then another layer of nail varnish and more bandage. It did the job but took about a year to come off!

Dickie Jeeps and the captaincy of England were always on a collision course and he began a run of 13 consecutive matches in charge against Wales in 1960 but there were moments when the relationship looked likely to self destruct.

I suppose I was a bit of a rebel really. I got in real hot water on one occasion before a final trial. I was chosen to captain the England XV and decided to write to the players in the team advising them that in my experience most of those who appeared in the senior team at the final trial could expect to be selected for international duty. Perhaps it would be a good idea if we met up before the match and went through a few routines. I had no idea where to send the letters so I asked Frank Prentice, secretary of the RFU, if he would mind forwarding them on.

Later, I got a phone call from Prentice and he gave me a right rollicking, 'This is not the sort of thing we do. It's professionalism … we don't do this, we don't do that…' He'd obviously opened one of the letters but I went ahead anyway. I'd arranged with Richmond that we could use the ground so the players turned up and we had an hour or so together and after the trial most of them were selected to play for England. I didn't see anything wrong with that; we were all spending the night at Richmond and I thought it was a good initiative.

Dicky Jeeps led England for three seasons; 13 matches that included the Springboks in 1961 and it was to South Africa that the British Lions headed in 1962 with Jeeps included for his third tour. Once again he proved irrepressible playing in the four Tests bringing his total to 13 added to which he led the Lions in the final Test in the absence of injured skipper

Arthur Smith. This final season of first class rugby saw him captain Northampton, England and ended with him leading the British Lions; there was only one place to go. 'I went back to Cambridge City. We had a record season only losing one match to Kettering 5–0. I still try to watch Cambridge a few times a season and often meet up with a couple of the lads from back then. It was a nice way to end.' Of course it didn't end at Cambridge. The RFU weren't going to let Jeeps go quietly and rebel or not he became a national selector in 1965 remaining in office for six years. In 1976 he was elected president of the RFU.

Dickie Jeeps is a remarkable man. The car park at the Bedford Lodge Hotel in Newmarket resembles no rugby ground on the planet but to watch Jeeps break into a shimmy and throw a few dummies as he makes his way back to his car suggests that to him everywhere is a rugby field. He has a very sharp recollection of his playing days and in his mind's eye seems capable of reproducing those great moments at the drop of a hat—he has his very own Field of Dreams.

Dickie Jeeps was one of 10 new caps introduced against Wales in 1956. Another making his debut in the match was fellow Northampton player, prop forward **Ron Jacobs** but unlike Jeeps who spent the rest of the season playing second fiddle to Johnny Williams, Jacobs kept his place and was a fixture in the front row for three years. Like Jeeps, Ron Jacobs also earned his living off the land. He studied agriculture at Nottingham University before returning to his native Cambridgeshire and a life on the farm which undoubtedly served as good preparation for his lengthy service in the Northampton front row.

Ron Jacobs was one of only 12 forwards used by England in the 13 matches played between 1956–58. He was also one of five players retained throughout the period and this almost unprecedented period of consistency displayed by the selectors certainly paid off producing the Grand Slam under Eric Evans' leadership in 1957 and an unbeaten team in 1958 but the following season the selectors replaced the front row en bloc. Bedford's Larry Webb and Gordon Bendon of the Wasps suddenly finding themselves the preferred choices at prop. Their selection allowed Ron Jacobs to focus his attention on Northampton leading the club in one of its finest seasons in which only six of the 39 matches played were lost.

With his club form speaking for itself Jacobs was selected for the opening match in 1960 and enjoyed another long run of nine matches before again deemed surplus to requirements. He was now 31, an age when many would argue prop forwards were likely to produce their best rugby, but the selectors showed a preference for 'youth' when opting for 28 year old Phil Judd to replace him against Wales and after winning 22 caps it appeared Ron Jacobs' international days were over.

Northampton enjoyed another successful season in 1961–62, once again only losing six games. But this was an aging team and the following season saw a significant fall from grace. This did not deter the England selectors looking to the club for reinforcements when several players who had featured in the 1963 Championship were unavailable for the tour to New Zealand and Australia in the summer. Full-back Roger Hosen won his first cap against New Zealand a few weeks short of his 30th birthday. There was a shock recall for Frank Sykes who at 35 played in two Tests, eight years on from his last appearance in the team. There was also a return to international duty for Ron Jacobs who played in the three Tests alongside Phil Judd and Bert Godwin in an all Midlands front row which earned its fair share of plaudits from the not always generous local media.

For the arrival of the Fifth All Blacks at Twickenham at the start of the new year the selectors reverted to the front row unit which was in place at the end of the 1963 Championship, Judd, Godwin and Nick Drake-Lee. Two weeks later Jacobs returned and he played throughout the Five Nations taking over the captaincy after a draw with Wales and defeat by Ireland. An away victory in Paris saw the team unchanged for the journey to Edinburgh where Scotland proved too strong, winning a match which marked the end of no less than nine England careers. Among those who played their last game that day were full-back John Willcox, centre Malcolm Phillips, hooker Bert Godwin and prop Ron Jacobs. England needed some new blood and a new captain when the next campaign got under way.

England's first visit to the antipodes highlighted many issues future tour organisers would have to address. Nothing could be done about the distances involved or the effects of jet lag but the itinerary was one area that could be reviewed. When England visited Australia for an eight match tour in 1988 with a stopover in Fiji scheduled on the return leg, there was a certain balance to the fixtures. The two Tests were a fortnight apart. This was an advantage, and there were matches against minor opposition that would allow the tourists to find their feet. Thought had also been given to the travel arrangements, so that the team followed a logical route through the country. Added to this, a medical officer and physiotherapist were included in the party. All these were positives, but despite winning six of the games played England actually fared little better than the 1963 tourists.

Leading England in Australia was **John Orwin**, a second-row forward who won his first cap against Romania in January 1985, played in the four Championship matches that followed and toured New Zealand during the summer in a squad led by Paul Dodge, playing in both Tests. Orwin was a serving officer in the RAF in 1985, a veteran of 20 Inter Services matches which began in 1976, but as with most RAF players he enjoyed much of his rugby elsewhere. Gloucester was his choice and he won those first seven caps as a representative of the RAF and the West Country club. When he next appeared on international duty John Orwin was playing for Bedford.

Wade Dooley, Maurice Colclough, Steve Bainbridge and Nigel Redman are some of the names which accounted for Orwin's absence from international rugby in 1986 and 1987. But after the disappointment of the first World Cup changes were made for the 1988 Championship and together with new caps Will Carling, Jeff Probyn and Mickey Skinner there was also a recall for the lock forward. In four matches, two England captains saw their international careers come to an end. After two defeats, Mike Harrison was dropped and the baton passed to Nigel Melville who fared much better leading England to victories over Scotland and Ireland but he suffered a bad injury against the Irish that forced him to leave the field and exit the international game. With a second match against Ireland scheduled in April as part of the Dublin Millennium celebrations the selectors needed a new captain. The contenders may have included full-back Jon Webb, front row men Probyn and Brian Moore or possibly wing forward Gary Rees but it was John Orwin who led England out at Lansdowne Road and after another victory was invited to lead the team in Australia.

Defeated in both Tests, England headed for Fiji and a chance to end the tour on a high. There was no place in the team for John Orwin who had played in seven matches in Australia and the captaincy was handed to scrum-half Richard Harding. By this time England had played eight capped matches in the first six months of the year under four captains all of whom saw their international aspirations come to an end. England played one more match in 1988, a November meeting with Australia at Twickenham when another name was added to the list of captains. This name would be around for a while—Will Carling was no short term fix.

Twenty years on John Orwin remains the last Bedford player to captain England. He didn't appear again following the 1988 tour but it was a very different story for two other players from the club who travelled 'down under' in 1963 and survived to tell the tale; not only did they survive but both went on to captain their country. One of the stars of the tour was number 8, **David Perry**. It was unfortunate that injuries necessitated him packing down in the second-row for the last three matches rather than in his preferred position at the back of the scrum. But needs must and the enforced change didn't detract from Perry enjoying a good tour in a country where they know all about loose forward play.

I played some rugby at school but when I did my National Service with the Parachute Regiment much of the time was spent in Cyprus and Jordan. I hardly played during the two years and only really got back into the game when I went up to Cambridge but I only stayed a year because I failed the first part of the economics tripos. In those days, one's parents were paying and though I could have gone back to study for a BA in estate management and agriculture my father suggested that as I had won a Blue perhaps I should have a few job interviews.

Harlequins signed me up while I was still at school so it was natural that I should play for the club when the opportunity eventually presented itself. I was a second-row forward but John Currie and David Marques were at the club so in my first match I was selected at number 8. Our hooker had his nose broken and had to leave the field which meant one of the props taking over. The logical thing would have been for Currie to move up to prop and me into the second-row. Currie was a big, physically strong man, older than I was and with a lot more experience and he would have managed perfectly well at prop forward but I was told to take over. We were playing Bath, they had a chap called Parfitt who was a beast of a man, immensely powerful and he absolutely murdered me. He turned me inside out and I could barely walk from one scrum to the next; that was my introduction to first class rugby.

I began working for a company that had an office in Leicester. The

Sales Director's only real interest in me was that I played rugby and it was decided I should move to Leicester and join the Tigers. I went on the Easter tour and played a few more matches then the company moved me to Luton. That ruled out Leicester and I joined Bedford which was much nearer. The club had a wealth of second-row forwards but were short in the back row so I settled down at number 8 alongside Budge Rogers.

In 1959 David Perry was selected for two England trials but that was as far as it went until four years later when he was called up for his first cap. The 1963 Championship had started promisingly enough with an away victory in Cardiff followed by a scoreless draw in Dublin and while the backs remained unchanged the pack was fine tuned which saw the introduction of the Bedford number 8 against France at Twickenham. Two John Willcox penalties got England home and when Scotland were beaten at Murrayfield, England could depart for a first major overseas tour as the reigning European champions. That tour and its problems have been discussed elsewhere but for some players it was an education that would stand them in good stead in the future. Competing against the likes of Colin Meads, Waka Nathan and Kel Tremain was tough but where better to learn one's craft?

We weren't a bad side and for the first time enjoyed something resembling a professional approach to the game. Back home we all had jobs and rugby couldn't come first but on tour there was nothing to interrupt our preparation; we trained well, the levels of fitness went up and as a result a lot of the team performed really well. We were leading in the first Test by 11–3 with 20 minutes to go and lost 21–11; missed tackles let them in for two tries but to lose from that position…can you believe it?

We lost the second Test 9–6 but were very unfortunate. Don Clarke made a mark and opted to kick at goal which you could do back then. The Law stated the opposition couldn't charge the kick until the ball was put on the ground. He got his brother Ian to hold the ball and told him not to place it knowing that Bert Godwin and Phil Judd who were the prescribed 10 yards away would probably charge when he began his run up which of course they did. Clarke pointed out to the referee that the ball hadn't been placed and he was awarded a penalty which he converted. It was tragic.

When the Fifth All Blacks arrived in Britain many of the names who had played against England in the summer were included and it wasn't long before Perry was renewing some old acquaintances. He captained the London Counties against the tourists at Twickenham, New Zealand comfortable winners by 27–0. England fared little better but as the tour neared its conclusion, Perry had a third opportunity to upset the odds. Injuries robbed the South-Eastern Counties of key players in the days leading up to what was the final match of the tour before a sojourn in France and the traditional finale against the Barbarians. This did not prevent Perry and his team raising their game and giving the All Blacks something of a fright at a packed King's Park in Bournemouth. Poor goal kicking by the usually consistent Don Clarke certainly helped the home cause but that aside it was two tries apiece with a Clarke penalty deciding the outcome.

This reunites us with the selectors in their search for some new blood and a new captain following the departure of Ron Jacobs. The new blood arrived in the shape of seven players who made their international debuts against Wales in Cardiff; forwards Tony Horton, Steve Richards and Nick Silk together with a new three-quarter line made up of David Rosser, Geoff Frankcom, Edward Rudd and Colin Simpson and asked to lead this new look 15 was David Perry. It was tough; away defeats in Cardiff and Dublin were followed by a victory against France so there was only a Calcutta Cup and some pride at stake when Scotland arrived at Twickenham for a match that ended in a draw but produced the defining moment of the season—Hancock's last gasp try.

Whenever any of us who played in that match get together we always joke about that try. Hancock wasn't really that quick, neither could he kick but he was physically very strong and could run and run and run. We reckon Scottish wing Ian Laughland had two attempts at tackling Andy; failing with the first attempt but having the time to get back up and make another tackle as the try was scored. I remember the dressing room after the match. Hancock had just scored an amazing try and the president of the RFU came in, went up to him and asked why he hadn't touched down behind the posts; the man had just run the length of the pitch and I think he burst into tears, he was absolutely exhausted. I suppose if he had put the ball down under the posts, even Don Rutherford might have converted it!

My final game was in Paris. Budge [Rogers] had taken over the captaincy and I got a fairly bad knee injury which forced me to leave the field. Of course there were no replacements back then and Andy Hancock had already departed with a torn hamstring so we were now down to 13 men. I went back on but every time I tried to run the knee collapsed, I was doing it no good at all. I didn't know at the time but the femur had come off at the knee joint and when we got home I immediately went into hospital for an operation which was done by a chap called Scottie Law, the RFU's nominated surgeon. He came round to see me the following day. There was no suggestion of any bedside manner or thought of letting me down gently, he just came out with it, '…you'll never play again…you're lucky not to have a stiff leg for the rest of your life…' It was absurd that you didn't have proper medical advice at the time, I should never have been allowed to continue.

I was given a video a few years ago which showed 100 great English tries. The first two were scored in matches I played in and they were the only ones in black and white—Hancocks' and Sharp's against Scotland. I showed the family and the younger members were horrified; firstly that the film was black and white and secondly that it all looked so long ago. When England won the World Cup my grandsons were at Hill House, a prep school in London. Rugby was a major topic of conversation and Josh rather proudly told his friends that his grandpa had captained England; this was met with great derision and disbelief which quite upset him. When he told his mother what had happened she produced a photograph of myself and Scotland captain Stewart Wilson being introduced to the Queen before the Calcutta match. He took it to school and showed it to the doubting Thomas who had accused him of telling lies. The boy studied the picture quizzically for some time and then asked, 'How do I know that is the Queen?' Priceless!

When the RFU celebrated its centenary in 1971, England's most capped player was **Budge Rogers**. He joined Bedford from school and remained at the club throughout his record-breaking career but it might all have been so different; a brief flirtation with football as a youngster and ideas of being a scrum-half could possibly have led him astray but for the vision of one of rugby football's unsung heroes—the sports master.

I went to Bedford School and played soccer until the age of 10. When I moved into the lower school I was introduced to rugby and played for the Under 12s as a wing forward but the school coach decided to convert me to scrum-half and I went through the Under 13s, Under 14s, Under 15s and Colts in that position. Then I had to compete for a place in the firsts or seconds. But there were two good scrum-halves ahead of me and the coach, a chap called Murray Fletcher who was probably the best scrum-half not to have played for England in the 1940s and 1950s, took me aside and explained that of the three scrum-halves available to him I was the worst and perhaps I should play at wing forward.

Before the start of the season I turned out for a scratch team made up of pupils and masters against the potential first XV and shortly after had a game for the firsts where I remained for the next two years. Bedford had a traditional Boxing Day fixture against Old Paulines which wasn't a particularly difficult match and it was usual for them to include a couple of pupils from Bedford Modern and Bedford School. I was invited along with a couple of others but that was normally it, a one off. A couple of weeks later they asked me to play against US Portsmouth which was fine because it was still the school holidays but when they invited me to play against Leicester we were into the new term and Murray wouldn't allow it.

During the next holiday I played four or five times for Bedford Seconds and when I left school it was natural that I should join the club and I stayed there for 20 seasons playing 484 matches which will probably always be the club record. I lived for the game, loved every minute of it, the playing and the training; I used to train a lot on my own because fitness was such a big part of my game.

In my first season I played for the East Midlands. A lovely man called Don White was coming to the end of his career so they played me on the open side and Don moved to the blind side but every so often we would swap roles. The great thing was that after every game he would sit me in a corner and talk to me about my performance—what I'd done wrong, what I'd done right. After leaving school he was the only man ever to do that—he was fantastic.

I had my first England trial in 1959 playing for the Colours against the Whites at Banbury. Bev Risman had just come back from the Lions tour and he led me a right dance, more often than not leaving me face down in the mud. I remember telling my parents in the car going home that it would be the first and last trial I'd be asked to take part in but the following year I got another chance. I played for the Probables at Coventry but didn't have a great game and was in the Rest for the final trial at Twickenham when I came up against Richard Sharp.

There is always this confrontational element between wing forwards and outside-halves and on that particular day I got the better of Sharp; then Bev came on for the second-half and I played well against him. It was a good trial but more importantly, earlier in the season I'd had a really good game for the Midland Counties against the Springboks at Leicester. We drew that match and apart from the Barbarians were the only team they didn't beat. I wasn't selected in the England team that lost to South Africa nor against Wales but after that game was lost I was picked to play in Dublin.

I received an itinerary advising to meet at King's Cross Station; I wondered what on earth we were doing meeting at King's Cross for a trip to Dublin. We got the train to Holyhead then the boat to Dublin over that wretched sea but I was new to all this and kept quiet. Later I asked one of the players why on earth we had travelled by train and boat rather than fly and he told me that Colonel Prentice, a commanding figure in his brown homburg and trench coat and secretary of the RFU at the time, didn't like flying.

Budge Rogers made a try scoring debut at Lansdowne Road. It wasn't enough to avoid a third consecutive defeat in five weeks but it probably helped him remain in favour and only injury brought a run of six appearances to an end when he had to stand down for the visit to Murrayfield at the end of the following season. Injury aside he had done enough to earn his place in the 30 strong British Lions party that spent the summer in South Africa where he further enhanced his growing reputation playing in 12 matches including the first and fourth Tests. England enjoyed a successful Five Nations in 1963 before touring New Zealand and Australia, Rogers playing in the three tests which brought his total number of caps to 13 and the following season Bedford elected him club captain, his first experience of the extra responsibility.

I enjoyed it a lot. The captain ran training, helped pick the team and had a big say in how the game was played. I had a philosophy that in a 35 game season you were probably going to get beaten so I suggested that we play the rugby we wanted to play and on that basis we might actually enjoy games we lost; and we did. Sometimes we'd win a game and be less satisfied; it was all about quality and moving the ball, getting everybody to participate, not just about kicking for touch.

David Perry was the incumbent England captain and he took over the captaincy at Bedford in the 1965 season whereupon quite ironically I was immediately asked to succeed him as England captain. That was very different. It was amazing how little input there was from the selectors once the team had been picked, none really. I was sitting alongside Dickie Jeeps on the coach on our way to Murrayfield. Dickie had joined the selectors and we started discussing how we should play the game before being interrupted by Tom Berry, the chairman of selectors, 'Now, now Dick. Budge stands and falls by his own judgement.' I got no support from anybody. This was only to be expected because I had seen previous captains have the same experience but it was still an exciting thing to do.

I once arranged for the players to come down to Richmond on the Thursday before a match at Twickenham so that we could have an extra run around. I got a phone call from RFU secretary Robin Prescott. 'Budge, I want to be able to assure the president that this will not take place.' To be fair I think that the International Board rules stipulated teams were not to meet up more than 48 hours before the match so that was knocked on the head straight away.

What made it most difficult were the number of changes from one game to the next; the team was forever changing. I must have played with six blind sides and four number 8s in my first few seasons with England. I know of instances when players were carrying an injury, nothing too serious but enough to stop them playing flat out, and they wouldn't drop out of the team because they knew that if they did they may never get back in. You also always knew that if the team lost there would be changes.

Win or lose, on his return to England duty in 1963 Rogers played in 20 consecutive matches which included his first four as captain. The run came to an end following defeat by Australia in January 1967 and although three more caps were won during the year bringing his total to 30 he didn't play for England in 1968 and Wavell Wakefield's record which had stood for almost 40 years looked safe. His recall against Ireland at the start of the 1969 Championship brought him level with Wakefield and when Dick Greenwood had to withdraw from the team to play France Rogers replaced him as captain and led England out at Twickenham to become England's most capped player. He continued as captain winning two more caps increasing the record to 34 where it stayed before being improved on by John Pullin five years later. With his playing days behind him, Budge Rogers became an England selector and later chaired the committee. There were some lessons he learnt as a player which he was keen to bring to the table but not all of them went down well.

I always remembered those players who were reluctant to declare themselves unfit because they were afraid that they wouldn't get back in the team. When I was made chairman of selectors I introduced a policy whereby if any player had to withdraw from the side for whatever reason, no matter how well his replacement played the man originally selected would get his chance in the next match. It all came home to roost in 1980 when before my first Championship match as chairman Maurice Colclough dropped out of the team to play Ireland and was replaced by Nigel Horton. Nigel had a good game and at the dinner in the evening I congratulated him but also told him that he wouldn't be playing in the next match; he wasn't best pleased. I hadn't seen Nigel for a long time but we met at a function a few years ago and the first thing he did was remind me of that decision, 'Remember that bloody game when you dropped me.' But that sort of policy allowed players to be more honest about their condition, whether they were fit enough to play or not. I was never one to chop and change just because a match was lost because if you picked what you thought was the best team one week then with very few exceptions it was still likely to be the best team the next week.

Bill Beaumont was captain at the time—one of England's finest—along with Carling and Johnson. I think Carling was underestimated as a player but Beaumont and Johnson were wonderful players and that is what made them good leaders, men you would go into the trenches with. All three had good teams, good men around them but they all added something extra. We were preparing for the Irish match at Twickenham in 1982 when Bill rang me to say he was sorry but he couldn't play anymore, his doctor had advised against it. The team were meeting for a practice at Stourbridge on the Monday evening and I told Steve Smith he was going to take over. Typical Steve, he said, 'We won't miss him as captain but we won't half miss him as a player.' That was slightly unfair but on the other hand there was an element of truth in it because Bill led by example. As did Johnson, as did Carling.

When asked, Budge Rogers was in two minds about using a wing forward as captain:

It's not bad but I think scrum-half is a better position to lead from. Dickie Jeeps was a natural captain; a hugely competitive, great player. I always remember him whenever I went off a line, drifted away from things. There would be this voice coming up behind shouting, 'Tackle! Tackle! Tackle!'. Dick had stopped coming to the matches at Twickenham but he started again a couple of years ago. I was sitting along the row from him and midway through the game I heard this 'Tackle! Tackle! Tackle!' coming from his direction—I roared.

Unlike many of his contemporaries Budge Rogers still follows England home and away. He and his mates do World Cups and Lions tours; someone organises the golf; somebody else sorts out food and the more important wine; and there will be someone on hand to look after the music. As for Budge, he organises the trip and drives the motor; sounds as if his pals are in good hands.

Budge Rogers and David Perry played in the England back row together 10 times. Don Manley, Vic Marriott, Peter Ford, Nick Silk and Dick Greenwood were among the various players to join them. Against Wales in 1966 it was Northampton's **Bob Taylor** who made up the trio. Like Rogers before him, Bob Taylor also learned much about his craft from Don White but this was a week in, week out education at Northampton rather than the infrequent hours Budge enjoyed in his mentors' company when representing the East Midlands.

Bob Taylor hails from Cumbria but the family moved to Northampton in the 1950s. This took him to the local grammar school before heading to Winchester where he studied physical education. His first job saw him return to the area when he followed in Jeff Butterfield's footsteps as PE master at Wellingborough Grammar School. And it was only natural that he should also follow Butterfield's well trodden path to Franklin's Gardens.

Budge Rogers highlighted the many vagaries shown by the selectors when it came to choosing the back row and from as early as 1963 when he was in contention for a place on the England tour, Bob Taylor was another name which had to be added to the conundrum. Such was the uncertainty that existed in the selection process during the 1960s when the team to play Wales in 1966 was announced there were only six survivors from the same fixture a year earlier. Considering that the season was not going particularly well for Northampton it was a surprise to see three of the club's players chosen to win first caps; Keith Savage on the wing, prop forward David Powell and blind side flanker Bob Taylor. Wales won at Twickenham and the selectors set about the task of reshaping the team for the visit of Ireland and while Savage and Powell were spared, Taylor was dropped. Joining him on the sidelines was another player who had won his first cap against the Welsh, Bristol's John Pullin. Time would prove that Taylor was in distinguished company when the selectors so unceremoniously discarded him. Pullin had to wait two years before his recall but Bob Taylor returned to the team the next season winning another four caps before disappearing without trace in 1968 until he was included in the British Lions party to tour South Africa.

Several places on the tour were still up for grabs two weeks before the squad was due to be announced and an impressive performance for the East Midlands against the Barbarians in the Mobbs Memorial Match was good enough to convince the selectors he should be included. Bob Taylor didn't disappoint playing in 14 matches including the four Tests but come the following season the England selectors again chose to ignore his claims leaving him out of the team to play Ireland and but for Dick Greenwood's unfortunate eye injury it is not certain he would ever have regained his place.

He may have been back in the team but this time there was a difference; Bob Taylor was no longer a blind side specialist, England opting to play the wing forwards as left and right. This saw Taylor and Budge Rogers literally at sixes and sevens when Wales ran riot at the Arms Park in the final match of the Championship. Greenwood didn't play for England again after his unlucky injury and with the cap record under his belt Budge Rogers also departed the international arena. This left Bob Taylor as the senior back row forward available and his services were called upon in all five matches in the 1969–70 season which began with England's first victory over South Africa and ended in defeat at Stades Colombes, the match in which Bob Taylor made his one appearance as England captain.

The following season celebrated the centenary of the RFU and the first of a series of matches commemorating the occasion saw England and Wales play Scotland and Ireland at Twickenham. England's most recent captain led the Anglo-Welsh combination in the match which ended in a draw but the captaincy was passed on for the start of the Championship and Northampton, after seeing four of the club's players lead England since 1959 would have to wait almost 30 years for the next to come along.

According to the *Concise Oxford Dictionary*, a dummy is a pretended pass one of several definitions but this is the only one that is relevant to rugby. On 21 June 1997 at Newlands, Cape Town a player 'threw' a pretended pass of such preposterous proportions that it took the assembled throng with it. A cross between a Mexican Wave and a giant Wimbledon occurred—necks were put out! More importantly it took Springbok scrum-half Joost van der Westhuizen and back row forwards Ruben Kruger and Gary Teichmann by surprise and the way to the try line opened up for the instigator of such an outrageous pretended pass. This was the first Test of the Lions tour and the resultant try put the visitors 20–16 ahead with little more than 10 minutes remaining on the clock. But for injury **Matt Dawson** would probably not have been on the field, first choice scrum-half Robert Howley's tour had ended seven days earlier, but his replacement more than came up to the mark.

Matt Dawson joined Northampton in 1991 and remained at the club for the next 13 seasons. The mid 1990s saw Dewi Morris and Kyran Bracken jousting for the scrum-half berth in the England team leaving Steve Bates, Andy Gomarsall, Austin Healey and Dawson to contest a place in England A. Of that quartet, Dawson had the first chance to play for the senior side when he was selected against Western Samoa in December 1995. Northampton outside-half Paul Grayson also made his debut that day and the pair were retained for the 1996 Championship helping England win a Triple Crown following a narrow defeat in Paris which put an immediate end to thoughts of anything more.

It had been a good season for Dawson; he'd won five caps and helped

Northampton gain promotion to National Division One but the club found adjusting to the higher level difficult meaning Dawson slipped down the international pecking order and had to watch on as Gomarsall and Healey were given their chances. While they were impressing the England selectors, Dawson made his mark on club coach Ian McGeechan, chosen to head the Lions coaching team on the forthcoming tour. The Scot knew the exact profile of the players he wanted to take to South Africa and although initially it looked as if Dawson was included in the party as third choice behind Howley and Healey at least he was on the plane when it left Heathrow.

Howley's unfortunate injury opened the door and Dawson was chosen for the first Test. A solid performance ensured he was included a week later when the Lions wrapped up the three match series in Durban and Dawson won his third Lions cap in the final Test at Ellis Park, Johannesburg; now it was time for a well earned rest. Or so one would have thought but England had a fixture to fulfil in Sydney. Dawson was one of a dozen Lions who headed for Australia from South Africa. Seven days after the third Test he played in a beaten England team in what for most of the players was quite simply a match too far—stop the world I want to get off!

British Lion or not, Dawson's place in the England team was far from assured with Kyran Bracken having become his greatest rival after Healey was switched to the wing. The pair shared the scrum-half duties during the 1997–98 season but when captain Lawrence Dallaglio needed repair work done on his shoulder it meant missing the summer tour to Australia, New Zealand and South Africa. Asked to lead a squad that included several uncapped players was Matt Dawson but it was a thankless task; all seven matches were lost and the record books needed rewriting after some horrendous reversals—stop the world I want to get off!

The competition between Dawson and Bracken raged on but for the warm up matches in the build up to the 1999 World Cup, Dawson edged in front and he went into the tournament as first choice with Austin Healey included as a utility back. England's tournament ended at the quarter-final stage but the Martin Johnson era was under way, things would improve. Injury forced the new captain out of the first Six Nations Championship and the mantle of leadership once more found its way to Dawson; Ireland, France, Wales and Italy were well beaten but for the second year in succession England missed out at the final hurdle, Scotland only too pleased to spoil the party.

With Johnson back at the helm, the 2001 Championship was going along swimmingly. England won four matches but an outbreak of foot-and-mouth meant the team would have to postpone the away game in Dublin until later in the year by which time the Matt Dawson version of foot-and-mouth would have taken rugby onto the front pages.

The Lions were in Australia and things weren't going well; that was Dawson's opinion and he shared his thoughts with the nation through an article written for a daily newspaper back home. The coaching staff, training schedules and much else besides were openly criticised and there was plenty of humble pie to be eaten before equilibrium was restored. To his eternal credit Dawson continued talking (but only on the pitch) and who would have envied him as he lined up what would be a match winning conversion of a last minute Austin Healey try against the ACT Brumbies. The relief shown on his face when the kick struck home expressed much more than a game won—Dawson had already paid his dues but that kick was for the management and players who had stood by him in his hour of need.

With Johnson again sidelined Matt Dawson led England for the ninth and final time when the team headed for Dublin in October to play the outstanding fixture from the previous season. Wales had upset the form book in the last match in 1999; Scotland had done the same in 2000; now it was Ireland's turn. The Celtic nations were having a ball at the expense of their arch rival. For the second time as England skipper Dawson had the Grand Slam and Triple Crown snatched from his grasp but everything comes to he who waits. When England finally did the business in 2003 Matt Dawson featured in three of the matches; the icing on the cake arriving later in the year when he was a member of the elite group that lifted the World Cup. Joining him in the England squad were fellow Northampton players Ben Cohen, Paul Grayson and Steve Thompson but for the 2004–05 season it would be squad members Stuart Abbott, Lawrence Dallaglio, Josh Lewsey, Simon Shaw and Joe Worsley who he would play alongside in the Premiership.

After 13 years at Northampton, Matt Dawson joined Wasps where he spent two seasons before retiring from the game in 2006. There was a third Lions tour in 2005 and he won 14 more caps from his new club taking the total to 77. This sees him in fifth position in the list of England's most capped players and won during a period when competition for the scrum-half jersey was fierce. His seven Lions caps must also be included in the final reckoning. But where do ex-players go in search of the next pay cheque once their playing days have come to an end?

In 2004 Dawson became one of the regular team captains on the BBC's long running sports quiz *A Question of Sport*. For Kyran Bracken now read Ally McCoist, the Scottish footballer replacing the scrum-half as Dawson's immediate rival, a role later taken on by cricketer Phil Tuffnell. Then in 2006 Matt Dawson displayed another of his many talents when showing television viewers his culinary skills; the pancetta, pasta, and pesto; lamb, langoustine and lemon grass; chicken, coulis and coriander. None of it stood a chance as Dawson boiled, roasted and seared his way to the *Celebrity Masterchef* title. Then it was to the dance floor where only cricket's Mark Ramprakash bettered his flair for the rumba, waltz and tango in the hugely popular *Strictly Come Dancing*.

Matt Dawson is not going to go away. Be it on television or radio, this one time England rugby captain seems to have found his vocation in life. With Kyran Bracken now established on the ice rink thanks to another popular television programme there may yet be a renewal of their rivalry—the mind boggles.

Matt Dawson headed south from Northampton; the environs of north London and the Wasps his destination. Bracken was already there playing for Saracens. It is these two clubs that will bring our journey to an end but there is one outstanding destination before that final chapter can begin. More accurately there are nine players who led England while associated with the club that in the professional era has been the most consistent in the land. This takes us to Welford Road—home of the Leicester Tigers.

10

THE TIGERS' LAIR

Leicester

Since rugby union joined the ranks of professional sport Leicester has become the biggest club in England. If any statement is guaranteed to raise the hackles of supporters elsewhere then this is it—Leicester are the biggest club in England. One of the Guinness Premiership clubs has to be bigger than the rest so why not the Welford Road outfit. More people turn out to watch the club than are seen elsewhere which is a good indication of the Tiger's standing in the local community and sufficient evidence to support the claim. If further proof is required it is not difficult to find.

Since 1995 Leicester has won six Premiership titles and secured the runners-up spot four times; won the senior cup competition twice and been beaten finalists twice; and lifted the Heineken Cup, Europe's foremost club trophy twice and come unstuck at the final hurdle on two further occasions. No English club can match these statistics in the professional era and it is not surprising that people descend on Welford Road in droves.

So why is Leicester entitled to join Blackheath, Harlequins and Richmond in having a chapter to itself? Nine captains is the simple answer. Nine men have led England while playing their club rugby at Leicester; fewer than Blackheath and Richmond and with one player included here who later led England from the Harlequins less than that London based club but still sufficient to allow it stand alone status.

Some disgruntled individuals associated with the Harlequins probably threw this book away in disgust when one of the all time greats of English rugby didn't appear in the chapter devoted to the club. It was with good reason that **William Wavell Wakefield** was absent as he was most certainly playing his club rugby at Leicester when he first captained England.

'I had by now come down from Cambridge and resigned my commission in the Air Force, but as this season of 1923–24 found me working in the North and Midlands I could not spare time to travel down to play with the Harlequins, and I therefore joined Leicester, who made me captain for the year... As far as International football went, that season was a great one for England...It was in that year that I took over the captaincy on Davies' retirement.' This statement taken from *Rugger* by W.W. Wakefield and H.P. Marshall, confirms the chronological order in which his tenure as England captain runs and Leicester's claim must take precedence over his nine appearances as captain when he returned to the Harlequins.

Sedbergh School can lay claim to several leading rugby players among its alumni; John Spencer and Will Carling spent their formative years there, as did William Wavell Wakefield some time earlier. A school steeped in rugby tradition, Sedbergh was the ideal destination for the young Wakefield who by the time he was 16 had played himself into the first XV and the earliest experience of captaincy came in his final school year.

Born in 1898, Wavell Wakefield came of age during the war years and enlisted with the Royal Naval Air Service where his ability with a rugby ball at his feet was noticed. He was a powerfully built, athletic man, especially quick for a forward at a time when, generally speaking, forwards were a one dimensional bunch of individuals. Wavell Wakefield was the first to recognise that by bringing a semblance of speciality to forward play a pack could become a different force altogether. No longer made up of eight individuals who each approached the game in the same way but a collective in which every player had a different function to perform.

The Royal Naval Air Service and the Royal Flying Corps merged to become the Royal Air Force during the latter stages of the First World War. Following the armistice Wavell Wakefield was responsible for organising a rugby team to represent the new service, one that could compete with the Army and Royal Navy in the newly introduced Inter Services tournament. He set about his task with some vigour and by the time he resigned his commission in 1923 the Royal Air Force Rugby Union was established and Wavell Wakefield had captained the team in the first seven Inter Services matches in which the RAF took part.

The time spent at Cambridge University was at the instigation of the RAF and he attended a course specifically related to the Service. This meant his rugby was divided between the RAF and Cambridge with the Harlequins, the club he joined in 1919, lucky if there was a free Saturday when he could don the multi-coloured jersey. And of course there was England; Wavell Wakefield was one of the 11 new caps introduced in the first post war international. Whereas many of the inductees would soon fall by the wayside here was an especially talented player who would go on to win 29 consecutive caps. After a brief break he added two more in 1927 making him the most capped England player, a record he would hold until Budge Rogers improved on it in 1969.

We have already seen how English rugby quickly got into its stride following the First World War with Grand Slam success in 1921 and 1923. When a third was delivered in 1924, it was the Leicester based Wavell Wakefield who led the team to four convincing victories from the second-row. Back to back Grand Slams are rare enough but what made England's achievement in 1924 all the more remarkable was that the team had undergone a major overhaul behind the scrum since the previous year. A new full-back, new names on the wing and untried partnerships in the centre and at half-back were all introduced. That the team scored 17 tries and only called upon the services of the same number of players speaks volumes as to how well Wavell Wakefield's pack performed. The All Blacks ended the winning run at Twickenham in January 1925 and it was following this defeat that Wavell Wakefield dropped back to number 8 from which position he won his last 10 caps.

Records tell us that Wavell Wakefield's playing career ended in 1930 and that his last game for the Harlequins was quite appropriately against one of his former clubs, Cambridge University. Following his retirement he was always likely to continue his association with the game in an administrative capacity and represented the RAF and Middlesex on the general committee of the RFU. His association with Middlesex continued until 1951 by which time he had come through the ranks of vice-president and senior vice-president and was elected as the 42nd president of the RFU for the 1951–52 season.

They say never mix sport and politics or politics and sport—whichever. Either way, Wavell Wakefield did exactly that when he was elected to Parliament in 1935 as the Conservative member for Swindon, remaining in office until 1945. The Second World War obviously impacted on this new career and Wavell Wakefield returned to the RAF where he served as a pilot before taking up a position at the Air Ministry from where his political standing and RAF experience were fully utilised.

Following the war Wavell Wakefield moved constituencies becoming Conservative candidate for Marylebone, London. He was elected to office in the General Election of 1945 which saw a landslide victory for Clement Atlee's Labour Party consigning Wavell Wakefield to the opposition benches. When Winston Churchill returned to Number 10 in 1951 Wakefield held his seat and remained an MP until 1963; 12 years of Tory government under Churchill, Anthony Eden and Harold Macmillan. Wavell Wakefield was created a Knight Bachelor in 1944 and on his retirement from politics became the first Baron Wakefield of Kendal.

As is only to be expected of such an upstanding and highly respected individual, once Lord Wakefield moved away from the sharp end of politics he was soon in great demand elsewhere. For many associations and companies, having a high profile personality as a figure-head or director is extremely desirable. He held several such appointments in his later years but probably the one position which he regarded above all others was that of president at the Harlequins which he retained for 30 years, standing down three years before his death on 12 August 1983.

A Harlequin then. Without any doubt, Wavell Wakefield was primarily a Harlequin and within that club's colourful history, he ranks at the very top. Others may have won more caps or led England on more occasions but even in this age of mass media attention and some extraordinarily talented players, few can be elevated to the heights reached by this grand English gentleman. His association with Leicester, however brief that may have been, is one the club must cherish and never allow to be forgotten.

The second New Zealand All Blacks brought an end to England's recent run of success when they defeated Wavell Wakefield's team at Twickenham in 1925 and went on to finish the tour unbeaten. The next representatives from the country found life much more difficult and by the time they arrived at Twickenham to play England, had already lost to Swansea and Wales and Ulster had held them to a creditable draw in the rain and mud at Ravenhill, Belfast. Included in the Ulster pack that day was an Army lieutenant currently serving in the province who had already come up against the tourists when they struggled to overcome the Combined Services 6–5 in similar conditions at Aldershot and at Twickenham, Leicester prop forward **Douglas 'Joe' Kendrew** enjoyed the 'third time lucky' experience.

Kendrew knew a bit about New Zealand rugby after touring with the 1930 British Lions but he hadn't featured in any of the Tests which is not surprising as he celebrated his 20th birthday on tour, a particularly young age to be included in such a gathering. All of which meant that the three matches in 1935–36 were his first encounters with the All Blacks. Not many players on the circuit could later claim to have played for three different teams against New Zealand registering a victory, a draw and a defeat by the smallest of margins.

Doug Kendrew had won two England caps before he went on the tour in 1930 and on his return, the next six seasons would see eight more added to the total. Ten caps over seven seasons may seem a small return for a player who obviously showed much promise but with Ray Longland and Henry Rew available, England were not lacking in the front row department. Both these men were older than Kendrew and fine exponents of a position where players were once expected to mature with age but in 1935 another bout of 'out with the old, in with the new' saw nine new caps chosen in the team to play Wales with Kendrew selected as captain.

This must have come as a surprise. He was not a recognised captain at club or county level, neither had he led the Army in the Inter Services tournament and with Longland apparently assured of his place in the team he would have seemed to be the obvious choice but the selectors elected to go with Kendrew. Many captains would have settled for a draw with Wales and a comfortable win against Ireland but what appears to have been a temporary appointment ended when Bernard Gadney, the player he had taken over from, returned to lead England in Edinburgh.

Douglas Kendrew was a professional soldier. In the Second World War he served with the Royal Leicestershire Regiment in North Africa and Italy in which campaigns he was awarded the DSO with 1st and 2nd bars added and there would be a 3rd some years later when he saw action in Korea. Kendrew attained the rank of Brigadier and there were many decorations which recognised an outstanding military career; Companion of the Order of the Bath, Commander of the Order of the British Empire, Knight Commander of the Order of St Michael and St George, Knight of the Order of St John. These are fitting tributes to an extraordinary man, who accepted one final appointment when he took over as Governor of Western Australia in 1964.

When Doug Kendrew was asked to return the England captaincy to his predecessor, it didn't travel far. **Bernard Gadney** was the Leicester and England scrum-half who led his country to the Triple Crown in 1934. On his return to the side he enjoyed another five games as captain all of which meant that for three consecutive seasons, 1934–36, England were led by a player based at Welford Road.

Since the heady days of the 1920s, England had struggled at half-back. Five outside-halves and seven scrum-halves were selected between 1929 and 1932 with many combinations tried, none of which bedded in. After losing to South Africa and Wales in January 1932, the selectors convened to choose a team to travel to Ireland with the problem at half-back uppermost in their thoughts. They were brave in choosing the uncapped Walter Elliot at outside-half and also gave a first cap to Bernard Gadney but such adventure often pays off and England came away with an 11–8 victory and delivered a second when beating Scotland a few weeks later, the new half-backs continuing in harness.

Gadney was tall and well built for a scrum-half which would have helped him in the contact areas around the scrums and lineouts. He was also deceptively quick and satisfied the most important criteria by which all scrum-halves are measured—he had a good pass. When the selectors invited him to captain England against Wales at the start of the 1934 Championship they included the customary glut of new caps. And they seemed to have decided that it was no longer a prerequisite of team selection to include a recognised goal kicker, a policy first introduced in the previous season and one which they remained faithful to throughout the next campaign. This meant that if England were to win matches they had to score tries putting additional pressure on the new captain who was going to have to be on top of his game and make all the right decisions, which he obviously did, England winning a 10th Triple Crown.

Gadney took over from Kendrew for the final match in 1935 and led England in 1936. This season included the famous victory over New Zealand. This is how Gadney recalled the start and end of that encounter, 'We kicked off, a long one. Touch. We took a scrum—not such a solid one as we had planned, but Nicholson got the ball. I ran with it, and was tackled and held on to the ball. The "boots" which I expected never came…Not least in our enjoyment was the pleasure which our victory seemed to have brought to various distinguished gentlemen in bowler hats. They must have travelled very quickly from their seats to our changing-room.' As scrum-half, Gadney appears to have been prepared for a tough time which didn't materialise and as captain, the hint of sarcasm at the expense of the selectors is not wasted.

Wavell Wakefield, Bernard Gadney and Doug Kendrew helped to keep Leicester on the rugby map between the wars but after Gadney it was the best part of 50 years before another player from the club led England.

Following the Second World War other than William Moore, Bob Stirling, Phil Horrocks-Taylor, Nick Drake-Lee and Alan Old few Leicester players rattled the selectors' cage in their quest for international recognition. Then in 1971, a recent arrival at the club set about putting the record straight.

Peter Wheeler was the only Leicester player included in the England squad of 23 that set off for the Far East in the summer of 1971. He played in four of the seven matches and in doing so laid down his marker for the hooker's berth in the following season but there was a stumbling block, one which he would not be able to overcome until 1975—it was called John Pullin. By 1971 Pullin was something of a veteran with 21 caps to his name who was spending the summer with the British Lions in Australia and New Zealand, one of several high points in an international career that had a long way to run—Wheeler was going to have to wait.

It has been said before and it is worth repeating here; if Richmal Crompton had taken her young hero through to maturity and William Brown had taken up the union game then he would have been a hooker. One only has to look at the wonderful artwork of Thomas Henry to see the look of innocence, the 'Who me?' expression, and then visit any rugby ground in the land and watch the hooker. Peter Wheeler did his work in the tight well but it was around the field that he was most prominent; in the loose where he was constructive in attack and destructive in defence and whenever he fell foul of the referee as all good forwards do he was a master of the 'Who me?' expression.

Leicester favoured him with the captaincy in 1973 and he was invited to continue for a second term in which the wait finally ended with his selection in the England team to play France. Injury forced him to leave the field against Wales and effectively ended his first taste of international rugby. His inclusion against Australia the following January finally elevated him to first choice and Wheeler played in 28 of the next 31 matches missing out once through injury and the two Tests in Argentina in 1981 when he was unable to tour.

It was a busy six seasons. In addition to England duty Wheeler toured New Zealand with the British Lions in 1977 playing in three Tests and went to South Africa in 1980 when he featured in all four. After a break of three seasons, he was reunited with the captaincy at Leicester leading the club to victory in the John Player Special Cup in three consecutive years, 1979–81 a run of success that confirmed Leicester as one of the leading clubs in the land. Dusty Hare, Paul Dodge, Clive Woodward, Les Cusworth and Robin Cowling would all join Wheeler in the England team and after a long period of underachievement the show was back on the road. But even the most optimistic of supporters could not have foreseen where it would eventually take the club.

When Peter Wheeler led the Midland Division to a resounding victory over New Zealand at Welford Road in November 1983 included in the team were seven Leicester players, increased to eight when Dean Richards joined the fray as a replacement. The England team selected to meet the tourists 11 days later included six of the eight who had represented the Midlands and Wheeler was chosen to captain his country for the first time. It was a dream start; England gained a third victory over New Zealand giving the new captain good reason to look forward to the Five Nations but when Scotland won convincingly at Murrayfield the wheels started to come off. Ireland were beaten at Twickenham thanks largely to the boot of Dusty Hare but even that trusty weapon was unable to stop France and Wales taking the spoils and after his five matches as captain and a total of 41 caps Peter Wheeler departed the international arena.

Twenty five years on he is still at Welford Road or more accurately at offices nearby. He is no longer found in the depths of the scrum but behind a desk in his role as Chief Executive of the club he has been associated with for the best part of 40 years. Since the arrival of professional rugby, Peter Wheeler has fought the corner of the Premiership clubs in their regular spats with the governing body and must take some gratification knowing that the dust appears to have settled in what has been at times a fiercely contested battle. Now he can focus on ground developments at Welford Road that will see the capacity increased to 30,000 reconfirming the club's position in the English game and making the home of the Tigers an even more daunting prospect for visiting teams.

Peter Wheeler can rightly be viewed as the highest profile player produced by Leicester during the 1970s but many other well known names were also playing for the club at the time. Several were introduced at a young age through a thriving Academy system that still serves Leicester well today. Age was never a barrier aspiring players had to concede to, Leicester have always been prepared to give youth its head, satisfied that if a player was good enough, he was old enough. One player who came through this system and went on to achieve great success was centre **Paul Dodge**. His is a story that begins in a very familiar way and one has to ask if all the soccer mad youngsters who were reluctantly converted to rugby by enthusiastic school masters had been allowed to continue in their preferred sport would English football be in the mess it is?

I went to Roundhill High School on the outskirts of the city. Up until then I had preferred soccer but Dave Lyons, the PE teacher, was a keen rugby man and it was through him that I came into the game. Dave helped set up the Leicester youth team which I joined when I was 15 and two years later, I played my first game for the club, away to Bedford. It all happened a bit quick; I didn't think anyone was taking any notice of me.

It certainly did happen quickly. Still only 17, Paul Dodge played for a Midland Counties (East) team that beat the 1975 Wallabies at Leicester and a year later he was in the North & Midlands combined team that played Argentina also at Leicester, another scalp and still only 18 years old. Such performances didn't go unnoticed beyond the environs of Welford Road. Dodge had his first taste of international rugby in 1977 playing for the England Under 23s in Canada and later in the year against France. He was selected for an England XV that played the USA at Twickenham under the captaincy of Bill Beaumont and if such matches were uncapped they were certainly taken seriously as four months later and 18 days short of his 20th birthday Paul Dodge made his England debut against Wales. Senior honours did not preclude him from continuing to play for the Under 23s and in April that year he captained an England team for the first time in Hilversum, Holland paired in the centre with a player from the Harlequins.

I had a good partnership with Clive Woodward at Leicester and with England. We played in the centre together for England 14 times and obviously there were a lot of games for Leicester. When I joined the 1980 British Lions tour in South Africa as a replacement Clive was already there having been chosen in the original party but we were never paired together. I played in a couple of matches when he was selected on the wing but Ray Gravell was my centre partner. Grav was a great man, a great character. He was always your best friend; a sad loss.

Dodge played under six England captains; Bill Beaumont, Roger Uttley, John Scott, Peter Wheeler, Steve Smith and Nigel Melville—four forwards and two scrum-halves. When he was chosen to lead the team in 1985, it was the first time for 13 years that the captaincy had gone beyond the scrum-half and he welcomed it with a certain amount of foreboding.

I'd captained Leicester for two seasons but felt that if the England job came along it was an indication that you would soon be out of the team; certainly that seemed to be the case in my era. My first match as captain was against Romania at Twickenham in 1985. Some young players were introduced and we won but didn't play very well and then it was straight into the Championship. It was a very cold winter and some matches were postponed which meant we played France and Scotland at home before travelling to Dublin and Cardiff. We drew with France and beat Scotland but lost both the away matches.

That summer England toured New Zealand. I really enjoyed it but it was tough. New Zealand is a great country to tour but as in South Africa, rugby is front page news, sometimes taking over the first few pages if there are Tests being played. The first Test against the All Blacks was quite close—the second Test wasn't. We could have won the first Test, there were a few penalties we should have put over but typical New Zealand, if you don't catch them when they are cold the chance is gone and a week later they put us away easily. That was my last game for England; last as captain and last as a player.

My record may suggest otherwise but I think that centre is a good position to lead from. You get a good balance of how the game is going. You're not tied up in the forwards and I think it is probably very difficult to do it from either full-back or on the wing. You get a good feel for the game in the centre and can keep your head up, see what is going on. Nowadays there tends to be a couple of leaders on the field, maybe a forward and a back which is something they use with good effect at Leicester.

But the game has moved on. I'm often asked if I would prefer to have played now and I have to say I would love to have been a professional rugby player but when I weigh it up against all the good times I enjoyed and all the friends I made along the way I'd take the career I had. I loved playing and you have to accept that rugby is a business now and it has become very cutthroat. There are some big squads which mean that certain players only get a couple of games a season; I couldn't stand that.

If this book has been flung around a bit and is looking worse for wear, Paul Dodge is the man to restore it to its former glory. Since leaving school, he has worked in the family book binding business now nearing its 50th anniversary. In his spare time, he works with the Under 16s at the Leicester Academy where he is ever searching for the next player who may be good enough to play for the Tigers or even captain England. Dodge makes a case for centre as a good position from which to lead a team. As the player who has led England more than any other is also a centre then perhaps he is right. But there are four Leicester players who became England captains still to discuss. These players all have one thing in common—they were all forwards.

Ask the public to name an England rugby union player and the chances are they will come up with Jonny Wilkinson. There is nothing wrong with that; Wilkinson is a fine player, a good example to youngsters coming into the game and any PR executive's dream. Jonny is a great ambassador for rugby. Ask the same question of those who follow the game religiously, and the likelihood is that the answer will be different; most will come up with lock forward **Martin Johnson**.

There are players who have won more caps than Johnson; captained England in more matches; scored more tries and certainly kicked more goals. So what is it about Martin Johnson that elevates him above all his contemporaries? Why has this comparatively shy and unassuming individual off the field become such a legend in his own lifetime for deeds performed on it? Why does he make the title of this book seem like a load of old hokum? He would strongly suggest otherwise of course, but it cannot be denied that Martin Johnson is one of a very small group of captains who, through no designs of their own, were considered men apart: John Eales of Australia; New Zealand's Sean Fitzpatrick; and the great man from Ballymena, Willie John McBride. It would be easy to extend the list but that would surely lead to argument. However, it is doubtful that anyone would question the credentials of Eales, Fitzpatrick, McBride and Johnson.

Between 14 November 1998 and 22 November 2003 Martin Johnson led England 39 times. It started at Huddersfield with two qualifying matches for the 1999 World Cup before the captaincy was returned to Lawrence Dallaglio. On Dallaglio's fall from grace Johnson took over the reins and only injury, periods of rest, his involvement with the Lions or the occasional ban prevented him from carrying out his duties. These duties lasted a total of five years and eight days and may have begun in West Yorkshire but ended in Sydney with England the newly crowned champions of the world.

Unlike Paul Dodge, Martin Johnson had to wait until he was 19 before making his debut for the Tigers. That was in 1989 but no sooner had he begun to make his mark at the club than he left for New Zealand where he enjoyed two seasons playing in the second division of the Inter-Provincial Championship and toured Australia with the New Zealand Colts in 1991— what might have been! On his return to Leicester, Johnson was quickly picked up by the England selectors and played for the Under 21 and B teams in the 1991–92 season but it was in 1993 that things really started to happen.

Preparing to play for England A against France A at Welford Road on the eve of the senior international at Twickenham, Johnson was drafted into the England team when an injury forced Wade Dooley to withdraw. It was an impressive debut, England winning 16–15, but Dooley rightly returned for the remainder of the Championship and together with fellow lock Martin Bayfield toured New Zealand with the British Lions in the summer. The sudden death of his father saw Dooley return home and an unfortunate set of circumstances unfold which revealed much that needed addressing in the administration department. These were difficult times without doubt but Dooley was originally told he could rejoin the tour later only for the red tape and bureaucratic engines to intervene and dictate that this could only be in a non-playing capacity which he declined. The outcome of this unfortunate incident saw Martin Johnson join the tour as Dooley's replacement and play in four matches including the second and third Tests, an unexpected early taste of things to come.

By the end of the 1996–97 season Martin Johnson had won 30 caps. He had achieved much in the past four years but there was little to suggest that here was a man with great leadership qualities; one capable of extracting that last ounce of energy from a player long since running on empty. Those who chose Martin Johnson to lead the Lions in South Africa were inspired, bold even, because their choice of leader had little experience of captaincy other than taking over at Leicester in the latter part of the season when Dean Richards was absent through injury. This was not exactly the background of previous Lions skippers but Johnson's selection proved an inspired and bold decision—it was also the right one. Manager of the 1997 Lions was Fran Cotton, a veteran of three previous tours, two to South Africa. He was a man who knew exactly what was needed.

There were some great candidates around: Ieuan Evans, Rob Wainwright, Jason Leonard. I was at the rugby writers' dinner and Peter Wheeler asked if any decision had been made. He told me that Martin Johnson was leading Leicester in Dean's absence and that all the feedback from the players was positive; his presence in the dressing room, his decision making—everything was good. He was a certainty for the tour and was going to be included as first choice at lock; my main criteria for the captain was that he was guaranteed his Test place and in Martin's case the answer was yes so I started doing a bit of research on him as a bloke.

I went to see Bob Dwyer, the Leicester coach, who also gave him great reviews in what he was doing as captain and then I thought who knows him better than his mother, so I rang his mother. I started talking to her about Martin, about his various qualities and asked her to give me just one real quality that she saw in him, something that marked him out as being a bit special. She told me the one thing that particularly stood out was that he would always look you in the eye and tell you the truth; in other words he was a very honest guy—Martin knew nothing of this at the time. I spoke to Ian McGeechan and Jim Telfer, the Lions coaching team, and we agreed that a physical presence was very important in South Africa. Psychologically that was a very big part of the game; would you prefer a small wing knocking on the dressing room door to say you were ready or a big 18 stone second-row forward; mind games really but we agreed that Martin Johnson was the man.

He led the Lions to a famous victory in the Test series and on his return took over as club captain at Leicester. Clive Woodward favoured Lawrence Dallaglio for the role of England captain and Johnson waited until the following year before being asked to lead the team in the two World Cup qualification matches in place of the injured Dallaglio. Things soon returned to normal; Johnson continuing in the second-row with a fully fit Dallaglio running the show from number 8 but all that changed one Sunday morning when Lawrence was on the front pages of the newspapers for all the wrong reasons and completely out of the blue England needed a new captain. Woodward did not have to look far for his replacement, Johnson taking over at very short notice for a one-off Test against Australia in Sydney, part of the build up to the World Cup played later in the year. But for England, the tournament proved to be a big disappointment. When injury ruled Johnson out of the Six Nations, the enforced period of inactivity was not to the captain's liking. Nothing if not resilient, Johnson was fit to lead England to South Africa in the summer where the team won a precious Test victory to add to those achieved in a different jersey three years earlier. That autumn England beat Australia and South Africa at Twickenham and suddenly the mystique that for so long had surrounded the southern hemisphere giants was broken—bring on the All Blacks!

England won four matches in the Championship but this was the season the visit to Lansdowne Road was postponed due to the foot-and-mouth outbreak. The match would be played later in the year but before England's focus could be placed on Grand Slams and the like there was another major event in the rugby calendar to be addressed. The four year cycle between Lions tours comes around far too quickly; now Australia was bracing itself for the arrival of the Barmy Army and many thousands more. When he was chosen to captain the tourists a second time, Martin Johnson became the only player to have done so but this time the champagne wouldn't taste so good. The Wallabies recovered from losing the first Test to win the second and third and in turn the series.

The new season got under way with some unfinished business. A hand injury prevented Johnson leading the team in Dublin where dreams of a Grand Slam came unstuck in the face of a typical Irish onslaught led by the indomitable Keith Wood. Any aspirations of repairing the damage in 2002 also went up in smoke in Paris, England beaten in the only Championship match lost when Johnson was captain. These two reverses aside, the signs were good, the team was coming together well. In the autumn of 2002, three glorious Saturdays in November saw New Zealand, Australia and South Africa all defeated at Twickenham and England installed as one of the favourites for the World Cup scheduled to take place in Australia in 12 months—time to get the bets on. The elusive Grand Slam was finally delivered in 2003. And when New Zealand and Australia were beaten in their own back yards in the summer, Martin Johnson and his men became firm favourites for the World Cup—the odds dramatically shortened.

The day after the World Cup final, two photographs were prominent in every English newspaper; one showed Jonny Wilkinson's winning drop goal and the other a jubilant England captain holding the William Webb Ellis Cup aloft with an expression on his face that said more than any words could possibly have done. The journey was over. The captain knew that this was the peak of his career and things could only go one way from here. After winning 84 caps and leading his country 39 times, Martin Johnson retired from international rugby. The England team was regaled the length and breadth of the country: honours were handed out; there were open bus celebrations; and for a few months, the euphoria generated refused to go away. Leicester supporters had more of his time before Johnson finally called it a day but his legacy at a club which he helped win so many cups and titles will always be there, something for others to aspire to.

Martin Johnson's appointment as England team manager in 2008 will see a return to the sharp end of things. Perhaps it is not a role for which he is best prepared having no previous experience in either management or coaching, both these areas will fall under his remit. But those who welcomed the news with cautionary remarks need only go back to 1997 when some inspired men chose him to lead the Lions with little more than the utmost faith in his ability to back their selection. One suspects that an element of déjà vu will arrive; such is the stature of the man. If any doubts remain then seek out someone who knows him as a player, as an individual and who has shared the odd scrum with him—ask Jason Leonard.

The secret to Martin Johnson is that he will never ask anyone to do anything that he wouldn't do himself and everyone respected that. We'd finish heavy training sessions leaving kit bags, tackle bags, balls, jerseys, water bottles, whatever, strewn all over the pitch; highly paid professional rugby players all thinking we'd done our training and were looking forward to getting some recovery time, a massage. Martin would ask us where we were going, point out that we only had one kit man and that we were no better than him; he'd tell us to give him a hand. Your Jonny Wilkinsons and Lawrence Dallaglios would just say 'OK Johnno,' and get on with it.

People have questioned his new role, wondering if he has the necessary experience in management and coaching but as a player he showed his leadership skills and his man management skills every day. Whether it was with the players, Clive Woodward or the RFU be it on or off the field he was always using those skills and I think he'll be a success. As long as Martin sticks to the core values that made him a great player he won't go far wrong. I wish the guy the best and I'm sure he'll do a fantastic job.

For five years the England captaincy was Martin Johnson's but inevitably there were matches when he was not available giving other players the chance to lead their country, a wonderful rugby opportunity. All those who stood in for Johnson knew they were not going to be there for the long haul, that it was only a temporary appointment but the honour is none the less for that. Two Leicester players led England under such circumstances; wing forward Neil Back and hooker Dorian West.

Neil Back was one of those players who stood out on a rugby field. Small in stature he may have been but here was a wing forward who was never far from the ball, his pace and shrewd reading of the game more than making up for any missing inches. Not everyone agreed and caps proved hard to come by as coaches showed a preference for taller men; Ben Clarke, Steve Ojomoh and later Lawrence Dallaglio and Richard Hill all contested the positions on the side of the scrum with their contribution at the tail of the lineout giving each of them a perceived advantage over the shorter man.

After winning his first cap against Scotland in 1993, Neil Back only had three caps to his name come the start of the 1997–98 season. New coach Clive Woodward had different ideas; he saw the benefit of a fast open side wing forward in a sport where the outcome was becoming more and more influenced by events at the breakdown. A quick man around the park was crucial to his requirements. Neil Back fitted the bill and from playing against South Africa in the autumn internationals in 1997 until the World Cup final six years later, he featured in 63 of the 73 matches—not bad for a short guy!

His club career at Leicester mirrored that of Martin Johnson. Back was there on all the big occasions; the Heineken Cup matches; successful Premiership campaigns; knock out cup competitions—when Dean Richards or Martin Johnson were picking up the trophies Neil Back was invariably there. He is revered at Welford Road but don't mention him in Limerick or Cork, cities which play host to Munster, the Irish province. The Munster supporters will never forgive Back for what they remember as a piece of skulduggery on the fringe of a scrum which may have cost their team the Heineken Cup.

The Millennium Stadium was packed to the rafters for the 2002 final, a sea of red matched by a mix of red, white and green. It was a wonderful setting for a great occasion but with minutes remaining and Leicester 15–9 ahead a Munster scrum deep in the Tiger's half saw Back flick the ball out of the Irish scrum-half Peter Stringer's hands and any danger there may have been went with it. The referee didn't see the incident, neither did the touch judges and that 30,000 Irishmen had didn't count for anything—meanwhile nobody from Leicester gave a hoot and the trophy was lifted.

Neil Back first captained England against Australia in 2001, Johnson was injured and his Leicester team mate led the side to a 21–15 victory and followed it up a week later with a resounding 134–0 defeat of a hapless Romania. Four months on, he had his second stint. This time Johnson had fallen foul of the referee and was serving a suspension but Back carried on the good work and England beat Wales and Italy with something to spare. Four outings as England captain, four games won and as we have seen, many ex-captains would like those statistics alongside their name.

Back played in two Tests for the Lions in South Africa and won two more Test caps in Australia in 2001 and although having announced his retirement from international rugby he undertook a third Lions campaign when he travelled to New Zealand with Clive Woodward and his entourage in 2005. This time there was no Johnson and the wheels came off big time but it was one last opportunity to play Test rugby and despite the odds Neil Back once again stood up to the plate.

Since retiring, Neil Back has remained at Leicester in a coaching capacity. For many players this is the obvious and preferred choice when they can no longer hold down a place in the team. With player contracts greatly outnumbering coaching positions those who land a job often have to leave the club they have played for if they want to continue in the game and for Dorian West this meant a move to one of Leicester's greatest rivals—Northampton.

Just as W.J.A. Davies chose to play for England when his roots were based in west Wales so too did **Dorian West** make the same choice. Born in Wrexham, West could have laid his store out with the land of his birth but after moving to the Midlands he became part of the Leicester movement initially as a wing forward. Such was the strength of the squad at the time opportunities were scarce and he decided to join Nottingham, continuing at wing forward but eventually converted to hooker in which position he soon established himself as one of England's rising stars.

All players had an important decision to make when the game turned professional in 1995—stick with the day job and play 'recreational' rugby or give it a go. For many the decision was straightforward, they were either good enough or they were not, but for some there was much soul searching to be done and for a 27 year old who was making his way in the local constabulary there was a lot at stake. West decided to gamble, throw his hat in with Leicester again and keep everything crossed. It was a brave decision; Richard Cockerill was first choice hooker at the club and would soon win his first cap while elsewhere, Phil Greening and Mark Regan had established themselves in the pecking order but there was to be no u-turn and Dorian West set about getting his name included in the mix.

He did well. By 1998, West had made his mark with the Tigers taking every opportunity to impress when Cockerill was away on international duty or recovering from injury and recognition finally came when he was selected on the bench against France for the opening match of the Five Nations. Mark Regan had replaced the injured Cockerill and when he was forced to leave the field, Dorian West ran on to win his first cap. He was 30 years old and had waited 10 years for what amounted to little more than 10 minutes of international rugby but it was worth it.

Early international matches were contested between teams made up of 20 players with the reduction to 15 introduced in 1877. Now it is not unreasonable to say that rugby union is a 22 man game; there are only 15 allowed on the field at any one time but the way the bench of seven players is used reaches well beyond the need to replace those forced to depart through injury. Tactical substitutions can be the difference between winning or losing and a strong bench is now an essential part of team selection.

Dorian West won 21 caps but he only started 10 matches. The other 11 saw him brought on at various times to either replace an injured player or introduce a fresh pair of legs to the forward effort. In those 11 appearances West didn't spend more than 150 minutes on the field; didn't spend the equivalent of two full matches in action, but in the modern game such contribution has to be equally compared with a player who started and finished any of the games. This is rugby in the 21st century and excepting the instances when the value of a cap is totally diminished by a coach who introduces a player in a game's dying moments for no apparent reason other than to maybe increase said player's pay cheque all other caps won by replacements are well earned.

Dorian West was nearing the end of his career when Clive Woodward asked him to lead England against France in a game played in Marseilles as part of the series of warm up matches in the build up to the 2003 World Cup. His experience leading England A stood him in good stead and with places still up for grabs in the 30 man squad to travel to Australia to be announced a week later there was a lot to play for. England did not travel mob handed and only three of the starting line up would be in the team selected to play the same opponents in the semi-final at the tournament. In contrast, the French team was not far from a first choice selection and 12 of the players would start the match in Sydney which makes England's 17–16 defeat all the more creditable. The result brought to an end a 14 match winning run that extended back to March 2002. Once again it was the French who gained the upper hand and but for a last minute drop goal attempt by Paul Grayson which missed by a matter of inches the unbeaten run would have eventually stretched to 25 matches—the full strength England only just getting into its stride.

West made the cut and travelled to the World Cup, one of three hookers included in the squad. He played against Uruguay in the group stages and replaced Steve Thompson in the closing minutes of the semi-final which proved to be his last appearance in an England jersey. Although one of the substitutes chosen for the final that was one match in which he didn't get among the action.

In 2007, Dorian West took over as forwards coach at Northampton Saints. The club had just been relegated from the Guinness Premiership and for such a big player (and payer) in the domestic game, competing in National Division One was not an option. The Saints went through the 2007–08 season undefeated and added the EDF Energy National Trophy to the cabinet but now the real work would begin; West would find out once and for all whether the right decision was made when he opted to become a professional sportsman.

England used 19 players during the 2003 World Cup final; three of the replacements had to sit it out hoping that Clive Woodward would tell them to get ready to go on but the word never came. This was cruel luck especially when remembering that the final went into extra time but like West, **Martin Corry** was well used to life on the bench; at the time of the final, he had won 18 of his 29 caps as a substitute.

Corry made his England debut in Buenos Aries on England's tour to the Argentine in 1997. With the Lions in South Africa, there were many leading names missing from the England squad. It was Corry's lot to keep the blind side position warm for Lawrence Dallaglio who returned to the team for the autumn internationals. Not only did the immovable beast that is Lawrence want his place back, he was now captain making Corry's future inclusion more doubtful. Even the big boys are knocked about and when the captain was unable to lead England in the two qualifying matches played at Huddersfield, Martin Corry was included at number 8. In Argentina, Corry had been a Bristol player; this time around, he was accredited as a Leicester Tiger and the games at Huddersfield marked the start of another Leicester-England connection that would run and run.

Corry came through the qualifiers and made the squad for the World Cup where his appearances were restricted to three as a replacement and the pattern continued during 2000 when he won seven more caps, all from the bench. Again in 2001 he played against Wales, Italy and France off the bench and with such limited game time, it was no surprise when he did not tour Australia with the Lions. England's summer tour to North America provided some consolation for Corry and he set off for Canada with a suitcase full of summer clothes and sun block.

When a butterfly flaps its wings there is a reaction somewhere distant—something to do with the chaos theory apparently. So it follows that when in Perth, Western Australia Simon Taylor took a knock to the knee in the first match of the Lions tour bringing his journey to a premature end. In Toronto a chap named Steve White-Cooper was probably doing cartwheels because Martin Corry had been summoned to Australia thereby opening the door for him to sample Test rugby. Such is the life of a professional sportsman, ever full of its ups and downs. Late out of the blocks he may have been but once in Australia Corry set about the task in hand with some intent and won three Lions caps, starting the first and third Tests and going on as a replacement for Richard Hill in the second.

With such a stop-start international career, it is to be expected that Corry's leadership qualities first reared their head at Leicester when he inherited the captaincy from the retired Martin Johnson in 2004. Jason Robinson was the incumbent England captain come the start of the 2005 Six Nations but when injury ruled him out of selection against Italy it was Martin Corry who was chosen to replace him as captain. Successive victories against Italy and Scotland got him off the mark and when the Lions squad to tour New Zealand was announced the new England captain was included—the butterflies could take the day off. Three Test appearances, two as a replacement, brought the total to six and life was good.

England retained Corry as England captain for the autumn internationals and he continued through the 2006 Six Nations but a chance to recharge the batteries was long overdue and he stood down from the summer tour to Australia. As reigning world champions, England were looking anything but the part. There was a lot going on behind the scenes prompting much speculation with talk of replacing coach Andy Robinson never far from the sports pages. The public were expecting much more from their team with the next World Cup only 12 months away. When it failed to deliver, something that was happening all too often, scapegoats were sought; people to place the blame on.

Argentina claimed a first victory at Twickenham in November which was also a seventh consecutive defeat for England. Although England beat South Africa a week later, the following Saturday the Springboks produced a winning performance that helped coach Jake White stave off the mounting pressure he was being subjected to. But it marked the end for Andy Robinson. Assistant coach Brian Ashton was given the responsibility of taking England to the World Cup, the responsibility of ensuring the champions would go down fighting and he wanted a new captain at the helm. This meant that nine months before the defence of the title began it was all change at the top.

Martin Corry led England three times in France taking over from Phil Vickery, Ashton's choice as leader, when he was suspended in the early part of the tournament. Those matches brought his number of games as captain to 17, a figure only bettered by Carling, Johnson, Dallaglio and Beaumont. For all that he will never be regarded in the same esteem as that quartet. Quite simply captains have to produce and goodness knows, we have discussed enough who failed to do so, but with Martin Corry a feeling of guilt creeps in when looking to criticise his tenure. No England captain has ever given more of himself in the cause that is English rugby. Corry did more than just lead by example; he bled for the team. Those mandatory after match interviews with a losing captain who had just given so much were painful to watch. How he managed to be so polite in the face of a stream of such inane questioning tells us much about the man; he couldn't have given any more and soon after the 2007 World Cup he announced his retirement from international rugby.

To say that Leicester were poor in the EDF Cup Final in 2008 is to flatter a team which can rarely have played worse but to suggest that was also the case in the 2007 Heineken Cup Final when they were summarily turned over would be doing London Wasps a grave injustice. London Wasps led by one of Corry's greatest rivals out-thought and out-played Leicester. It would have been a bitter pill to swallow but Lawrence Dallaglio would not have cared one iota about that!

11

A STING IN THE TALE

Gipsies, Kings College Hospital, Marlborough Nomads, Old Merchant Taylors', Old Millhillians, Saracens, St Mary's Hospital, Wasps

Back to the metropolis; the hustle and bustle of the city amid all its splendour and ever-changing skyline. This final chapter brings together clubs which play the game in the top tier, clubs that no longer exist and some that fall somewhere in-between. That the names of a bygone era, the Nomads and the Gipsies (sic), could have been used in recent years as addendums for the London Wasps and the Saracens is true, such has been the wanderlust displayed by both clubs, but there any similarity ends. And there are representatives of the public school network; Old Merchant Taylors' and Old Millhillians still turn out teams and joining them is St Mary's Hospital. All in all this is a veritable ménage with which to conclude.

London Wasps play at Adams Park in High Wycombe which immediately poses the question—why wasn't the club included earlier? If, by playing at Reading, London Irish was deemed to be sufficiently distanced from London to be excluded from the opening chapters then surely the same criteria should be applied in the case of the Wasps. The explanation is simple; in Mike Catt, London Irish has its sole claim on the England captaincy and as Catt only played for the club after it had decamped to Reading, it would have been illogical to include it elsewhere. Not so with the Wasps; four players who went on to captain England were involved with the club while it was based at Sudbury as was the fifth. But when this fifth player became England captain the wanderlust had begun to rear its head and the journey which ended at High Wycombe via Loftus Road, the home of Queen's Park Rangers FC, was under way. Therefore, if not for one particular individual High Wycombe need only have been mentioned in passing but the same could never be said about **Lawrence Bruno Nero Dallaglio**.

Lawrence Dallaglio was the player the public loved to hate; not English followers of the game, just those found everywhere else. Be it at any of the world's major stadia or on a park's ground, if the location was outside England then people treated the name Dallaglio with scorn. Why? Because Lawrence Dallaglio was a mighty fine rugby player; a brute of a man that anybody, anywhere would have preferred to have playing for than against them. Even beyond the environs of the Wasps, English supporters struggled to take the man on board when he was piling in amongst their own particular favourites but when he pulled on the British Lions jersey, English, Irish, Scottish and Welsh alike joined the same bandwagon and hailed his praises from on high—for a few weeks at least. When the tour was over and the rugby calendar resumed its normal agenda Lawrence became the villain of the piece again—the player the public loved to hate—a true sign of greatness!

Dallaglio first gained international recognition not in the 15 man game but the shorter version, seven-a-side rugby. He was a member of the England team that won the Rugby World Cup Sevens at Murrayfield in 1993. He was also in the Wasps' seven that took the Middlesex title in the same year. Comfortable with ball in hand and very mobile, the back row forward was an ideal sevens player, a game in which speed prevails above all else, but without the ball the fleetest of foot are redundant and Dallaglio's presence ensured a regular supply would reach the men with pace.

His inclusion in the England Under 21s and England A teams confirmed he was a contender and following the 1995 World Cup Dallaglio was chosen as a replacement for the match against newly crowned world champions South Africa at Twickenham. He went on in place of Tim Rodber and played out the last 10 minutes, one of the rare occasions he would be capped from the bench until near the end of his career when he was used as an impact player, a complete reversal to how Martin Corry's international career unfolded.

Following that brief appearance Dallaglio started the next 10 matches, the run ending when injury prevented him lining up against Wales in the final match of the 1997 Championship. An automatic choice for the Lions tour to South Africa, Dallaglio played in the three Tests, however maybe there were a few raised eyebrows when Clive Woodward chose him as England captain for the series of autumn internationals with Martin Johnson also included in the team. Dallaglio's introduction to the job could not have been more demanding; on consecutive Saturdays England drew with Australia, were beaten by New Zealand and South Africa and after letting a 17 point advantage slip away had to settle for a 26–26 draw in a second meeting with the All Blacks.

The 1998–99 season started with defeat in Paris but England were too strong for the Celtic nations and won a fourth consecutive Triple Crown giving out a clear message; the top end of international rugby could be divided into two divisions. England were either at the bottom of the first or top of the second. Eight competitive international matches in five months and a tough season of club rugby rarely leave the big men in one piece. Come June Dallaglio needed some repair work, in particular a shoulder problem needed attention, and he decided the summer would be best spent undergoing surgery and taking the necessary time to make a full recovery. The captain missed the tour to the southern hemisphere and the World Cup qualifying matches giving Tony Diprose, Matt Dawson and Martin Johnson the chance to lead England but he was back in harness for the visit of Australia and South Africa later in the year. A one point defeat to Australia was followed by victory over the Springboks bringing to an end a record equalling run of 17 consecutive Test wins then it was back to that most unpredictable of tournaments—the Five Nations. The last three Championships had seen France deny England the Grand Slam but when Scotland and Ireland were beaten and the French bogey laid to rest at Twickenham, only Wales stood in the way of Dallaglio and his team realising the dream.

In the space of a couple of months, two totally unrelated incidents brought Lawrence Dallaglio's rugby career back to earth with an almighty bang. First Wales proved a much tougher nut to crack than most pundits predicted. The match was played at Wembley while the Millennium Stadium was under construction. With few minutes remaining on the clock, England were leading 31–25 and awarded a kickable penalty. Even if the reliable Wilkinson missed, it would at least have helped run the clock down. Dallaglio ignored that option preferring to kick for position and rely on the forwards to do the rest; bring the Grand Slam home in style. Wales survived and won a penalty taking them back into England's half; battled on and won a lineout inside the 22 from which Scott Gibbs danced over leaving Neil Jenkins to add the two points for victory.

Poor judgement? Over confidence? An attempt to keep possession and see out the final moments with the ball up the jumper? Call it what you like but the result paled into insignificance when a second incident took the England captain from the relative safety of the back pages to banner headlines on the front—drugs were the issue but it was Lawrence who was the dope. In an interview with journalists from a Sunday newspaper he was apparently quite open about some drug related incidents in his past. This was big news; a sports story guaranteed to sell extra copies when it was splashed across the front pages and the England captain was summarily hung out to dry. In rugby circles, this could mean only one thing; Dallaglio fell on his sword, stood down from the captaincy of his country and braced himself for the worse. It was a sad day. Never one to run and hide, he faced the music, confronted his critics and then proceeded to get on with what he did best.

This indiscretion broke as England prepared to travel to Australia for a one off Test and Dallaglio was immediately replaced in the squad and the captaincy passed to Martin Johnson. Common sense prevailed and he was back in the team for the World Cup warm up matches going on to make 21 consecutive appearances before his selection for a second Lions tour effectively brought the run to an end. His inclusion in the squad to visit Australia was in the balance after injuring a knee in a club fixture but the Lions management were prepared to gamble, wrap him in cotton wool for a couple of weeks and introduce him later in the tour. Dallaglio did get to play in two matches but a knock on the problem knee in the feisty encounter with the New South Wales Waratahs ended his tour prematurely and in New Zealand four years later he suffered similar misfortune, dislocating an ankle in the opening match.

The knee problem kept him sidelined for the rest of the year and he played little international rugby in 2002. Clive Woodward wanted a fit Lawrence Dallaglio at his disposal in 2003 and was prepared to give the player as long as it took, gradually reintroducing him into the fray from the bench. It paid off, Dallaglio the only England player involved in every minute of the World Cup; seven matches in which he wasn't replaced or more importantly yellow carded. The knee was better.

With Johnson retired England were in need of a new captain and almost five years after turning down a kick at goal at Wembley Stadium, Lawrence Dallaglio was once again chosen to lead his country. Ireland were first to beat the world champions followed by France, New Zealand twice and Australia; unfamiliar results in recent years but a reminder of how things were back in 1998 when Lawrence was first appointed captain. At the start of the 2004–05 season Dallaglio announced his retirement from international rugby but Clive Woodward had other ideas. Woodward was selected head coach of the British and Irish Lions for the upcoming tour to New Zealand and was keen to have Dallaglio in the squad. He got his man and although the experience was short and painful it served to remind

Dallaglio what he was missing and albeit future appearances were from the bench he returned to international rugby finally bowing out after the 2007 World Cup final in which he won his 85th cap.

A full and satisfying international career then; no glaring omissions. Dallaglio's involvement at the Wasps was equally rewarding; three time winners of the knock out cup competition; league champions twice and in recent seasons, winners of four Premiership play off finals. The team won the Parker Pen European Challenge Cup in 2003 and the more prestigious Heineken Cup in 2004 and again in 2007. Well into his 36th year Lawrence Dallaglio called it a day at the end of the 2007–08 season in grand style leading the London Wasps to victory over Leicester in the Premiership final played in front of a record attendance for a club match. When he left the field for the last time with 10 minutes remaining on the clock 81,000 stood and applauded one of the true greats of the modern game; a most fitting end to the magnificent career of a man who spent 18 years with one club and would seriously dispute suggestions regarding Leicester's standing made in the preceding chapter.

Enmities of old. We are not talking Leicester and London Wasps here, rather rivalries that go back to time immemorial. We are talking about the local derby; the annual encounters between teams that are inextricably linked by their proximity to each other. Football has Manchester United and Manchester City; Liverpool and Everton; and in north London, Arsenal and Tottenham Hotspur. For rugby, take any permutation from the Bath, Bristol and Gloucester triumvirate; Leicester and Northampton; and in north London, Wasps and Saracens were once friendly neighbours until the attractions of ground sharing with leading football teams put some distance between them.

One of the moneymen to arrive with professionalism was Nigel Wray, a Saracens supporter of old who set about ploughing part of his vast fortune into the club in an effort to take it to areas never previously visited. Established in 1876 the Saracens was a club still waiting for its first piece of silverware but with Wray on board that was about to change. Philippe Sella, Michael Lynagh and Francois Pienaar were all signed up on lucrative contracts and as the 1997–98 season entered its final weeks the Saracens were chasing what would once have been viewed as a highly improbable double. The club may have had to settle for the runners-up position in the league, losing out by a point to the equally cash rich Newcastle, but it had progressed to the final of the Tetley's Bitter Cup where the Wasps would provide the opposition—a match made in heaven.

Leading Saracens was not one of the game's superstars but a homegrown talent, a number 8 with a handful of caps to his name who had previously captained the England A team. **Tony Diprose** was one of several outstanding back row forwards in England in the 1990s but he would be restricted to 10 caps having to accept that no matter how good a player he was there were some around who were better. At Twickenham on 9 May 1998, Diprose led Saracens against a Wasps 15 that included the current England captain who would also lead his team from the middle of the back row. Saracens picked up that elusive first trophy by trouncing Lawrence Dallaglio and his men 48–18. This was a big score which gave the victors much cause for celebration and Diprose was no doubt in good heart when he set off with the England squad headed for Australia and the other tri-nation countries a few weeks later.

Someone had to do it. Somebody has to be remembered as England's captain in her darkest hour; captain when a record score was posted. Matt Dawson had been appointed tour captain but was unable to take his place in the opening match against Australia and the honour was handed to Tony Diprose. With many leading players left at home to recharge the batteries or get some necessary repair work done to their battered bodies the England team that took the field in Brisbane was well under strength. For the five players winning their first caps and Diprose in his first outing as captain the game was an especially sobering experience. Australia won 76–0, a score not likely to be removed from the record books in the foreseeable future, and Tony Diprose would not captain his country again. Such a desperately disappointing performance and outcome is a shared experience and there is no reason why the captain should be burdened with any additional responsibility but Tony Diprose will remain in the record books until an even worse day at the office is witnessed; or until Hell freezes over—a much more likely prospect.

So, what if Hell did freeze over, or a new Ice Age descended on the planet? This is highly improbable with the threat of global warming but if it did, **Kyran Bracken** would be all right. Kyran Bracken, champion of *Dancing on Ice* and star of *Holiday on Ice*; one time England scrum-half and captain. More accurately, Kyran Bracken was 51 times England scrum-half and three times England captain.

Dublin born Bracken might have qualified to play for Ireland but having left the Emerald Isle at the age of four he threw his lot in with England. Bristol University led to the Memorial Ground where he learnt his craft before moving to London and linking up with the Saracens, another to join the club on the advent of professional rugby. That was in 1996, Nigel Wray's intentions confirmed with another spend which brought more leading players to the new ground at Enfield.

Bracken was a seasoned international player by the time he arrived in north London. Richard Hill, Richard Harding and Nigel Melville had come to the end of their England careers leaving Dewi Morris as first choice but when illness forced his late withdrawal from the team to play New Zealand, Bracken was called up to win a first cap. This was in November 1993 and the All Blacks were touring England and Scotland on the back of their success in the Test series against the Lions earlier in the year. Eight of the England team had played in that series and were still smarting from some dubious refereeing decisions—it was payback time!

A few minutes into the match back row forward Jamie Joseph stamped on Bracken's ankle, a blatant foul which could have had a more damaging outcome but the scrum-half was strapped up and continued, going on to play a significant part in England's famous victory. For two more years Bracken and Morris contested the scrum-half duties until Morris retired from international rugby after the 1995 World Cup thereby opening the door for Matt Dawson and Andy Gomarsall to join the quest for international honours; now there were three players chasing the position and Austin Healey was never going to go away.

In the summer of 1997 Bracken was on tour with England in Argentina when he received a call asking him to join the Lions in South Africa following Rob Howley's injury—the butterflies were back. Matt Dawson was already there of course, about to announce his arrival on the international stage in spectacular fashion after the unfortunate Howley's departure but there was time for Bracken to make one appearance and be named on the score sheet. Four years on Bracken was again overlooked by the Lions selectors, however he was invited to lead England on the summer tour to North America. As expected, England won the two Tests in Canada and one against the USA giving Bracken a perfect record in his short tenure as England captain. Even if defeat against either country would have been unthinkable this was no mean achievement as so many first choice players were in Australia with the Lions. It was in North America that Ollie

Barkley, Ben Kay, Lewis Moody and Jamie Noon all won first caps under the leadership of a captain who ensured their introduction to international rugby was a smooth one.

A member of England's World Cup squad in 2003, Kyran Bracken was another player who chose to bow out of international rugby following the tournament. Among English scrum-halves only Matt Dawson has won more caps but there must be more about the number nine jersey than is apparent from the touchlines; something which allows these men to change direction once they have called it a day. They seem to replace the rugby ball with a fit young woman and start throwing her about with as much concentrated effort and skill as is ever required at the base of the scrum. While Dawson went dancing, Bracken chose to take to the ice. He got out the blades, the skin tight outfit, skated to success in television's *Dancing on Ice* and suddenly a whole new career opened up for him; coming to a rink near you—Kyran Bracken in *Holiday on Ice*.

Tony Diprose and Kyran Bracken are the only Saracens players to captain England and both took their place in the Tetley's Cup Final in 1998 that helped thank Nigel Wray for his financial commitment to the club. Time has shown Wray not to be one of those who went in search of any short term benefits rugby had to offer only to disappear when nothing was forthcoming. He has stayed the course with little more on his agenda than seeing the Saracens thrive. With the club reaching the semi-final of the 2008 Heineken Cup there is ample reason to believe that the dream lives on. Rugby union needs the Nigel Wrays of this world because without their commitment it is doubtful if teams like the Saracens would continue to play at the top level. Good on him.

Time now to consider two clubs which had their origins in London but eventually fell by the wayside. To do this we have to go back to the beginning; the founding of the RFU, the late nineteenth century and the public schools. Marlborough College and Tonbridge School were the establishments that led to the formation of the Marlborough Nomads and the Gipsies Football Club. Both saw the light of day in 1868, Marlborough Nomads establishing themselves in Blackheath before moving to Surbiton but of the Gipsies there is no record as to where the club may have played its home matches, perhaps the name telling us all we need to know.

Albert St George Hammersley attended Marlborough College before moving to London. On arrival in the city he started out on a legal career and decided to pursue his sporting interests at the club recently founded by ex-pupils from his college. Hammersley was the only member of the Nomads to play in the first international in 1871 but a year later, in an England team much more representative of the strength of club rugby, he was one of four Marlborough old boys included. He featured in England's first four matches and became the second captain when he took over from Fred Stokes in 1874, leading the side to victory against the Scots at the Kennington Oval.

And that was it. English rugby had seen the last of Albert St George Hammersley. At 26 years of age he packed his bags and went in search of adventure; fame and fortune would follow. He decided to go as far as possible, see what New Zealand could offer a young man with a good education and a professional qualification to his name and made his way to the South Island, settling on the east coast in the Canterbury lowlands. Rugby in New Zealand can trace its origins back to 1870 with the founding of a club in Nelson. Others soon followed but when Hammersley arrived in 1874 the region was yet to join the movement and he is credited as one of those responsible for the formation of the South Canterbury Football Club. Next stop was Canada and in particular Vancouver which, like South Canterbury, was also without a rugby club; shortly after Hammersley's arrival the matter was rectified and the formation of the British Columbia Rugby Union soon followed.

When Albert Hammersley arrived in London from College he was automatically accepted by the Marlborough Nomads but for **Francis Luscombe** fresh from Tonbridge there was no such club for that educational establishment's former pupils to affiliate with. Luscombe and two other old boys set about addressing the issue and were successful in recruiting sufficient like minded individuals to make the venture viable. The Gipsies Football Club quickly established itself as one of the most successful teams in London remaining unbeaten throughout its first season. It is highly probable that Luscombe and Hammersley would have come across each other in the forward exchanges when the Gipsies and the Nomads met.

Fred Luscombe was one of those who supported the concept of a governing body and he also played a big part in arranging the first international but for all his close involvement he was absent from the team in Edinburgh. He had to wait until the following year before he was capped. England played eight matches during the 20-a-side era and when Francis Luscombe became the fourth man to captain the team he was also the last before teams were reduced to 15 players. He led England to victories over Ireland and Scotland but there was no place for him among the forwards once they were restricted to a maximum of 10. Luscombe was the last player from the Gipsies to play for England before the club was disbanded and the Nomads would also see their representative honours greatly reduced as the balance of power slowly shifted; something that would be a regular occurrence in the years to come.

As the club network expanded and strengthened those coming from a public school background had to reappraise where they should play if they held any aspirations of becoming involved in the game at the highest level. The Old Boys clubs were no longer likely to provide the level of competition needed but for all that there were some who viewed things differently. **Ronald Cove-Smith** was one such player who, once his days at Merchant Taylors' School and Cambridge University were over, immediately headed to Croxley Heath, home of Old Merchant Taylors', and would famously become an exception to the pattern that was developing around him.

Intelligence and discipline are quintessential if one is to achieve success in any walk of life. The same applies on the rugby field where what is essentially a simple game can become the most complex of pursuits if a player hasn't the intelligence to know that all he has to do is stay on the right side of the ball. Naturally, there is much more which has to be considered; a player has to be able to handle the ball, kick the ball, have the ability to tackle and jump through hoops if necessary. All of which can be learned on the training ground but if he enters the arena devoid of intelligence and short of self discipline then a player quickly becomes a liability. Of course he will get away with it in the murky depths of the extra-fifths or the veterans; the world of Michael Green if such a place still exists, but he won't get away with it at Twickenham in front of 80,000 people with millions more watching on television.

There can be little doubt that these two particular qualities have played a big part in the selection of England captains and in Ronald Cove-Smith we arrive at another who came from a public school and Oxbridge background. A first-class honours degree in natural sciences led to a career in medicine and in 1923, at the comparatively young age of 25, Cove-Smith became a Member of the Royal College of Surgeons. First selected to play for England in 1921, he won five caps during his time at Cambridge but he joined Old Merchant Taylors' on coming down from university, eventually becoming the club's most capped player.

All pre-war tours to the southern hemisphere undertaken by the home union countries had been in the guise of British teams or on one occasion an Anglo-Welsh team. For the first venture following the First World War the sobriquet 'Lions' was introduced and Ronald Cove-Smith was invited to lead the squad on a 21 match tour of South Africa in 1924, a player equally capable at prop or in the second-row, statistically this was a poor tour; one of the worst on record. Only nine of the matches were won and the Test series lost; injuries, poor preparation, long journeys and, if some reports are to be believed, much fine wining and dining, all contributed to the poor results but for Cove-Smith the experience reached way beyond the playing field.

> The hospitality extended to us throughout was extraordinary—in fact, almost excessive; to such an extent, that embarrassment was felt in having to refuse so many invitations and entertainments…The success of such a tour, however, cannot be merely measured by the points gained or lost, but more by the points of contact that can thereby be established between men of different upbringing and outlook. In this direction there can be little doubt that the tour was satisfactory…

Cove-Smith was now an international captain but it would be more than three years before he was chosen to lead England. That responsibility came against New South Wales at Twickenham in January 1928, a match that immediately preceded the Five Nations. England beat the visitors in a match that the Australian Rugby Union would later award full international status and it set the tone for what was to follow. Two narrow victories in Swansea and Dublin were followed by a good performance against France leaving only Scotland standing between England and a fourth Grand Slam in the space of eight years. Cove-Smith became the fifth captain to lead England throughout a Grand Slam winning season when the Scots were defeated at Twickenham. The sole survivor of the 1921 and 1923 teams Ronald Cove-Smith played in 14 of the 16 matches that secured the four Grand Slams of the 1920s, a record no other English player has come close to equalling.

The next season Cove-Smith played his club rugby with King's College Hospital and his last two appearances as captain and player introduced another name to the list of clubs associated with the England captaincy. Wales were beaten but Ireland ended the winning run with a 6–5 victory at Twickenham; England had won six matches under his leadership and with 29 caps to his name he stood second in the list of the most capped England players behind Wavell Wakefield.

The average rugby player can expect 10 years at the top. Ten years in which to make it at club level, break into the national side, maybe play in a couple of World Cups with the chance of a Lions tour possible for the very best. Some will last longer and some won't, the threat of injury never far away in such a physical sport but that aside, the 10 year cycle which most would enjoy has varied little. When 1929 rolled into 1930 it is not surprising that the players asked to pick up the pieces after the war years were all replaced and the next period of rebuilding was under way. The new decade needed a new England and the selectors brought in the customary draft of players to win their first caps. There were a few of old stagers retained among the forwards, Harold Periton who took over the captaincy from Cove-Smith together with Sam and Bill Tucker but the other dozen players could only rustle up a grand total of four caps between them.

Peter Howard was among those introduced against Wales in 1930. Here was an Oxford undergraduate who didn't graduate, leaving the university with little more to his name than two rugby Blues and an England cap. When it came to finding a suitable club Howard adopted the same philosophy as Cove-Smith. A former pupil at Mill Hill School, Howard joined Old Millhillians and is the only England captain associated with the club. His day came against Ireland in 1931 but unfortunately he led a beaten team and a month later Carl Aarvold took over, Howard retained in the back row for two more games but after winning eight consecutive caps in two seasons his international rugby came to an end.

A respected political journalist, Peter Howard spent his later life working with the Moral Re-Armament movement which was founded by American evangelist Frank Buchman who instructed that by observing the highest moral standards as an individual will ultimately be to the benefit of all. Howard was pre-eminent in this movement and expected to take over as leader when Buchman died but he only outlived his mentor by four years and was denied the opportunity to take the movement further.

But for Peter Howard, Old Millhillians would not be included here and the same can be said about **Harold Owen-Smith** and his connection with St Mary's Hospital. No matter how much the rugby map of England has changed over the years it has never included Rondebosch, that leafy suburb of Cape Town overlooked by the Rhodes Memorial, a constant reminder of Cecil Rhodes and his importance in the history of South Africa. Beyond the diamonds and gold, Rhodesia and the infamous Jameson Raid, Cecil

Rhodes is best remembered for the academic scholarships that bear his name. These give outstanding students from the Commonwealth, the United States and to a lesser extent Germany the opportunity to study at Oxford University where Rhodes himself was a scholar. One of the beneficiaries of this foundation was Harold Owen-Smith and like Leonard Brown, another recipient of a Rhodes Scholarship, he too became England captain. Sam Woods was the first overseas born player to tread this ambiguous route to sporting acclaim and just as he had played Test cricket for the country of his birth so too did Owen-Smith don the whites for South Africa.

'Tuppy' Owen-Smith was a full-back, a player for whom tackling was a pleasure, an aspect of rugby which he not only delighted in but was also particularly adept at. He won his first cap while still at Oxford, playing throughout the 1934 Triple Crown season. When the selectors invited him to take over the captaincy, Owen-Smith was finishing his studies at St Mary's Hospital. Whilst Nim Hall and E.K. Scott would go on to lead England they had left the hospital by the time of their appointment and Owen-Smith remains the institution's only England captain. Narrow victories they may have been but by defeating Wales 4–3, Ireland 9–8 and Scotland 6–3 in the 1937 Championship, Owen-Smith led England to an 11th Triple Crown. This was his final season with England and he ended his career with 10 caps, only a scoreless draw with Wales and a 6–3 defeat at Lansdowne Road spoiling an outstanding record.

The addition of St Mary's Hospital brings the number of clubs directly associated with the captaincy to 54. This is a high figure when only 42 clubs make up the Premiership and National Divisions 1 and 2, and only 23 of these clubs are included in the total. The book discusses the various reasons for the demise of the other clubs and all that remains is a final visit to Wasps to look at the remaining four players who will bring the story to its temporary conclusion.

Teams do not win Triple Crowns easily; Grand Slams are even harder to come by. To date England has won 23 Triple Crowns and 12 Grand Slams. No country has won more, but following the 1937 Triple Crown 17 years passed before the next arrived. In 1951 England beat Scotland but lost to Ireland and Wales; a year later England beat Ireland and Scotland but Wales took the spoils at Twickenham; then in 1953 only a draw in Dublin prevented not only a Triple Crown but also a Grand Slam. These results showed a progression and suggested that in 1954 the team should go one step further and at the very least claim a 12th Triple Crown.

Present throughout the four seasons was prop forward **Bob Stirling** who won 13 caps as a Leicester player and five in his last season of international rugby by which time he was playing for the Wasps. Stirling was a late arrival winning his first cap at 31 years of age but with Eric Evans and Walter Holmes he made up a front row which laid the foundation for England's rise from also-rans in 1951 to champions in 1953 and winners of the Triple Crown a year later. His RAF career, which took him from the junior ranks during the Second World War to Wing Commander on his retirement in 1969, placed additional demands on his playing time as he also featured in several Inter Services matches from 1948 to 1954.

Captaincy was not something with which Bob Stirling was overly familiar, his only experience of the role being with the RAF and at county level. This limited exposure to leadership on the field didn't prevent him leading the Combined Services and the Midland Counties against Bob Stuart's 1953 All Blacks. The matches were played within the space of five days and a month later Stirling led England out at Twickenham for his third encounter with the tourists. There was no repeat of Doug Kendrew's good fortune, New Zealand winning all three matches.

England's 12th Triple Crown brought a fitting end to Bob Stirling's international career but the team were unable to go that one step further in the final match of the season in Paris. Stirling was well into his 35th year when he played his last representative match, one of England's older captains who also played in a position not often favoured by selectors or coaches when deciding who should lead the team. Taking those two factors into consideration suggests that despite his advancing years and the time spent in the depths of scrums and mauls Stirling possessed the necessary leadership qualities that those around him would respond to, qualities without which the art of captaincy becomes a forlorn cause.

Three years after winning his first cap, Bob Stirling took over as England captain. For **Nigel Melville**, the two landmark events arrived on 3 November 1984. It seems a case of being thrown in at the deep end to see if he would sink or swim, however, a second glance at the scrum-half's past record suggests otherwise. Melville had previously led England B and the Wasps in the 1983–84 season in which the club only lost six of the 41 matches played. He had also been involved with the England Schools, Under 19 and Under 23 levels but the story actually began in Yorkshire where his great potential was first recognised.

I'd finished school and spent a year working on a building site. I was playing for Otley at the time but the opportunity to play for the Wasps presented itself and that tied in with my going to North East London Polytechnic. I first became involved with the senior England team in Argentina in 1981 and the following season captained England B against France B. On finishing college I returned to Yorkshire hoping to rejoin Otley but the club wasn't considered to be of a sufficiently high standard and it was suggested that I look elsewhere which took me to Wakefield.

It was as a Wakefield player that Nigel Melville toured North America with England in 1982 but his appearances were restricted as he had to be content with being the number two choice behind tour captain, Steve Smith. During what would prove to be a short return home Melville helped Yorkshire reach the County Championship Final for the first time in 20 years but it was the semi-final that had most bearing on his future. Yorkshire met Middlesex for a place in the final, the match played at Sudbury, home of the Wasps. In the summer it was reported that he would be returning to the Wasps for the start of the new season and would captain the club.

The British Lions toured New Zealand in 1983. The Five Nations saw England struggle, a draw with Wales helping to avoid a whitewash. This poor campaign meant that only Dusty Hare, John Carleton and Clive Woodward of the backs were selected for the tour. At this time Melville was probably third in the England pecking order behind Steve Smith and Nick Youngs making his call up as replacement for the injured Terry Holmes totally unexpected. It was something which should have kick started his international career but in fact delayed it by a year as the injuries that would plague the rest of his career began to take their toll.

I played my first game of the tour against Southland at Invercargill. It went well, the Lions won and I scored a couple of tries. Then I was included in the team to play North Auckland at Whangarei in the week following the second Test. We were awarded a penalty for a scrum infringement and as I picked up the ball their blind side came around and thumped me on the side of the head—I suffered a bit of whiplash but decided to play on. At the next lineout the ball came off the top but when

I went for it I couldn't move my arm—that was the end of my tour.

The following season I was back at Wasps. During some pre-season training two guys landed on me as I was scoring and my knee was badly damaged. It required surgery and the cartilage was removed but from then on I suffered a lot of knee problems and eventually had to have the other cartilage out. This was all before the advent of keyhole surgery so they had to take the whole thing out which meant quite a long recovery period; the knee was never quite the same again.

The sequence of injuries and the periods of rehabilitation greatly disrupted Melville's playing career but he kept coming back for more and his determination was eventually rewarded. Circumstances dictated that Fred Stokes did it in the first international, 20 years later Fred Alderson became the second and Joe Mycock, in the first match following the Second World War joined a very short list. In November 1984 Nigel Melville was selected to play against Australia at Twickenham and in addition to winning his first cap was also chosen as captain, thereby extending the number of players to have led England on their debut to four. It proved to be rather an inauspicious start, Australia winning 19–3, and Melville missed three matches before returning to the team against Ireland and Wales at the end of the Championship.

Paul Dodge had replaced him as captain and led the team on the summer tour of New Zealand. The opening match was against North Auckland at Whangarei which undoubtedly brought back some painful memories but Melville could not ignore the chance to exorcise the ghosts and he was among the try scorers in a 27–14 victory.

On a bit of a roll he played in four matches but injury forced him to leave the field in the second Test; a pulled hamstring the latest in what was becoming an impressive list. Reunited with the captaincy in 1986 the Championship went well until the final match in Paris when once again the knee presented further problems which proved serious enough to keep him out of the team for the next two years. So much time was spent on the sidelines that it is a pleasure to be able to report that when he was once again asked to captain England Nigel Melville was rewarded with victories over Scotland at Murrayfield, and in what proved to be his final appearance, England beat Ireland at Twickenham—the captain forced to leave the field early.

I returned to Yorkshire and became player-coach at Otley. I learnt my trade at the club and was Director of Rugby when the game turned professional. The Wasps were looking for somebody to perform a similar role; I applied, got the job and spent another seven years at the club. Then followed a spell at Gloucester followed by a year with Reading Football Club where I was employed to help out with the coaching. I really enjoyed my time with Reading and the season ended with the club gaining promotion into the Premiership which made it particularly gratifying.

Nigel Melville returned to rugby in 2006 when he accepted the job of Chief Executive Officer and President of Rugby Operations with USA Rugby. Sixteen months on it looks as if he has settled well into his new position and is hopeful of staying in America until the 2011 World Cup. This American connection brings us to a man not remotely connected with the captaincy of England but who has also made the USA his home after moving there over 20 years ago.

Historical fiction is a popular genre; books that are based around actual events but which introduce fictional characters who stay long in the memory after the final page has been read. If successful another book can be written taking the characters further until a series of books has been produced. Television companies may become interested in adapting the novels for the small screen and with that added impetus, what was once a figment of someone's imagination can become a household name. But where do these names come from? How are they arrived at? Surely such invention can't have been influenced by a rugby player, an England captain?

'It is true. When I began writing the first book I wanted to find a really interesting name for the hero—something like Horatio Hornblower. I just could not find one so I decided to use the (slightly amended) name of one of my great heroes—Richard Sharp, the rugby player of Cornwall and England.'—Bernard Cornwell, February 2008.

So it was that Richard Sharpe entered the ranks of the best seller lists and was equally successful when he made the transition onto the small screen; the medium of television that many years earlier introduced his namesake to a wider public than could possibly be contained within the portals of HQ.

First time visitors to St Ives in Cornwall are immediately taken by the colour of the sea. The blue tones promise warmer waters than maybe exist but with an equally blue sky above an idyllic scenario is created and where better to live than within easy walking distance of the harbour and the coastal paths. It is in this westerly region of England that **Richard Sharp** now resides but the story began in Mysore, a city to the south of Goa on India's west coast.

My father was a mining engineer. He attended Camborne School of Mines but jobs were hard to find following the depression so he and my mother went to India where I was born in 1938. My mother's family home was in Redruth and following the war my father sent us back to England, back to Cornwall. My great love for rugby began at Redruth. As a seven or eight year old I used to go and watch the club where my heroes were Bill Phillips, a big back row forward and full-back Frank Partridge. I remember collecting their autographs after every game; they were always very kind and that was the start of a lifelong love of the game.

I first played rugby at Montpelliers Prep School in Paignton. I started at scrum-half and continued in the position when I went to Blundell's School. Graham Parker, who was England full-back in 1938, ran the first XV and in my last year he decided to switch me and I played my first game at fly-half against Cheltenham in 1956. On leaving Blundell's I began two years' National Service in the Royal Marines but broke my collar bone before joining up and immediately broke it again after not giving it sufficient time to mend properly. Any hopes I had of playing for the Navy were put on hold and I didn't play any rugby to speak of for the whole of the 1957–58 season. In my second year I did get to play for the Marines and the Royal Navy with the occasional game for Cornwall then, my National Service behind me, I went up to Oxford in September 1959.

Sharp celebrated his 21st birthday shortly before arriving at Oxford. With his previous experience the university immediately installed him in the rugby team but he injured his heel in the early part of the season and was looking a doubtful starter for the Varsity Match in December. Malcolm Phillips, the England centre and Oxford captain showed faith in his outside-half, keeping the position open until the last possible moment and after one game against London Scottish, Sharp took his place at Twickenham.

I've always been grateful to Malcolm for the faith he showed in me at that time. Shortly after the Varsity Match I was selected as a reserve in the second England trial held at Exeter. At half-time the selectors moved Mike Weston into the centre for the Possibles and I was brought on at fly-half and then to my great surprise and joy I was selected to play for the Rest in the final trial at Twickenham. I was partnered with Johnny Williams, a British Lion in 1955, and the press all seemed to be of the opinion that we had out played Jeeps and Risman but I always felt that at that time they were the better players; both were heroes of mine and they were rightly selected to play against Wales.

I was included as a non travelling reserve but when I returned to Oxford after the holiday there was a telegram from my father saying that I had been asked to report to Richmond on the Friday afternoon. I travelled down on the Thursday evening and found myself sharing a room with Ron Jacobs who had also been called up. At Friday's training session I learnt that poor Bev Risman had pulled a hamstring and was extremely doubtful and he was withdrawn later that afternoon. The selectors called me over and told me that I was going to play and I had literally 10 minutes to practice with Dickie Jeeps—little more than a few passes.

It was Dicks' first game as captain and I will never forget his team talk before the match. He said that the team had two enforced changes, 'Richard is in for Bev and Ron is in for Larry Webb, but these two changes haven't weakened the team at all.' I have never forgotten that. What a nice thing to say, particularly for a chap who was sitting there feeling rather nervous and thinking that he really shouldn't be in the side at all. The game went well and I kept my place. It was a wonderfully successful season; we won the Triple Crown and drew in Paris and what made it all the more memorable was the fact that the same 15 players featured in every match.

Bev was chosen against South Africa and Wales in 1961 before I was included in the team to play Ireland, Bev moved into the centre. I played against the French and was selected for the last match of the season against Scotland but had to withdraw. The week before, Oxford University had travelled to Dublin to play Trinity College. John Wilcox was captain and not wanting to let him down I went against the RFU guidelines and played. The instructions to selected players were that if it was your first cap you weren't supposed to play in the seven days before the match and for everyone else you couldn't play in the week of the match. I pulled a hamstring playing against Trinity, I could hardly walk and was a bit concerned that I wouldn't be selected again. I saw a specialist who confirmed that I couldn't possibly play so I turned up at the training session and cried off, Phil Horrocks-Taylor chosen to take my place. A year later the same thing happened. We were in Edinburgh and the night before the match I went down with flu; Phil was called up to replace me for the second time.

Richard Sharp toured South Africa with the British Lions in the summer of 1962. He played in 11 of the 25 matches; a good record after a fractured cheekbone sidelined him for a month. He recovered in time to play in the third and fourth Tests and remarkably finished the tour as the second highest points scorer only 12 short of John Willcox's total. The May departure and the duration of the tour meant postponing his final exams for 12 months. The college was happy to allow him to do this with the proviso that he took a part time job at St Edward's School in Oxford for the next academic year. It was this which finally took him to the club he had been destined to play for from a particularly young age.

I became a member of the Wasps when I was six weeks old. My father Freddie Sharp and his brother Ivan both played for the club in the 1920s so I always had an emotional attachment with the Wasps and I had a very enjoyable couple of seasons playing there. Early on in the 1962–63 season I alerted the England selectors that I wouldn't be able to travel to New Zealand the following summer as I had to take my finals but that didn't seem to make any difference in their selections for the Championship. I played in the trials which went well and I ended up captaining England against the Rest in the final trial which alerted me that I was possibly being considered as England captain.

The 1963 Championship began in Cardiff on a pitch frozen solid in one of the harshest winters for many years. England won and went to Dublin looking to build on the ideal start that an away win presents. Incessant rain in the build up to the match meant that it was played on a quagmire and the England captain considers his team fortunate to have come away with a scoreless draw. The Irish front five were all British Lions: Sid Millar, Ronnie Dawson, Ray Mcloughlin, Willie John McBride and Bill Mulcahy. We struggled for possession and if it hadn't been for our back row, with

Budge Rogers playing an outstanding game, and John Willcox at full-back catching everything they threw at him we would have lost. We hung on and survived…'

England beat France but the draw in Dublin meant there would be no Triple Crown. However, there was still the Championship and Calcutta Cup to play for which England had held since 1951. Scotland were beaten 10–8 at Twickenham; England were champions, undefeated in the four matches and the Calcutta Cup was retained for another year. For those at the ground and for the large television audience, there was one moment in the game that would live long in the memory. Bernard Cornwell has written about *Sharpe's Devil*, *Sharpe's Enemy*, *Sharpe's Gold* and much else besides but at Twickenham on 16 March 1963 all that was talked about following the match was Sharp's try.

In those days the backs were allowed to stand in line with the front row at a scrum; they weren't offside. We decided that there wasn't a lot you could do from a set scrum that was orthodox as this allowed the opposing backs to be up on you so quickly, you had to have some variation and either a dummy or scissors move could create some uncertainty. It was our put in at a scrum on the 25 to the right of the posts and I arranged with Mike Weston that we should try a scissors move. I received the ball and Mike came towards me but I threw a dummy and managed to break through the mid-field leaving me with the full-back to beat. It later came out that a lot of people thought I was a bit greedy not passing the ball. I had every intention of passing to Jim Roberts, was just about to pass in fact, but I could see that the full-back Blaikie had already bought a dummy which I hadn't started to throw; he was gone, moved on to cover Jim and it was his anticipation which enabled me to score under the posts.

Richard Sharp was a hero, everybody wanted a piece of him but they were wasting their time. Sharp received letters requesting interviews, magazines wanting to do a feature on the England captain, from journalists looking for that one off quote. The demands on him suddenly escalated but he answered every enquiry with a polite but firm no. 'The reason I did that was primarily because I didn't want the skipper to become the centre of attention. I didn't want one person in the team to get the publicity; we were a team and I wanted everyone to know that all we had achieved was down to the team effort. I didn't want to be regarded as more important than anyone else.'

On completion of his finals Sharp took a position at Sherburn School in Dorset. Recently married and with a new job his priorities changed and he began to view his rugby career as all but over.

Teaching at a boarding school is all encompassing. Lessons go through to Saturday lunchtime and because of my sporting background I became involved with the school rugby teams. I carried on playing with the Wasps but I could never train with them and it just meant going up to London on a Saturday morning and heading home immediately after the game. It was far from practical and with great reluctance I decided I had to leave the club. I looked for somewhere nearer home which took me to Bristol where I played for a season but that proved to be just as difficult, particularly the away matches. It got to the point where I wasn't enjoying it any more so I restricted myself to the odd charity game with the occasional appearance for Bristol and it was in that final season the England selectors chose me to captain the team against Australia which was more or less the last game I played.

In 2007 the London Wasps held a dinner to mark the induction of the first eight players into a Hall of Fame. Three were included posthumously but five were on hand to receive the plaudits of club officials, players past and present and supporters. Among the gathering there would have been some who could recall the silky skills of the outside-half now sitting among them and for those who hadn't previously seen it, Sharp's try was shown on the big screen. Joining Richard Sharp at the top table was another player included among the eight inductees; another outside-half who once made his mark on the field but now holds an equally exposed position within the corridors of power, a man who definitely enjoys being at the sharp end of things.

It has taken the best part of 100 years but Twickenham is finally finished. From humble beginnings that started when England met Wales in the first international played on the ground back in 1910 to the 80,000 plus all seating arena it has become, Twickenham is now among the game's finest stadia. From an office block sitting in the shadows of the East Stand the RFU administers English rugby, a sport that has witnessed more significant changes in the last decade than occurred during the rest of its long history.

This is no place for the faint hearted; this is the focal point of what is now a business that reaches way beyond the playing fields that claim the attention for little more than two hours a week. Rugby football hasn't just become a business, it has become a big business, a place where dog eats dog and only the fittest survive—almost a sport played by men in suits.

Rob Andrew is the union's Elite Rugby Director—nothing new there then. For many years he directed rugby operations at the highest level but from the outside-half position rather than from behind a desk, his cultured boot regularly pinning back the opposition when it wasn't keeping the scoreboard ticking over. Whether it was preferable to face a rampaging back row than the press hordes that now so frequently descend on TW1 is debatable or maybe not so; surely most would prefer to take on the back row?

I was always a fly-half. I went to Barnard School as an 11 year old mad keen on soccer but that wasn't an option so it was rugby; I'd never seen a ball before then. It was a case of rolling up your sleeves and getting on with it, I didn't have any choice. Rory Underwood was at Barnard at the same time; we were in the same year, in the same house and played for the same school teams and from the very beginning I was always at fly-half and Rory was always on the wing. Later on I played the odd game at full-back or in the centre but from the age of 11 I was predominantly in the one position; I was a kicker, out of hand and at goal, probably a bit bossy and I ended up in that slot.

I went to Cambridge straight from Barnard. I studied geography and land economy, always regarded as the rugby players' degree. It had that reputation because a lot of post graduates went to Cambridge to do a second degree and it was the subject most chose. I was an undergraduate, specifically at Cambridge to get a degree, but sport quickly took over and I played a lot of rugby and cricket winning Blues in both. Fortunately I did get my degree which led to a career as a chartered surveyor and I eventually spent 10 years working in London.

During this extended period Rob Andrew played for the Wasps, the club with which he is most associated but in what became a long international career he represented several other clubs when he donned the England jersey and there can be few players who have represented England from six different clubs.

I was capped from Cambridge but my first senior rugby club was with

Middlesbrough, the club I joined when I was still at school. When I went up to Cambridge I maintained my affiliation with the club and played for them during the holidays. I played in the Varsity Match in December 1984 and won my first cap in January 1985 so technically I was playing for the two clubs at the time. Later that season I joined Nottingham. My first job took me to the area and although I actually ended up working in Leicester I stayed with Nottingham for the following season during which I won four caps.

Before moving to London I spent the summer of 1986 in Australia playing for the Gordon club in Sydney and it was on my return in September that I joined Wasps and apart from a season spent in France I stayed at the club until 1995. The break came after the 1991 World Cup; I'd always wanted to play in France and through various connections had got to know Pierre Villepreux. Somehow I managed to convince the company I was working for and Toulouse that it would be a good idea if I relocated and they both agreed; it was a brilliant experience, fantastic.

The Rob Andrew rugby C.V. was completed when he travelled to Australia in 1989 to join up with the British Lions as a replacement for the injured Paul Deans. Disappointed not to be included in the original selection he was quickly into action and played in the second and third Tests which the Lions won to pull off a remarkable series victory after being well beaten in the first Test. Many observers believed that his partnership with Robert Jones saw Andrew produce some of his best rugby but although both players were reunited on the 1993 tour to New Zealand, Andrew was partnered by Dewi Morris in the Tests.

One appearance in the 1987 World Cup was followed by six in 1991 when England reached the final only to lose to Australia and five more in South Africa four years later. As a leading player South Africa was the place to be in the summer of 1995, not necessarily for the rugby but more specifically for events off the field, events that would have far reaching repercussions on rugby football and everything that it stood for in sport. One of the last bastions of the amateur ethos was about to be breached.

Almost 100 years had passed since the issue of 'broken time' payments and the formation of the Rugby League. By the early 1990s it looked as if there would be a repeat of that defining moment in the game's history as once again the financial implications of being involved in a sport which had become particularly demanding on the players' time came to the surface.

Understandably, the unions and the IRB were reluctant to get embroiled in an issue which went against the values rugby union was so protective of. Because of their stand off attitude, the door opened for others to look at ways of hi-jacking the sport from under the very noses of those responsible for the day to day running of it—and they very nearly succeeded.

I always felt the game was going to go professional, that there was an inevitability about it. It was just a case of how that would happen, whether the governing body embraced it or if the move would come from elsewhere. As it turned out the pressure from outside eventually forced the IRB into declaring the game open but it could so easily have gone the other way. Had the people involved in trying to establish what would have amounted to a global franchise delivered contracts for signing at the World Cup in 1995 then I believe the game would have gone. The plan was in place and there were several discussions held but the mistake made was that they didn't nail people down while they were in South Africa, they allowed everybody to go home and then tried to do it from a distance. The momentum was in South Africa but they failed to capitalise on it.

It was the only topic of conversation among the players at the banquet which followed the final. The four semi-finalists were there, players from South Africa, New Zealand, France and England and it was all we talked about; South Africa had just won the World Cup in their own country and nobody was discussing it. 'Have you signed? What are you going to do?' And the general feeling was yes, the players were going to sign up. The money on offer wasn't exceptional but it was more than the market started at when the game went professional soon after. There were probably too many loose ends which was why it wasn't sorted in South Africa but had there been a bit more organisation and a bit more detail I think they would have got it away. By allowing everyone to leave South Africa they lost the moment. Then the IRB took the initiative and a few months later we had a professional sport.

It was instant. Newcastle were out of the blocks through the football club and Sir John Hall and I was up there within about three weeks of the game going professional; the World Cup was in June, the IRB opened the game up in August and I was in Newcastle in September. The football club bought Gosforth which at the time was struggling at the bottom of Division 2. Gosforth had a history and achieved some success in the late 70s when the likes of Roger Uttley and Peter Dixon were playing but overall it had all been a bit hit and miss. The drive for me was to try and establish a team in the north east, make it work and get something firmly embedded in the region. It was a leap into the unknown but at the same time very exciting.

It was a fascinating period; a bit like the Wild West for a few years, a real roller coaster, run from the back of a fag packet in many ways. The whole thing was on a knife edge for probably five years before people began to realise that this was here to stay by which time there were casualties. Richmond had gone, Sir John Hall pulled out and the football club sold Newcastle-Gosforth and a lot of other clubs suffered—West Hartlepool, Moseley, Coventry—but it was an interesting period.

By the time he moved to Newcastle, Rob Andrew had won 70 caps and captained England on two occasions. He made his debut against Romania in 1985 and when Will Carling was unable to lead the team against the same opponents in 1989 it was Andrew who took over as captain. The second opportunity came during the 1995 World Cup when he led England against Italy in the group stages of the tournament, Carling rested during what was a hectic first couple of weeks.

I never saw myself as the England captain. I wasn't going to have an extended tenure in the job because of Will but at the same time I was heavily involved in the running of the team because of the position I played, however I'm not convinced that fly-half is a good position to captain the team from. By the very nature of the position you are involved in the running of the game anyway and I don't feel that you need any additional pressure. Fly-halves are better off just focussing on the decision making, the tactical kicking, maybe the goal kicking and becoming a leader of sorts just by having number 10 on their back. If there is somebody else in the team who is able to take on the responsibilities that go with the captaincy then I believe they should be given the job. The fly-half is better off just getting on with playing fly-half; there is enough on their plate without somebody adding the tag 'captain' after their name. To be a really good captain you have to be able to think about everybody else in the team, what happens on and off the field and I feel that distracts from the role of fly-half. No disrespect to other positions but at number 10 you have probably got as much on your plate as any other player; managing the game, running the game, practicing the goal kicking if applicable. You've enough to think about without somebody saying, 'You're captain as well…make sure this is sorted, that's sorted…do the press…' You don't need to burden the fly-half with all that.

Eighteen months into his role as director of rugby at Newcastle Rob Andrew received a series of daily phone calls which eventually resulted in taking his tally of caps to 71. His departure from international rugby following the World Cup in 1995 was expected to be permanent so if a return to the big stage was not exactly of Frank Sinatra proportions his England recall certainly came as a surprise and gave the newspapers another angle to explore in the build up to the match against Wales in Cardiff.

I hadn't planned to retire following the World Cup but when I accepted the Newcastle job I felt it was time to draw a line under that part of my career; move on. I carried on playing at the club but my international days were over, then the phone started ringing. It was the last game of the 1997 Championship and it appeared England were struggling with injuries, particularly at outside-half. I had a couple of calls sounding me out, suggesting if there was a problem would I consider coming back. I thought that there must be somebody else but apparently not and as the week went on it became clear that there was a problem and I agreed to sit on the bench. It was the last match at the old Arms Park, they started knocking it down on the Monday, and I got on for the last 10 minutes. It was also Will Carling's and Jonathan Davies' last games and I enjoyed being involved again but it was a one off.

With his international career now definitely over Andrew continued to play club rugby until 1999 and then fully concentrated on his role as administrator, bringing together the last pieces of the rugby jigsaw that would equip him for the tasks that lay ahead. In 2006 he left Newcastle and returned south; returned to Twickenham the scene of so many of his international experiences but this time it was to an office on the first floor of Rugby House and the all encompassing role of Elite Rugby Director.

The job has got everything. I have to draw on all my experiences as a player both at club level and with England; the time spent as manager of a club; the involvement with a big football club and the board meetings; the coaching and management of leading players; and the business side of the game, I was on the board of Premier Rugby for three years. There isn't a lot I haven't seen and most importantly I understand the RFU. As a player I was involved with the union alongside Will and Brian Moore when we spoke on behalf of the squad, fought our corner. I know how the machine works but there are always curved balls coming at you. That's no different to when I was a player; the curved balls represent the biggest challenges. You have to plan, be as best prepared as possible but there will always be the curved balls and the key is how to deal with them—you know they are going to arrive but you're not quite sure where they are coming from.

Rob Andrew had his critics as a player and nothing has changed since he threw the boots away and started wearing a collar and tie to work. People in high profile positions are there to be shot at whoever they are and if Andrew wasn't sitting behind the desk at Rugby House someone else would be having to take the flak. But it is doubtful if there is anybody better qualified to handle the slings and arrows and the curved balls than England's current Elite Rugby Director.

There is no more appropriate place for this journey to end than sitting in Rob Andrew's office. From the Pall Mall Restaurant in Cockspur Street to Rugby House, Twickenham can be little more than 10 miles as the crow flies. By electing to take the scenic route the mileage was much greater; 1,200 miles maybe, probably more. The timescale covered by the book extended to 137 years; 54 clubs came into the reckoning; and most importantly, the book has discussed 122 captains. This number will increase with time but no matter how many names are added to the list the membership of English rugby's most elite club will never become anything less than exclusive. Teams will always need a captain; someone to lead from the front by example and make those all important decisions. When all is said and done, rugby union remains the greatest of team sports and the captain will always be one of 15 players who take the field. He will always be one among equals.

APPENDIX 1

The captains' records: capped matches
27 March 1871—31 May 2008

The captains are listed in chronological order with the games in which they appeared as captain annotated by number. For example, Fred Stokes led England against Scotland on 27 March 1871—match number 1. Rugby union uses a points scoring system that has been amended on several occasions. In 1890, the International Board provided a format that allowed the introduction of a points system and the results reflect this from match number 37. For consistency, the winning score is recorded first.

1   STOKES, FREDERICK - Forward - Blackheath - 3 matches
1	27 March 1871	Scotland	a	l	1 goal, 1 try to 1 try
2	5 February 1872	Scotland	h	w	1 goal, 1 drop goal, 2 tries to 1 drop goal
3	3 March 1873	Scotland	a	d	no score

2   HAMMERSLEY, ALBERT ST GEORGE - Forward - Marlborough Nomads - 1 match
4	23 February 1874	Scotland	h	w	1 drop goal to 1 try

3   LAWRENCE, HENRY ARNOLD - Forward - Richmond - 2 matches
5	15 February 1875	Ireland	h	w	1 goal, 1 drop goal, 1 try to nil
6	8 March 1875	Scotland	a	d	no score

4   LUSCOMBE, FRANCIS - Forward - Gipsies - 2 matches
7	13 December 1875	Ireland	a	w	1 goal, 1 try to nil
8	6 March 1876	Scotland	h	w	1 goal, 1 try to nil

5   KEWLEY, EDWARD - Forward - Liverpool - 3 matches
9	5 February 1877	Ireland	h	w	2 goals, 2 tries to nil
10	5 March 1877	Scotland	a	l	1 drop goal to nil
11	4 March 1878	Scotland	h	d	no score

6   MARSHALL, MURRAY WYATT - Forward - Blackheath - 1 match
12	11 March 1878	Ireland	a	l	2 goals, 1 try to nil

7   ADAMS, FRANK REGINALD - Forward - Richmond - 2 matches
13	10 March 1879	Scotland	a	d	1 drop goal to 1 goal
14	24 March 1879	Ireland	h	w	2 goals, 1 drop goal, 2 tries to nil

8   STOKES, LENNARD - Three-quarter - Blackheath - 5 matches
15	30 January 1880	Ireland	a	w	1 goal, 1 try to 1 try
16	28 February 1880	Scotland	h	w	2 goals, 3 tries to 1 goal
17	5 February 1881	Ireland	h	w	2 goals, 2 tries to nil
18	19 February 1881	Wales	h	w	7 goals, 6 tries, 1 drop goal to nil
19	19 March 1881	Scotland	a	d	1 goal, 1 try to 1 drop goal, 1 try

9   GURDON, CHARLES - Forward - Richmond - 1 match
20	6 February 1882	Ireland	a	d	2 tries apiece

10   HORNBY, ALBERT NEILSON - Full-back - Manchester - 1 match
21	4 March 1882	Scotland	h	l	2 tries to nil

11   GURDON, EDWARD TEMPLE - Forward - Richmond - 9 matches
22	16 December 1882	Wales	a	w	2 goals, 4 tries to nil
23	5 February 1883	Ireland	h	w	1 goal, 3 tries to 1 try
24	3 March 1883	Scotland	a	w	2 tries to 1 try

25	5 January 1884	Wales	h	w	1 goal, 2 tries to 1 goal
26	4 February 1884	Ireland	a	w	1 goal to nil
27	1 March 1884	Scotland	h	w	1 goal to 1 try
28	3 January 1885	Wales	a	w	1 goal, 4 tries to 1 goal, 1 try
29	7 February 1885	Ireland	h	w	2 tries to 1 try
32	13 March 1886	Scotland	a	d	no score

12 MARRIOTT, CHARLES JOHN BRUCE - Forward - Blackheath - 2 matches

| 30 | 2 January 1886 | Wales | h | w | 1 goal from a mark, 2 tries to 1 goal |
| 31 | 6 February 1886 | Ireland | a | w | 1 try to nil |

13 ROTHERHAM, ALAN - Half-back - Richmond - 3 matches

33	8 January 1887	Wales	a	d	no score
34	5 February 1887	Ireland	a	l	2 goals to nil
35	5 March 1887	Scotland	h	d	1 try apiece

14 BONSOR, FREDERICK - Half-back - Bradford - 1 match

| 36 | 16 February 1889 | Maoris | h | w | 1 goal, 4 tries to nil |

15 STODDART, ANDREW ERNEST - Three-quarter - Blackheath - 4 matches

37	15 February 1890	Wales	h	l	1–0
39	15 March 1890	Ireland	h	w	3–0
46	7 January 1893	Wales	a	l	12–11
48	4 March 1893	Scotland	h	l	8–0

16 HICKSON, JOHN LAWRENCE - Forward - Bradford - 1 match

| 38 | 1 March 1890 | Scotland | a | w | 6–0 |

17 ALDERSON, FREDERICK HODGSON RUDD - Three-quarter - Hartlepool Rovers - 5 matches

40	3 January 1891	Wales	a	w	7–3
41	7 February 1891	Ireland	a	w	9–0
42	7 March 1891	Scotland	h	l	9–3
43	2 January 1892	Wales	h	w	17–0
45	5 March 1892	Scotland	a	w	5–0

18 WOODS, SAMUEL MOSES JAMES - Forward - Wellington, Blackheath - 5 matches

44	6 February 1892	Ireland	h	w	7–0
47	4 February 1893	Ireland	a	w	4–0
52	5 January 1895	Wales	a	w	14–6
53	2 February 1895	Ireland	a	w	6–3
54	9 March 1895	Scotland	h	l	6–3

19 LOCKWOOD, RICHARD EVISON - Wing three-quarter - Heckmondwike - 2 matches

| 49 | 6 January 1894 | Wales | h | w | 24–3 |
| 50 | 3 February 1894 | Ireland | h | l | 7–5 |

20 TAYLOR, ERNEST WILLIAM - Half-back - Rockcliff - 6 matches

51	17 March 1894	Scotland	a	l	6–0
55	4 January 1896	Wales	h	w	25–0
56	1 February 1896	Ireland	h	l	10–4
58	9 January 1897	Wales	a	l	11–0
59	6 February 1897	Ireland	a	l	13–9
60	13 March 1897	Scotland	h	w	12–3

21 MITCHELL, FRANK - Forward - Blackheath - 1 match

| 57 | 14 March 1896 | Scotland | a | l | 11–0 |

22 BYRNE, JAMES FREDERICK - Full-back - Moseley - 3 matches

61	5 February 1898	Ireland	h	l	9–6
62	12 March 1898	Scotland	a	d	3–3
63	2 April 1898	Wales	h	w	14–7

23 ROTHERHAM, ARTHUR - Scrum-half - Richmond - 3 matches

64	7 January 1899	Wales	a	l	26–3
65	4 February 1899	Ireland	a	l	6–0
66	11 March 1899	Scotland	h	l	5–0

24 CATTELL, RICHARD HENRY BURDON - Half-back - Moseley - 1 match

| 67 | 6 January 1900 | Wales | | h | l | 13–3 |

25 DANIELL, JOHN - Forward - Cambridge University, Richmond - 6 matches

68	3 February 1900	Ireland	h	w	15–4
69	10 March 1900	Scotland	a	d	0–0
74	8 February 1902	Ireland	h	w	6–3
75	15 March 1902	Scotland	a	w	6–3
80	13 February 1904	Ireland	h	w	19–0
81	19 March 1904	Scotland	a	l	6–3

26 TAYLOR, JAMES - Centre three-quarter - West Hartlepool - 1 match

70	5 January 1901	Wales	a	l	13–0

27 BUNTING, WILLIAM LOUIS - Centre three-quarter - Moseley, Richmond - 2 matches

71	9 February 1901	Ireland	a	l	10–6
72	9 March 1901	Scotland	h	l	18–3

28 ALEXANDER, HARRY - Forward - Birkenhead Park - 1 match

73	11 January 1902	Wales	h	l	9–8

29 OUGHTRED, BERNARD - Half-back - Hartlepool Rovers - 2 matches

76	10 January 1903	Wales	a	l	21–5
77	14 February 1903	Ireland	a	l	6–0

30 KENDALL, PERCY DALE - Half-back - Birkenhead Park - 1 match

78	21 March 1903	Scotland	h	l	10–6

31 STOUT, FRANK MOXHAM - Forward - Richmond - 4 matches

79	9 January 1904	Wales	h	d	14–14
82	14 January 1905	Wales	a	l	25–0
83	11 February 1905	Ireland	a	l	17–3
84	18 March 1905	Scotland	h	l	8–0

32 CARTWRIGHT, VINCENT HENRY - Forward - Nottingham - 6 matches

85	2 December 1905	New Zealand	h	l	15–0
86	13 January 1906	Wales	h	l	16–3
87	10 February 1906	Ireland	h	l	16–6
88	17 March 1906	Scotland	a	w	9–3
89	22 March 1906	France	a	w	35–8
90	8 December 1906	South Africa	h	d	3–3

33 HILL, BASIL ALEXANDER - Forward - Blackheath - 2 matches

91	5 January 1907	France	h	w	41–13
92	12 January 1907	Wales	a	l	22–0

34 GREEN, JOHN - Forward - Skipton - 1 match

93	9 February 1907	Ireland	a	l	17–9

35 ROBERTS, ERNEST WILLIAM - Forward - RNEC Keyham - 1 match

94	16 March 1907	Scotland	h	l	8–3

36 KELLY, THOMAS STANLEY - Forward - Exeter - 1 match

95	1 January 1908	France	a	w	19–0

37 BIRKETT, JOHN GUY GILBERNE - Centre three-quarter - Harlequins - 5 matches

96	18 January 1908	Wales	h	l	28–18
107	19 March 1910	Scotland	a	w	14–5
108	21 January 1911	Wales	a	l	15–11
109	28 January 1911	France	h	w	37–0
110	11 February 1911	Ireland	a	l	3–0

38 HAMMOND, CHARLES EDWARD LUCAS - Forward - Harlequins - 1 match

97	8 February 1908	Ireland	h	w	13–3

39 SLOCOCK, LANCELOT ANDREW NOEL - Forward - Liverpool - 1 match

98	21 March 1908	Scotland	a	l	16–10

40 LYON, GEORGE HAMILTON D'OYLY - Full-back - United Services Portsmouth - 1 match

99	9 January 1909	Australia	h	l	9–3

41 DIBBLE, ROBERT - Forward - Bridgewater Albion, Newport - 7 matches

100	16 January 1909	Wales	a	l	8–0
101	30 January 1909	France	h	w	22–0
102	13 February 1909	Ireland	a	w	11–5

103	20 March 1909	Scotland	h	l	18–8
112	20 January 1912	Wales	h	w	8–0
113	10 February 1912	Ireland	h	w	15–0
114	16 March 1912	Scotland	a	l	8–3

42 STOOP, ADRIAN DURA - Half-back - Harlequins - 2 matches

104	15 January 1910	Wales	h	w	11–6
105	12 February 1910	Ireland	h	d	0–0

43 MOBBS, EDGAR ROBERT - Wing three-quarter - Northampton - 1 match

106	3 March 1910	France	a	w	11–3

44 GOTLEY, ANTHONY LEFROY HENNIKER - Scrum-half - Blackheath - 1 match

111	18 March 1911	Scotland	h	w	13–8

45 WODEHOUSE, NORMAN ATHERTON - Hooker - United Services Portsmouth - 6 matches

115	8 April 1912	France	a	w	18–8
116	4 January 1913	South Africa	h	l	9–3
117	18 January 1913	Wales	a	w	12–0
118	25 January 1913	France	h	w	20–0
119	8 February 1913	Ireland	a	w	15–4
120	15 March 1913	Scotland	h	w	3–0

46 POULTON, RONALD WILLIAM - Centre three-quarter - Liverpool - 4 matches
later POULTON-PALMER

121	17 January 1914	Wales	h	w	10–9
122	14 February 1914	Ireland	h	w	17–12
123	21 March 1914	Scotland	a	w	16–15
124	13 April 1914	France	a	w	39–13

47 GREENWOOD, JOHN ERIC - Forward - Cambridge University - 4 matches

125	17 January 1920	Wales	a	l	19–5
126	31 January 1920	France	h	w	8–3
127	14 February 1920	Ireland	a	w	14–11
128	20 March 1920	Scotland	h	w	13–4

48 DAVIES, WILLIAM JOHN ABBOTT - Outside-half - United Services Portsmouth - 11 matches

129	15 January 1921	Wales	h	w	18–3
130	12 February 1921	Ireland	h	w	15–0
131	19 March 1921	Scotland	a	w	18–0
132	28 March 1921	France	a	w	10–6
134	11 February 1922	Ireland	a	w	12–3
135	25 February 1922	France	h	d	11–11
136	18 March 1922	Scotland	h	w	11–5
137	20 January 1923	Wales	h	w	7–3
138	10 February 1923	Ireland	h	w	23–5
139	17 March 1923	Scotland	a	w	8–6
140	2 April 1923	France	a	w	12–3

49 BROWN, LEONARD GRAHAM - Prop - Blackheath - 1 match

133	21 January 1922	Wales	a	l	28–6

50 WAKEFIELD, WILLIAM WAVELL - Lock, Number 8 - Leicester, Harlequins - 13 matches

141	19 January 1924	Wales	a	w	17–9
142	9 February 1924	Ireland	a	w	14–3
143	23 February 1924	France	h	w	19–7
144	15 March 1924	Scotland	h	w	19–0
145	3 January 1925	New Zealand	h	l	17–11
146	17 January 1925	Wales	h	w	12–6
147	14 February 1925	Ireland	h	d	6–6
148	21 March 1925	Scotland	a	l	14–11
149	13 April 1925	France	a	w	13–11
150	16 January 1926	Wales	a	d	3–3
151	13 February 1926	Ireland	a	l	19–15
152	27 February 1926	France	h	w	11–0
153	20 March 1926	Scotland	h	l	17–9

51 **CORBETT, LEONARD JAMES** - Centre three-quarter - Bristol - 4 matches

154	15 January 1927	Wales	h	w	11–9
155	12 February 1927	Ireland	h	w	8–6
156	19 March 1927	Scotland	a	l	21–13
157	2 April 1927	France	a	l	3–0

52 **COVE-SMITH, RONALD** - Lock - Old Merchant Taylors', King's College Hospital - 7 matches

158	7 January 1928	N.S.Wales	h	w	18–11
159	21 January 1928	Wales	a	w	10–8
160	11 February 1928	Ireland	a	w	7–6
161	25 February 1928	France	h	w	18–8
162	17 March 1928	Scotland	h	w	6–0
163	19 January 1929	Wales	h	w	8–3
164	9 February 1929	Ireland	h	l	6–5

53 **PERITON, HAROLD GREAVES** - Wing forward - Waterloo - 4 matches

165	16 March 1929	Scotland	a	l	12–6
166	1 April 1929	France	a	w	16–6
167	18 January 1930	Wales	a	w	11–3
168	8 February 1930	Ireland	a	l	4–3

54 **TUCKER, JOHN SAMUEL** - Hooker - Bristol - 3 matches

169	22 February 1930	France	h	w	11–5
170	15 March 1930	Scotland	h	d	0–0
171	17 January 1931	Wales	h	d	11–11

55 **HOWARD, PETER DUNSMORE** - Wing forward - Old Millhillians - 1 match

172	14 February 1931	Ireland	h	l	6–5

56 **AARVOLD, CARL DOUGLAS** - Centre, wing three-quarter - Headingley, Blackheath - 7 matches

173	21 March 1931	Scotland	a	l	28–19
174	6 April 1931	France	a	l	14–13
175	2 January 1932	South Africa	h	l	7–0
176	16 January 1932	Wales	a	l	12–5
177	13 February 1932	Ireland	a	w	11–8
178	19 March 1932	Scotland	h	w	16–3
179	21 January 1933	Wales	h	l	7–3

57 **NOVIS, ANTHONY LESLIE** - Centre three-quarter - Blackheath - 2 matches

180	11 February 1933	Ireland	h	w	17–6
181	18 March 1933	Scotland	a	l	3–0

58 **GADNEY, BERNARD** - Scrum-half - Leicester - 8 matches

182	20 January 1934	Wales	a	w	9–0
183	10 February 1934	Ireland	a	w	13–3
184	17 March 1934	Scotland	h	w	6–3
187	16 March 1935	Scotland	a	l	10–7
188	4 January 1936	New Zealand	h	w	13–0
189	18 January 1936	Wales	a	d	0–0
190	8 February 1936	Ireland	a	l	6–3
191	21 March 1936	Scotland	h	w	9–8

59 **KENDREW, DOUGLAS ANDREW** - Prop - Leicester - 2 matches

185	19 January 1935	Wales	h	d	3–3
186	9 February 1935	Ireland	h	w	14–3

60 **OWEN-SMITH, HAROLD GEOFFREY** - Full-back - St Mary's Hospital - 3 matches

192	16 January 1937	Wales	h	w	4–3
193	13 February 1937	Ireland	h	w	9–8
194	20 March 1937	Scotland	a	w	6–3

61 **CRANMER, PETER** - Centre three-quarter - Moseley - 2 matches

195	15 January 1938	Wales	a	l	14–9
196	12 February 1938	Ireland	a	w	36–14

62 **TOFT, HENRY BERT** - Hooker - Waterloo - 4 matches

197	19 March 1938	Scotland	h	l	21–16
198	21 January 1939	Wales	h	w	3–0
199	11 February 1939	Ireland	h	l	5–0
200	18 March 1939	Scotland	a	w	9–6

63 MYCOCK, JOSEPH - Lock - Sale - 2 matches

201	18 January 1947	Wales	a	w	9–6
202	8 February 1947	Ireland	a	l	22–0

64 HEATON, JOHN - Centre three-quarter - Waterloo - 2 matches

203	15 March 1947	Scotland	h	w	24–5
204	19 April 1947	France	h	w	6–3

65 SCOTT, EDWARD KEITH - Centre three-quarter - Redruth - 3 matches

205	3 January 1948	Australia	h	l	11–0
207	14 February 1948	Ireland	h	l	11–10
208	20 March 1948	Scotland	a	l	6–3

66 KEMP, THOMAS ARTHUR - Outside-half - Richmond - 1 match

206	17 January 1948	Wales	h	d	3–3

67 WEIGHILL, ROBERT HAROLD GEORGE - Number 8 - Harlequins - 1 match

209	29 March 1948	France	a	l	15–0

68 HALL, NORMAN MACLEOD - Outside-half, full-back - Huddersfield, Richmond - 13 matches

210	15 January 1949	Wales	a	l	9–3
211	12 February 1949	Ireland	a	l	14–5
222	15 January 1952	South Africa	h	l	8–3
223	19 January 1952	Wales	h	l	8–6
224	15 March 1952	Scotland	a	w	19–3
225	29 March 1952	Ireland	h	w	3–0
226	5 April 1952	France	a	w	6–3
227	17 January 1953	Wales	a	w	8–3
228	14 February 1953	Ireland	a	d	9–9
229	28 February 1953	France	h	w	11–0
230	21 March 1953	Scotland	h	w	26–8
236	22 January 1955	Wales	a	l	3–0
237	12 February 1955	Ireland	a	d	6–6

69 PREECE, IVOR - Outside-half - Coventry - 6 matches

212	26 February 1949	France	h	w	8–3
213	19 March 1949	Scotland	h	w	19–3
214	21 January 1950	Wales	h	l	11–5
215	11 February 1950	Ireland	h	w	3–0
216	25 February 1950	France	a	l	6–3
217	18 March 1950	Scotland	a	l	13–11

70 ROBERTS, VICTOR GEORGE - Wing forward - Penryn - 1 match

218	20 January 1951	Wales	a	l	23–5

71 KENDALL-CARPENTER, JOHN MAC GREGOR - Number 8 - Oxford University, Penzance and Newlyn - 3 matches

219	10 February 1951	Ireland	a	l	3–0
220	24 February 1951	France	h	l	11–3
221	17 March 1951	Scotland	h	w	5–3

72 STIRLING, ROBERT VICTOR - Prop - Wasps - 5 matches

231	16 January 1954	Wales	h	w	9–6
232	30 January 1954	New Zealand	h	l	5–0
233	13 February 1954	Ireland		w	14–3
234	20 March 1954	Scotland	a	w	13–3
235	10 April 1954	France	a	l	11–3

73 YOUNG, PETER DALTON - Lock - Dublin Wanderers - 2 matches

238	26 February 1955	France	h	l	16–9
239	19 March 1955	Scotland	h	w	9–6

74 EVANS, ERIC - Hooker - Sale - 13 matches

240	21 January 1956	Wales	h	l	8–3
241	11 February 1956	Ireland	h	w	22–0
242	17 March 1956	Scotland	a	w	11–6
243	14 April 1956	France	a	l	14–9
244	19 January 1957	Wales	a	w	3–0
245	9 February 1957	Ireland	a	w	6–0

246	23 February 1957	France	h	w	9–5
247	16 March 1957	Scotland	h	w	16–3
248	18 January 1958	Wales	h	d	3–3
249	1 February 1958	Australia	h	w	9–6
250	8 February 1958	Ireland	h	w	6–0
251	1 March 1958	France	a	w	14–0
252	15 March 1958	Scotland	a	d	3–3

75 BUTTERFIELD, JEFFREY - Centre three-quarter - Northampton - 4 matches

253	17 January 1959	Wales	a	l	5–0
254	14 February 1959	Ireland	a	w	3–0
255	28 February 1959	France	h	d	3–3
256	21 March 1959	Scotland	h	d	3–3

76 JEEPS, RICHARD ERIC GAUTRY - Scrum-half - Northampton - 13 matches

257	16 January 1960	Wales	h	w	14–6
258	13 February 1960	Ireland	h	w	8–5
259	27 February 1960	France	a	d	3–3
260	19 March 1960	Scotland	a	w	21–12
261	7 January 1961	South Africa	h	l	5–0
262	21 January 1961	Wales	a	l	6–3
263	11 February 1961	Ireland	a	l	11–8
264	25 February 1961	France	h	d	5–5
265	18 March 1961	Scotland	h	w	6–0
266	20 January 1962	Wales	h	d	0–0
267	10 February 1962	Ireland	h	w	16–0
268	24 February 1962	France	a	l	13–0
269	17 March 1962	Scotland	a	d	3–3

77 SHARP, RICHARD ADRIAN WILLIAM - Outside-half - Wasps, Bristol - 5 matches

270	19 January 1963	Wales	a	w	13–6
271	9 February 1963	Ireland	a	d	0–0
272	23 February 1963	France	h	w	6–5
273	16 March 1963	Scotland	h	w	10–8
290	7 January 1967	Australia	h	l	23–11

78 WESTON, MICHAEL PHILIP - Centre three-quarter, outside-half - Durham City - 5 matches

274	25 May 1963	New Zealand	a	l	21–11
275	1 June 1963	New Zealand	a	l	9–6
276	4 June 1963	Australia	a	l	18–9
298	24 February 1968	France	a	l	14–9
299	16 March 1968	Scotland	a	w	8–6

79 WILLCOX, JOHN GRAHAM - Full-back - Harlequins - 3 matches

277	4 January 1964	New Zealand	h	l	14–0
278	18 January 1964	Wales	h	d	6–6
279	8 February 1964	Ireland	h	l	18–5

80 JACOBS, CHARLES RONALD - Prop - Northampton - 2 matches

| 280 | 22 February 1964 | France | a | w | 6–3 |
| 281 | 21 March 1964 | Scotland | a | l | 15–6 |

81 PERRY, DAVID GORDON - Number 8 - Bedford - 4 matches

282	16 January 1965	Wales	a	l	14–3
283	13 February 1965	Ireland	a	l	5–0
284	27 February 1965	France	h	w	9–6
285	20 March 1965	Scotland	h	d	3–3

82 ROGERS, DEREK PRIOR - Wing forward - Bedford - 7 matches

286	15 January 1966	Wales	h	l	11–6
287	12 February 1966	Ireland	h	d	6–6
288	26 February 1966	France	a	l	13–0
289	19 March 1966	Scotland	a	l	6–3
301	8 February 1969	France	h	w	22–8
302	15 March 1969	Scotland	h	w	8–3
303	12 April 1969	Wales	a	l	30–9

83   JUDD, PHILIP EDWARD - Prop - Coventry - 5 matches

291	11 February 1967	Ireland	a	w	8–3
292	25 February 1967	France	h	l	16–12
293	18 March 1967	Scotland	h	w	27–14
294	15 April 1967	Wales	a	l	34–21
295	4 November 1967	New Zealand	h	l	23–11

84   MCFADYEAN, COLIN WILLIAM - Centre-three quarter - Moseley - 2 matches

296	20 January 1968	Wales	h	d	11–11
297	10 February 1968	Ireland	h	d	9–9

85   GREENWOOD, JOHN RICHARD HEATON - Wing forward - Waterloo - 1 match

300	8 February 1969	Ireland	a	l	17–15

86   HILLER, ROBERT - Full-back - Harlequins - 7 matches

304	20 December 1969	South Africa	h	w	11–8
305	14 February 1970	Ireland	h	w	9–3
306	28 February 1970	Wales	h	l	17–13
307	21 March 1970	Scotland	a	l	14–5
311	27 February 1971	France	h	d	14–14
315	15 January 1972	Wales	h	l	12–3
316	12 February 1972	Ireland	h	l	16–12

87   TAYLOR, ROBERT BAINBRIDGE - Wing forward - Northampton - 1 match

308	18 April 1970	France	a	l	35–13

88   BUCKNELL, ANTHONY LAUNCE - Wing forward - Richmond - 1 match

309	16 January 1971	Wales	a	l	22–6

89   SPENCER, JOHN SOUTHERN - Centre three-quarter - Headingley - 4 matches

310	13 February 1971	Ireland	a	w	9–6
312	20 March 1971	Scotland	h	l	16–15
313	27 March 1971	Scotland	a	l	26–6
314	17 April 1971	RFU President's XV	h	l	28 –11

90   DIXON, PETER JOHN - Wing forward - Harlequins - 2 matches

317	26 February 1972	France	a	l	37–12
318	18 March 1972	Scotland	a	l	23–9

91   PULLIN, JOHN VIVIAN - Hooker - Bristol - 13 matches

319	3 June 1972	South Africa	a	w	18–9
320	6 January 1973	New Zealand	h	l	9–0
321	20 January 1973	Wales	a	l	25–9
322	10 February 1973	Ireland	a	l	18–9
323	24 February 1973	France	h	w	14–6
324	17 March 1973	Scotland	h	w	20–13
325	15 September 1973	New Zealand	a	w	16–10
326	17 November 1973	Australia	h	w	20–3
327	2 February 1974	Scotland	a	l	16–14
328	16 February 1974	Ireland	h	l	26–21
329	2 March 1974	France	a	d	12–12
330	16 March 1974	Wales	h	w	16–12
336	31 May 1975	Australia	a	l	30–21

92   COTTON, FRANCIS EDWARD - Prop - Coventry - 3 matches

331	18 January 1975	Ireland	a	l	12–9
332	1 February 1975	France	h	l	27–20
333	15 February 1975	Wales	a	l	20–5

93   NEARY, ANTHONY - Wing forward - Broughton Park - 7 matches

334	15 March 1975	Scotland	h	w	7–6
335	24 May 1975	Australia	a	l	16–9
337	3 January 1976	Australia	h	w	23–6
338	17 January 1976	Wales	h	l	21–9
339	21 February 1976	Scotland	a	l	22–12
340	6 March 1976	Ireland	h	l	13–12
341	20 March 1976	France	a	l	30–9

94 UTTLEY, ROGER MILES - Number 8 - Gosforth - 5 matches

342	15 January 1977	Scotland	h	w	26–6
343	5 February 1977	Ireland	a	w	4–0
344	19 February 1977	France	h	l	4–3
345	5 March 1977	Wales	a	l	14–9
351	3 February 1979	Scotland	h	d	7–7

95 BEAUMONT, WILLIAM BLACKLEDGE - Lock - Fylde - 21 matches

346	21 January 1978	France	a	l	15–6
347	4 February 1978	Wales	h	l	9–6
348	4 March 1978	Scotland	a	w	15–0
349	18 March 1978	Ireland	h	w	15–9
350	25 November 1978	New Zealand	h	l	16–6
352	17 February 1979	Ireland	a	l	12–7
353	3 March 1979	France	h	w	7–6
354	17 March 1979	Wales	a	l	27–3
355	24 November 1979	New Zealand	h	l	10–9
356	19 January 1980	Ireland	h	w	24–9
357	2 February 1980	France	a	w	17–13
358	16 February 1980	Wales	h	w	9–8
359	15 March 1980	Scotland	a	w	30–18
360	17 January 1981	Wales	a	l	21–19
361	21 February 1981	Scotland	h	w	23–17
362	7 March 1981	Ireland	a	w	10–6
363	21 March 1981	France	h	l	16–12
364	30 May 1981	Argentina	a	d	19–19
365	6 June 1981	Argentina	a	w	12–6
366	2 January 1982	Australia	h	w	15–11
367	16 January 1982	Scotland	a	d	9–9

96 SMITH, STEPHEN JAMES - Scrum-half - Sale - 5 matches

368	6 February 1982	Ireland	h	l	16–15
369	29 February 1982	France	a	w	27–15
370	6 March 1982	Wales	h	w	17–7
371	15 January 1983	France	h	l	19–15
372	5 February 1983	Wales	a	d	13–13

97 SCOTT, JOHN PHILLIP - Number 8, lock - Cardiff - 4 matches

373	5 March 1983	Scotland	h	l	22–12
374	19 March 1983	Ireland	a	l	25–15
380	2 June 1984	South Africa	a	l	33–15
381	9 June 1984	South Africa	a	l	35–9

98 WHEELER, PETER JOHN - Hooker - Leicester - 5 matches

375	19 November 1983	New Zealand	h	w	15–9
376	4 February 1984	Scotland	a	l	18–6
377	18 February 1984	Ireland	h	w	12–9
378	3 March 1984	France	a	l	32–18
379	17 March 1984	Wales	h	l	24–15

99 MELVILLE, NIGEL DAVID - Scrum-half - Wasps - 7 matches

382	3 November 1984	Australia	h	l	19–3
390	17 January 1986	Wales	h	w	21–18
391	15 February 1986	Scotland	a	l	33–6
392	1 March 1986	Ireland	h	w	25–20
393	15 March 1986	France	a	l	29–10
404	5 March 1988	Scotland	a	w	9–6
405	19 March 1988	Ireland	h	w	35–3

100 DODGE, PAUL WILLIAM - Centre three-quarter - Leicester - 7 matches

383	5 January 1985	Romania	h	w	22–15
384	2 February 1985	France	h	d	9–9
385	16 March 1985	Scotland	h	w	10–7
386	30 March 1985	Ireland	a	l	13–10
387	20 April 1985	Wales	a	l	24–15

388	1 June 1985	New Zealand	a	l	18–13	
389	8 June 1985	New Zealand	a	l	42–15	

101 HILL, RICHARD JOHN - Scrum-half - Bath - 3 matches

394	7 February 1987	Ireland	a	l	17–0	
395	21 February 1987	France	h	l	19–15	
396	7 March 1987	Wales	a	l	19–12	

102 HARRISON, MICHAEL EDWARD - Wing three-quarter - Wakefield - 7 matches

397	4 April 1987	Scotland	h	w	21–12	
398	23 May 1987	Australia	a	l	19–6	RWC
399	30 May 1987	Japan	a	w	60–7	RWC
400	3 June 1987	USA	a	w	34–6	RWC
401	8 June 1987	Wales	a	l	16–3	RWC
402	16 January 1988	France	a	l	10–9	
403	6 February 1988	Wales	h	l	11–3	

103 ORWIN, JOHN - Lock - Bedford - 3 matches

406	23 April 1988	Ireland	a	w	21–10	
407	29 May 1988	Australia	a	l	22–16	
408	12 June 1988	Australia	a	l	28–8	

104 HARDING, RICHARD MARK - Scrum-half - Bristol - 1 match

409	16 June 1988	Fiji	a	w	25–12	

105 CARLING, WILLIAM DAVID CHARLES - Centre three-quarter - Harlequins - 59 matches

410	5 November 1988	Australia	h	w	28–19	
411	4 February 1989	Scotland	h	d	12–12	
412	18 February 1989	Ireland	a	w	16–3	
413	4 March 1989	France	h	w	11–0	
414	18 March 1989	Wales	a	l	12–9	
416	4 November 1989	Fiji	h	w	58–23	
417	20 January 1990	Ireland	h	w	23–0	
418	3 February 1990	France	a	w	26–7	
419	17 February 1990	Wales	h	w	34–6	
420	17 March 1990	Scotland	a	l	13–7	
421	28 July 1990	Argentina	a	w	25–12	
422	4 August 1990	Argentina	a	l	15–13	
423	3 November 1990	Argentina	h	w	51–0	
424	19 January 1991	Wales	a	w	25–6	
425	16 February 1991	Scotland	h	w	21–12	
426	2 March 1991	Ireland	a	w	16–7	
427	16 March 1991	France	h	w	21–19	
428	20 July 1991	Fiji	a	w	28–12	
429	27 July 1991	Australia	a	l	40–15	
430	3 October 1991	New Zealand	h	l	18–12	RWC
431	8 October 1991	Italy	h	w	36–6	RWC
432	11 October 1991	United States	h	w	37–9	RWC
433	19 October 1991	France	a	w	19–10	RWC
434	26 October 1991	Scotland	a	w	9–6	RWC
435	2 November 1991	Australia	h	l	12–6	RWC
436	18 January 1992	Scotland	a	w	25–7	
437	1 February 1992	Ireland	h	w	38–9	
438	15 February 1992	France	a	w	31–13	
439	7 March 1992	Wales	h	w	24–0	
440	17 October 1992	Canada	h	w	26–13	
441	14 November 1992	South Africa	h	w	33–16	
442	16 January 1993	France	h	w	16–15	
443	6 February 1993	Wales	a	l	10–9	
444	6 March 1993	Scotland	h	w	26–12	
445	20 March 1993	Ireland	a	l	17–3	
446	27 November 1993	New Zealand	h	w	15–9	
447	5 February 1994	Scotland	a	w	15–14	
448	19 February 1994	Ireland	h	l	13–12	
449	5 March 1994	France	a	w	18–14	

450	19 March 1994	Wales	h	w	15–8	
451	4 June 1994	South Africa	a	w	32–15	
452	11 June 1994	South Africa	a	l	27–9	
453	12 November 1994	Romania	h	w	54–3	
454	10 December 1994	Canada	h	w	60–19	
455	21 January 1995	Ireland	a	w	20–8	
456	4 February 1995	France	h	w	31–10	
457	18 February 1995	Wales	a	w	23–9	
458	18 March 1995	Scotland	h	w	24–12	
459	27 May 1995	Argentina	a	w	24–18	RWC
461	4 June 1995	Western Samoa	a	w	44–22	RWC
462	11 June 1995	Australia	a	w	25–22	RWC
463	18 June 1995	New Zealand	a	l	45–29	RWC
464	22 June 1995	France	a	l	19–9	RWC
465	18 November 1995	South Africa	h	l	24–14	
466	16 December 1995	Western Samoa	h	w	27–9	
467	20 January 1996	France	a	l	15–12	
468	3 February 1996	Wales	h	w	21–15	
469	2 March 1996	Scotland	a	w	18–9	
470	16 March 1996	Ireland	h	w	28–15	

106 ANDREW, CHRISTOPHER ROBERT - Outside-half - Wasps - 2 matches

| 415 | 13 May 1989 | Romania | a | w | 58–3 | |
| 460 | 31 May 1995 | Italy | a | w | 27–20 | RWC |

107 de GLANVILLE, PHILLIP RANULPH - Centre three-quarter - Bath - 8 matches

471	23 November 1996	Italy	h	w	54–21	
473	1 February 1997	Scotland	h	w	41–13	
474	15 February 1997	Ireland	a	w	46–6	
475	1 March 1997	France	h	l	23–20	
476	15 March 1997	Wales	a	w	34–13	
477	31 May 1997	Argentina	a	w	46–20	
478	7 June 1997	Argentina	a	l	33–13	
479	12 July 1997	Australia	a	l	25–6	

108 LEONARD, JASON - Prop - Harlequins - 2 matches

| 472 | 14 December 1996 | Argentina | h | w | 20–18 | |
| 545 | 23 August 2003 | Wales | a | w | 43–9 | |

109 DALLAGLIO, LAWRENCE BRUNO NERO - Number 8, wing forward - Wasps - later London Wasps - 22 matches

480	15 November 1997	Australia	h	d	15–15	
481	22 November 1997	New Zealand	h	l	25–8	
482	29 November 1997	South Africa	h	l	29–11	
483	6 December 1997	New Zealand	h	d	26–26	
484	7 February 1998	France	a	l	24–17	
485	21 February 1998	Wales	h	w	60–26	
486	22 March 1998	Scotland	a	w	34–20	
487	4 April 1998	Ireland	h	w	35–17	
494	28 November 1998	Australia	h	l	12–11	
495	5 December 1998	South Africa	h	w	13–7	
496	20 February 1999	Scotland	h	w	24–21	
497	6 March 1999	Ireland	a	w	27–15	
498	20 March 1999	France	h	w	21–10	
499	11 April 1999	Wales	a	l	32–31	
555	15 February 2004	Italy	a	w	50–9	
556	21 February 2004	Scotland	a	w	35–13	
557	6 March 2004	Ireland	h	l	19–13	
558	20 March 2004	Wales	h	w	31–21	
559	27 March 2004	France	a	l	24–21	
560	12 June 2004	New Zealand	a	l	36–3	
561	19 June 2004	New Zealand	a	l	36–12	
562	26 June 2004	Australia	a	l	51–15	

110 DIPROSE, ANTHONY - Number 8 - Saracens - 1 match

| 488 | 6 June 1998 | Australia | a | l | 76–0 | |

111 DAWSON, MATTHEW JAMES SUTHERLAND - Scrum-half - Northampton - 9 matches

489	20 June 1998	New Zealand	a	l	64–22	
490	27 June 1998	New Zealand	a	l	40–10	
491	4 July 1998	South Africa	a	l	18–0	
508	5 February 2000	Ireland	h	w	50–18	
509	19 February 2000	France	a	w	15–9	
510	4 March 2000	Wales	h	w	46–12	
511	18 March 2000	Italy	a	w	59–12	
512	2 April 2000	Scotland	a	l	19–13	
525	20 October 2001	Ireland	a	l	20–14	

112 JOHNSON, MARTIN OSBORNE - Lock - Leicester - 39 matches

492	14 November 1998	Netherlands	h	w	110–0	
493	22 November 1998	Italy	h	w	23–15	
500	26 June 1999	Australia	a	l	22–15	
501	21 August 1999	United States	h	w	106–8	
502	28 August 1999	Canada	h	w	36–11	
503	2 October 1999	Italy	h	w	67–7	RWC
504	9 October 1999	New Zealand	h	l	30–16	RWC
505	15 October 1999	Tonga	h	w	101–10	RWC
506	20 October 1999	Fiji	h	w	45–24	RWC
507	24 October 1999	South Africa	a	l	44–21	RWC
513	17 June 2000	South Africa	a	l	18–13	
514	24 June 2000	South Africa	a	w	27–22	
515	18 November 2000	Australia	h	w	22–19	
516	25 November 2000	Argentina	h	w	19–0	
517	2 December 2000	South Africa	h	w	25–17	
518	3 February 2001	Wales	a	w	44–15	
519	17 February 2001	Italy	h	w	80–23	
520	3 March 2001	Scotland	h	w	43–3	
521	7 April 2001	France	h	w	48–19	
528	24 November 2001	South Africa	h	w	29–9	
529	2 February 2002	Scotland	a	w	29–3	
530	16 February 2002	Ireland	h	w	45–11	
531	2 March 2002	France	a	l	20–15	
535	9 November 2002	New Zealand	h	w	31–28	
536	16 November 2002	Australia	h	w	32–31	
537	23 November 2002	South Africa	h	w	53–3	
538	15 February 2003	France	h	w	25–17	
539	22 February 2003	Wales	a	w	26–9	
541	22 March 2003	Scotland	h	w	40–9	
542	30 March 2003	Ireland	a	w	42–6	
543	14 June 2003	New Zealand	a	w	15–13	
544	21 June 2003	Australia	a	w	25–14	
547	6 September 2003	France	h	w	45–14	
548	12 October 2003	Georgia	a	w	84–6	RWC
549	18 October 2003	South Africa	a	w	25–6	RWC
550	26 October 2003	Samoa	a	w	35–22	RWC
552	9 November 2003	Wales	a	w	28–17	RWC
553	16 November 2003	France	a	w	24–7	RWC
554	22 November 2003	Australia	a	w	20–17	RWC

113 BRACKEN, KYRAN PAUL PATRICK - Scrum-half - Saracens - 3 matches

522	2 June 2001	Canada	a	w	22–10	
523	9 June 2001	Canada	a	w	59–20	
524	16 June 2001	United States	a	w	48–19	

114 BACK, NEIL ANTHONY - Wing forward - Leicester - 4 matches

526	10 November 2001	Australia	h	w	21–15	
527	17 November 2001	Romania	h	w	134–0	
532	23 March 2002	Wales	h	w	50–10	
533	7 April 2002	Italy	a	w	45–9	

115 VICKERY, PHILIP JOHN - Prop - Gloucester, London Wasps - 15 matches

534	22 June 2002	Argentina	a	w	26–18	
551	2 November 2003	Uruguay	a	w	111–13	RWC
585	3 February 2007	Scotland	h	w	42–20	
586	10 February 2007	Italy	h	w	20–7	
587	24 February 2007	Ireland	a	l	43–13	
592	4 August 2007	Wales	h	w	62–5	
594	18 August 2007	France	a	l	22–9	
595	8 September 2007	United States	a	w	28–10	RWC
599	6 October 2007	Australia	a	w	12–10	RWC
600	13 October 2007	France	a	w	14–9	RWC
601	20 October 2007	South Africa	a	l	15–6	RWC
602	2 February 2008	Wales	h	l	26–19	
604	23 February 2008	France	a	w	24–13	
605	8 March 2008	Scotland	a	l	l5–9	
606	15 March 2008	Ireland	h	w	33–10	

116 WILKINSON, JONATHAN (JONNY) PETER - Outside-half - Newcastle Falcons - 2 matches

| 540 | 9 March 2003 | Italy | h | w | 40–5 | |
| 591 | 2 June 2007 | South Africa | a | l | 55–22 | |

117 WEST, DORIAN EDWARD - Hooker - Leicester - 1 match

| 546 | 30 August 2003 | France | a | l | 17–16 | |

118 ROBINSON, JASON THORPE - Full-back, wing three-quarter - Sale Sharks - 7 matches

563	13 November 2004	Canada	h	w	70–0	
564	20 November 2004	South Africa	h	w	32–16	
565	27 November 2004	Australia	h	l	21–19	
566	5 February 2005	Wales	a	l	11–9	
567	13 February 2005	France	h	l	18–17	
568	27 February 2005	Ireland	a	l	19–13	
590	26 May 2007	South Africa	a	l	58–10	

119 CORRY, MARTIN EDWARD - Number 8, wing forward, lock - Leicester - 17 matches

569	12 March 2005	Italy	h	w	39–7	
570	19 March 2005	Scotland	h	w	43–22	
571	12 November 2005	Australia	h	w	26–16	
572	19 November 2005	New Zealand	h	l	23–19	
573	26 November 2005	Samoa	h	w	40–13	
574	4 February 2006	Wales	h	w	47–13	
575	11 February 2006	Italy	a	w	31–16	
576	25 February 2006	Scotland	a	l	18–12	
577	12 March 2006	France	a	l	31–6	
578	18 March 2006	Ireland	h	l	28–24	
581	5 November 2006	New Zealand	h	l	41–20	
582	11 November 2006	Argentina	h	l	25–18	
583	18 November 2006	South Africa	h	w	23–21	
584	25 November 2006	South Africa	h	l	25–14	
596	14 September 2007	South Africa	a	l	36–0	RWC
597	22 September 2007	Samoa	a	w	44–22	RWC
598	28 September 2007	Tonga	a	w	36–20	RWC

120 SANDERSON, PATRICK - Number 8 - Worcester Warriors - 2 matches

| 579 | 11 June 2006 | Australia | a | l | 34–3 | |
| 580 | 17 June 2006 | Australia | a | l | 43–18 | |

121 CATT, MICHAEL JOHN - Centre three-quarter - London Irish - 3 matches

588	11 March 2007	France	h	w	26–18	
589	17 March 2007	Wales	a	l	27–18	
593	11 August 2007	France	h	l	21–15	

122 BORTHWICK, STEPHEN WILLIAM - Lock - Bath - 1 match

| 603 | 10 February 2008 | Italy | a | w | 23–19 | |

APPENDIX 2

Club representation of English captains in capped matches
27 March 1871—31 May 2008

The statistics are based on the total number of matches in which players representing the respective clubs captained England.

Club	Matches	Club	Matches
Harlequins	91	Cardiff	4
Leicester	87	Saracens	4
Wasps, London Wasps	53	London Irish	3
Richmond	42	Newport	3
Blackheath	30	Redruth	3
Northampton	30	St Mary's Hospital	3
Sale/Sale Sharks	27	Birkenhead Park	2
Bristol	22	Bradford	2
Fylde	21	Wanderers	2
United Services Portsmouth	18	Gipsies	2
Bedford	14	Gloucester	2
Coventry	14	Heckmondwike	2
Bath	12	Huddersfield	2
Waterloo	11	King's College Hospital	2
Moseley	9	Newcastle Falcons	2
Liverpool	8	Penzance-Newlyn	2
Broughton Park	7	Wellington	2
Hartlepool Rovers	7	Worcester	2
Wakefield	7	Exeter	1
Cambridge University	6	Manchester	1
Headingley	6	Marlborough Nomads	1
Nottingham	6	Old Millhillians	1
Rockcliff	6	Oxford University	1
Durham City	5	Penryn	1
Gosforth	5	RNEC Keyham	1
Old Merchant Taylors'	5	Skipton	1
Bridgewater And Albion	4	West Hartlepool	1

BIBLIOGRAPHY

Chester, Rod, McMillan, Neville and Palenski, Ron, *The Encyclopaedia of New Zealand Rugby*, Hodder Moa Beckett, 2000

Chester, Rod, McMillan, Neville and Palenski, Ron, *Men in Black*, Hodder Moa Beckett, 2000

Cleary, Mick, *Wounded Pride - The Official Book of the Lions Tour to Australia 2001*, Mainstream Publishing, 2001

Cooper, Ian, *Immortal Harlequin - The Story of Adrian Stoop*, Tempus Publishing Ltd, 2004

Fox, Dave, Bogle, Ken and Hoskins, Mark, *A Century of the All Blacks in Britain and Ireland*, Tempus Publishing Ltd, 2006

Frost, David, The Bowring Story of the Varsity Match, MacDonald Queen Anne Press, 1998

Godwin, Terry, *The International Rugby Championship 188-1983*, Collins Willow, 1984

Harding, Rowe, *Rugby: Reminiscences and Opinions*, Pilot Press, 1929

Hedley, Alan, *The Newcastle Rugby Story*, Tempus Publishing Ltd, 2000

Jenkins, Vivian, *Lions Rampant - The 1955 British Isles Rugby Tour of South Africa*, Cassell & Co Ltd, 1956

Jenkins, Vivian, *Lions Down Under*, Cassell & Co Ltd, 1960

Mace, John, *The History of Royal Air Force Rugby 1919-1999*, The Royal Air Force Rugby Union, 2000

Malin, Ian and Griffiths, John, *The Essential History of Rugby Union - England*, Headline Book Publishing, 2003

Marshall, Revd. F. (ed), *Football: The Rugby Union Game*, Cassell and Co. Ltd, 1892

Maule, Raymond, *The Complete Who's Who of England Rugby Union Internationals*, Breedon Books, 1992

McGeechan, Ian, *So Close to Glory - The Lions in New Zealand 1993*, Queen Anne Press, 1993

McGeechan, Ian with Cleary, Mick, *Heroes All - The Official Book of the Lions in South Africa 1997*, Hodder and Stoughton, 1997

McLean, Terry, *They Missed the Bus - Kirkpatrick's All Blacks of 1972/73*, A.H. & A.W. Reed Ltd, 1973

Moorhouse, Geoffrey, *A People's Game - The Official History of Rugby League 1895-1995*, Hodder and Stoughton, 1995

Reason, John, *The 1968 Lions*, Eyre and Spottiswoode, 1968

Reason, John, *The Unbeaten Lions - 1974 Tour of South Africa*, Rugby Football Books Ltd, 1974

Reason, John, *Lions Down Under - 1977 Tour of New Zealand*, Rugby Football Books Ltd, 1977

Reason, John, *Backs to the Wall - 1980 British Lions Tour of South Africa*, Rugby Football Books Ltd, 1980

Sewell, E.H.D., *Rugby Football Today*, John Murray, 1931

Thomas, Clem, *The History of the British Lions*, Mainstream Publishing, 1996

Thomas, J.B.G., *Lions Courageous*, Stanley Paul & Co Ltd, 1960

Thomas, J.B.G., *Lions Among the Springboks*, Stanley Paul & Co Ltd, 1963

Thomas, J.B.G., *Lions at Bay*, Pelham Books, 1966

Titley, U.A. and McWhirter, Ross, *Centenary History of the Rugby Football Union*, RFU, 1970

Townsend Collins, W.J., *Rugby Recollections*, R.H. Johns, 1948

Wakefield, W.W. and Marshall, H.P., *Rugger*, Longmans, Green and Co., 1930

Wakelam, Captain H.B.T. (ed), *The Game Goes On*, Arthur Barker Ltd, 1936

Yearbooks
(Various editions, publishers and editors)
Rugby Football Annual

Playfair Rugby Football Annual

Rothmans Rugby Yearbook

IRB International Rugby Yearbook

IRB World Rugby Yearbook

New Zealand Rugby Almanack

RFU Yearbook